THE BOOK OF PSALMS

"A PANORAMIC VIEW OF THE BIBLE"

National Baptist Convention, USA. Inc.
WHITE ROCK BAPTIST CHURCH
5240 Chestnut Street • Philadelphia, PA 19139-3488

William J. Shaw
President

April 29, 2005

Dear Reverend Duncan:

The officers and members of the National Baptist Convention, USA, Inc. join me in passing on well wishes and praying for you as you celebrate the publishing of your new book "The Book of Psalms–*A Panoramic View of the Bible*". I wish you much success in your future endeavors.

I pray that His joy will be yours.

In the Name of our Christ,

William J. Shaw

William J. Shaw, President
National Baptist Convention, USA, Inc.

"Dedicated to Improving the Total Quality of Life, Mind, Body & Spirit."

Shiloh Baptist Church & Community Life Center

Bishop Dr. James Washington, Senior Pastor

I am pleased to write this letter in support of the literary work of Rev. Joyce Duncan.

Rev. Duncan is a Spirit led Minister of The Lord; whose writings are aimed at Kingdom Building. The unique approach she utilizes places the word of God at The Forefront. Thus, allowing the true richness of the Holy Writ to be the focus; as opposed to any effort to interject personal opinion.

The Book of Psalms…"A Panoramic View of the Bible"; is an immensely thorough work. The new convert as well as the seasoned Saint of God can glean immeasurable benefit from the study of this author's labor.

I am extremely honored and proud of this daughter of The Shiloh Baptist Church, of Atlantic City, New Jersey. Rev Duncan is living proof of the Fruit of the Spirit that can be produced, when one Abides in the Lord and allows His Words to Abide in them (John 15:7-8)

It is my prayer, that the Lord will continue to Richly Anoint this mighty Woman of God.

Yours for the Up Building of His Kingdom,

Bishop Dr. James Washington

Church Motto "God's Way Is the Best Way" (Proverbs 3: 5-6)
701 Atlantic City, NJ 08401 * 609-449-1100 Church * 609-449-1103 fax
609-449-1105 Shiloh Community Life Center OR 1-888-SHILOH2
blessings@newshiloh.com **(email) *** www.newshiloh.com **(website)**

Mt. Sinai Institutional Baptist Church

111 Cambria Street

Conemaugh, Pennsylvania 15909

Dear Rev. Duncan:

In this contemporary Christian conscious day, I am filled with encouragement and appreciation to her book entitled, The Book of Psalms, " A Panoramic View Of The Bible" written by a believer that can meet the need of this hour without concession.

The content of her work witness hours of devotion before the Lord with prayerful study and preparation before putting pen to paper. Rev. Duncan's work qualifies as an oasis to every true seeker of Biblical information in this sometime dry wilderness walk.

The author painstakingly lays out a model of truths for teacher, student and every person involved in Christian Education. She cautiously provide for every reader confidence as they read her work; which has the Bible as the foundation.

I have known Rev. Duncan for a number of years and I have found her to be a student of the Word of God. She is also a person of indisputable character.

It is indeed a pleasure to present this work by Rev. Duncan. My desire is that the Lord blesses this labor of love for the work of the Kingdom of God.

May God Be The Glory.

Rev J. Hunter /pw

Pastor J. Hunter
Pastor of the Mt. Sinai Institutional Baptist Church

James S. Hall, Sr.
Pastor & Organizer

Cathy M. Johnson
Assistant Pastor

Triumph Baptist Church

1536-40 W. Wingohocking Street ¥ Philadelphia, PA 19140

Victory Through Christ

April 3, 2006

CONGRATULATIONS

TO THE REVEREND JOYCE M. DUNCAN on her book, THE BOOK OF PSALMS "A PANORAMIC VIEW OF THE BIBLE"

Though the Psalms are perhaps the most familiar portion of the Bible, they are also among the most difficult to interpret. Encountering this book of Psalms begins by examining the nature, structure and authorship of the Psalter and providing readers with specific principles for interpretation.

The Reverend Duncan has created this book to introduce readers to study and interpret the Psalms. This volume offers a study of the Psalms as an unique effort to plumb the depths of life's meaning and as a central part of ancient Israel theological achievement, Pastors/Preachers, laypeople will appreciate this helpful scholarship of THE BOOK OF PSALMS "A PANORAMIC VIEW OF THE BIBLE".

The author, The Reverend Joyce M Duncan is at her best in combining Biblical research and theological insights with her comprehensive background of scholarly training and experience as PREACHER, TEACHER AND PASTORAL COUNSELOR.

I highly endorse and recommend the reading of this BOOK OF PSALMS and commend to be used in your CHURCH'S BIBLE STUDIES and MINISTRY OF CHRISTIAN EDUCATION.

I Remain Yours In Christ,

Ronald King Hill

DR. RONALD KING HILL
DIRECTOR OF MINISTRIES
TRIUMPH BAPTIST CHURCH
PHILADELPHIA, PENNSYLVANIA

(215) 324-8036 • Fax (215) 324-8503

THE BOOK OF PSALMS

"A PANORAMIC VIEW OF THE BIBLE"

Rev. Joyce M. Duncan

Library of Congress Control Number: 2004099871
ISBN: Hardcover 978-1-4134-5857-2
Softcover 978-1-4134-5838-1

This book was printed in the United States of America.

Special Appreciation

First, I give honor to God and the Holy Spirit for guiding my hand to allow me to write His Word, For no one other than my LORD could give me directions and determination. I know now assuredly that God is able to do exceedingly above all that we ask or think. I felt a divine compulsion to write this Book. (God has magnified His Word above His own Name) Ps.138:2. As I encounter many obstacles, This has been the greatest calling during my short time in the Ministry as being His servant, I feel truly blessed! I thank God for my family, and friends who have given me encouragement in the writing of this Book.

TO GOD BE THE GLORY!

Thanks to the following persons

Dr. and Mrs. James Washington
Pastor and Mentor
Atlantic City, N.J.

Dr. Charles R. McCreary, Sr.
Mentor and Proofreader

Rev. Melvin Williams, Jr.
Benefactor
[For opening his pulpit freely]
as Guest Preacher

Dr. and Mrs. Sanat Mandal, Cardiologist
[My greatest encouragers]

Reginald and Lori Duncan
Technical Advisors

Bridget Duncan
Photographer

Tyrone C. Duncan
Advisor

Dedicated to My Children

Tyrone
Reginald
Christine
Bridget
Lori
Theodore Duncan Jr. (deceased)
Mark Duncan (deceased)

And to My Grandchildren

Tylar
Miles
Isaiah
Reginald Jr.
Desireé

TABLE OF CONTENTS

I. MESSIANIC PSALMS

II. PENITENTIAL PSALMS

III. IMPRECATORY PSALMS

Cries To God To Avenge

IV. ETERNALITY OF GOD, MAN'S FRAILTY

V. HALLEL OR HALLELUJAH PSALMS

SONG'S OF PRAISE

VI. IN PRAISE OF GOD'S WORD

VII. PILGRIM PSALMS-120-134

ASCENT JOY CAPTIVITY TO JERUSALEM

VIII. THANKSGIVING PSALMS 118 AND 136

IX. THE SUMMATION

APPENDIX

INDEX TO ANNOTATIONS

BOOKS OF THE OLD AND NEW TESTAMENT AND THEIR ABBREVIATIONS

Old Testament

Book	Abbreviation	Book	Abbreviation
Genesis	**Gen.**	**Ecclesiastes**	**Eccl.**
Exodus	**Ex.**	**Song of Solomon**	**Song**
Leviticus	**Lev.**	**Isaiah**	**Isa.—Is.**
Numbers	**Num.**	**Jeremiah**	**Jer.**
Deuteronomy	**Dt.—Deut.**	**Lamentations**	**Lam.**
Joshua	**Josh.**	**Ezekiel**	**Ezek.**
Judges	**Judg.**	**Daniel**	**Dan.**
Ruth	**Ruth**	**Hosea**	**Hos.**
1 Samuel 1	**Sam.**	**Joel**	**Joel**
2 Samuel	**2 Sam.**	**Amos**	**Amos**
1 Kings 1	**Ki.—1Kin.**	**Obadiah**	**Obad.**
2 Kings	**2 Ki.—2Kin.**	**Jonah**	**Jon.**
1 Chronicles	**1 Chr.**	**Micah**	**Mic.**
2 Chronicles	**2Chr.**	**Nahun**	**Nah.**
Ezra	**Ezra**	**Habakkuk**	**Hab.**
Nehemiah	**Neh.**	**Zephaniah**	**Zeph.**
Esther	**Est.—Esth.**	**Haggai**	**Hag.**
Job	**Job**	**Zechariah**	**Zech.**
Psalms	**Ps.**	**Malachi**	**Mal.**
Proverbs	**Prov.**		

New Testament

Matthew	**Mt.—Matt.**	**1 Timothy**	**1 Tim.**
Mark	**Mk.—Mark**	**2 Timothy**	**2 Tim.**
Luke	**Lk.—Luke**	**Titus**	**Ti.-Titus**
John	**Jn. John**	**Philemon**	**Phil.-Philem**
Acts	**Acts**	**Hebrews**	**Heb.**
Romans	**Rom.**	**James**	**Jas.—James**
1 Corinthians	**1 Cor.**	**1 Peter**	**1 Pet.**
2 Corinthians	**2 Cor.**	**2 Peter**	**2 Pet.**
Galations	**Gal.**	**1 John**	**1 Jn.-1 John**
Ephesians	**Eph.**	**2 John**	**2 Jn.-2 John**
Philippians	**Phil.**	**3 John**	**3 Jn.-3 John**
Colossians	**Col.**	**Jude**	**Jude**
1 Thessalonians	**1 Th.—Thess.**	**Revelation**	**Rev.**
2 Thessalonians	**2 Th.—Thess.**		

Special Abbreviations

compare = cp. for example = e.g. Authorized King James Verse =KJV literally= lit. verse = v. verses =vv. New Testament = N.T. Old Testament =O.T. two or more verses following reference =ff.

HOW TO USE THE MARGINAL REFERENCES

My Dear Friends:

Today, I Plan to introduce to you a unique method of reading and understanding the Scripture. It is the Marginal Reference Method.

First, have available a Reference Bible, preferably, a Scofield Reference Bible. This method selects verses of Scripture and Highlights the words, phrases, names, or subjects by letters of the alphabet such as a, b, c, d, etc. and placing these letters in center, right, or left margin of the Bible and comparing them to related Scriptures or Parallel Scripture.

There maybe multiple references or just one; These references are related to the Scripture being read greatly amplifies and simplifies the Word. This method applies to any or all the Books of the Bible. Also, annotations (notes) are designated by numbers such as 1, 2, 3, 4, etc. these notes give valuable information and should add to your understanding.

Editor's Note: The words in BOLD letters are the sayings of Jesus.

FOREWORD

This Book was dictated by the Wisdom of God under the Guidance and Inspiration of the Holy Spirit and prepared by the Author and Scribe,

Rev. Joyce M. Duncan

This Book is presented to all who love reading the Bible, especially, those who have difficulty in reading the Bible with a clear understanding.

This Book is a practical and instructional tool, toward giving a Panoramic view of the Scriptures.

How I arrived at the title of this Book.

A number of years ago I had the privilege of visiting my relatives in the State of Virginia. One day they took me for a ride up on the Blue Ridge Mountains, Skyline Drive, to it's highest peak, a place called Panorama. We went to a Lookout and viewed the entire Shenadoah Valley as far as the eyes could see. It was the most exciting and beautiful scene I have ever experienced. After reading the 34th chapter of Deuteronomy, I could very well empathize with Moses when God took him from the plains of Moab unto the mountain of Nebo, to the top of Pisgah, that is over against Jericho, And the LORD showed him all the land of Gil'ead, unto Dan, God gave Moses a Panoramic View of the Promise Land (A Full View) of the land. The LORD did not allow him to enter. So it is with us, No one can know all of the Bible, but we can have a Panoramic View.

It follows the formats of such notable Reference Bibles as the

Scofield Reference Bible, the Nelson King James Study Bible and the Thompson Chain Reference Bible.

The exciting new feature of this Book is the addition of the actual texts of the referred passages in full.

Everyone who desires a clearer understanding of the scripture should purchase this Book..

1. No more thumbing through the Bible looking for Books and marginal references.
2. The Books and marginal references have been researched and located by the Author and Scribe, the Rev. Joyce M. Duncan.
3. The references are written out in their entirety to give their relationship to the Book of Psalms. This amplifies and simplifies your reading.
4. The Author urges all Persons who purchase this Book, to have available for study and reading, a good Reference Bible, preferably, The Scofield Reference Bible, or the Nelson King James Study Bible. The Book of Psalms is the best Book to accomplish the task described.

[The Mighty God, even the Lord Has Spoken] ! Psalms 50:1

The Book of Psalms tells a story from the beginning to end of God dealing with His people, it is indeed a summary of the Old Testament and New Testament.

The Psalms are quoted in every Book of The Old Testament; and more frequently in The New Testament than any other Book of The Old Testament. There are 186 quotations from the Psalms in The New Testament.

Read the Book of Psalms, especially the Messianic Psalms, you will become more intelligible of the Gospels for it deals with the Ministry of Humiliation / Rejection of Christ. It is indeed, Christocentric.

Read the Book of Psalms and you will add to your knowledge of Paul's Epistles, for it deals with Christ's Ministry of Exaltation. Read the Book of Psalms, especially the Hallelujah Psalms, and you will receive a clearer understanding of the Songs of Praises and Triumph in the Book of Revelation.

Read the Book of Psalms and you will see that it covers the whole Bible from Genesis to Revelation.

INTRODUCTION

The Book of Psalms was chosen for this Comprehensive Study. The Psalter is generally divided into five Books, each concluding with a doxology.

The Book of Psalms is considered as a Book of Hebrew Poetry, a Book of Songs used Temple Worship and a Book of Prayers, but it is more then these, it is God's Directory, through His Covenants, Laws, Ordinances, Testimonies, and Precepts. This is God speaking to His chosen people Israel, and to man through out all the ages. I. Psalms 1—41; II. Psalms 42—72; III Psalms 73—89; IV Psalms 90—106 V Psalms 107—150.

This Book was chosen because of it's character, Principles, Divine Affections, Divine Life, and Holy Power, which reflects God's dealing with His Peculiar People, that they may become a Holy and Righteous People.

The Author, Rev. Joyce M. Duncan, has separated these five Books into eight different types of Psalms, for the purpose of this Study; the types are as follows, namely:

I MESSIANIC PSALMS — 2; 6; 8; 16; 21; 22; 23; 24; 40; 45; 68; 69; 72; 75; 89; 102; 110; 118. These Psalms speak in whole, or in part of the Messiah—Christ.

II THE PENITENTIAL PSALMS — Cries for Mercy. These are: 6; 32; 38; 51; 102; 130-143.

III THE IMPRECATORY PSALMS — Cries to God for Avenge. 35; 52; 55; 58; 59; 79; 137; 139.

IV GOD'S ETERNALITY — Man's Frailty.
90 — 106

V HALLEL or HALLELUJAH SONG'S — SONGS of PRAISES.
111 — 118.

VI PSALM OF THE WORD OF GOD. 119.

VII PILGRIM PSALMS—SONGS of ' ASCENT '
From Captivity to Jerusalem;
120 – 134

VIII THANKSGIVING PSALMS
118 – 136

IX SUMMATION OF GOD'S PRAISE—PSALM 150

I

MESSIANIC PSALMS

CHRIST THE COMING KING

PSALM 2

v.1 (2) Why do the (b) | nations | rage, and the people imagine a vain thing? 2 (2:1) Psalms 2; 8; 16; 22; 23; 24; 40; 45; 68; 72; 89; 102; 110; 118 are generally considered Messianic. These Psalms, either in whole or in part, speak of the Messiah. Undoubtedly many other Psalms also refer to Christ. Though the primary thrust of the Messianic Psalms is Christocentric, there is also much of instruction for the godly in their walk with God. See 118:29, note.

(b) KJV heathen

v.2 The Kings of the earth set themselves, and the (c) rulers take counsel together, against the Lord, and against his (d) anointed, saying,

(c) rulers
(c) Mt. 12:14 Mk11:18—Act (1) 4:25-27
(c) Mt.12 : 14

Then the Pharisees went out, and held a council against him, how they might destroy him.

(c) Mk.11:18

And the scribes and chief priests heard it, and sought how they might destroy him; for they feared him, because all the people were astonished at his doctrine.

(d) Anointed—Christ (The First Advent)

v.3 Let us break their bands asunder, and cast away their cords from us. (1) The rage and the vain imagination of the Jews and Gentiles against the Lord and His Anointed (vv.1-3). The inspired interpretation of this is in Acts 4:25-28, which asserts its fulfillment in the crucifixion of Christ.

Acts 4:25-28

v. 25 Who, by the mouth of thy servant, David, hast said, Why did the |nations| rage, and the peoples imagine vain things?

v.26 The Kings of the earth stood up, and the rulers were gathered together against the Lord, and against his Christ.

v.27 For of a truth against thy holy child, Jesus, whom thou hast anointed, both Herod, and Pontius Pilate, with the |nations|, and the people of Israel, were gathered together,

v.28 To do whatever thy hand and thy counsel determined before to be done.

[This was fulfilled in the crucifixion of Christ]

v.4 He who sitteth in the heavens shall laugh; the Lord shall have them in derision.

The derision of the Lord (v.4), that men should suppose it possible to set aside His covenant (2 Sam.7:8-17) and oath (Ps.89:34-37)

2 Sam.7:8-17

v.8 Now, therefore, so shalt thou say unto my servant, David, Thus saith the Lord of hosts, I took thee from the sheepcote, from following the sheep, to be ruler over my people, over Israel;

v.9 And I was with thee |wherever| thou wentest, and have cut off all thine enemies out of thy sight, and have made thee a great name, like unto the name of the great men who are in the earth.

v.10 Moreover, I will appoint a place for my people, Israel, and will plant them, that they made dwell in a place of their own, and move no more; neither shall the children of wickedness afflict them anymore, as |formerly|,

v.11 And as since the time that I commanded judges to be over my people, Israel, and have caused thee to rest from all thine enemies. Also the Lord telleth thee that he will make thee an house.

v.12 And when thy days be fulfilled, and thou shalt sleep with thy fathers, I will set up thy seed after thee, which shall proceed out of |thine own body. And I will establish his Kingdom.

v.13 He shall build an house for my name, and I establish the throne of his Kingdom forever.

v.14 I will be his father, and he shall be my son. If he commit iniquity, I will chasten him with the rod of men, and with the stripes of the children of men;

v15 But my mercy shall not depart away from him, as I took it from Saul, whom I put away before thee.

v.16 And thine house and thy Kingdom shall be established forever before thee; thy throne shall be established forever.

v.17 According to all these words, and according to all this vision, so did Nathan speak unto David. God's Oath cannot be set aside [annulled]

Ps. 89:34-37

v. 34 My covenant will I not break, nor will I after the thing that is gone out of my lips.

v.35 Once have I sworn by my holiness that I will not lie unto David.

v.36 His seed shall endure forever, and his throne as the sun before me.

v.37 It shall be established forever like the moon, and as a faithful witness in heaven. Selah.

v.5 Then shall he speak unto them in his wrath, and (e) vex them in his | great | displeasure.

(e) vex
(e) Tribulation (the great) vv. 1-5—See the above
Isa. 24: 20—Mt. 24:29
(Ps.2:5;Rev.7:14)

v.20 The earth shall reel to and fro like a drunkard, and shall be removed like a | booth | ; and the transgression thereof shall be heavy upon it, and it shall fall, and not rise again.

Mt. 24 :29

v.29 **Immediately after the tribulation of those days shall the sun be darkened, and the moon shall not give it's light, and the stars shall fall from heaven, and the powers of the heavens shall be shaken.**

Fulfilled in the destructions of Jerusalem, and the dispersion of the Jews at that time; yet to be fulfilled more completely in the tribulation. See the above v.5

Rev.7:14

v.14 And I said unto him, Sir, thou knowest. And he said to me, These are they who came out of | the great | tribulation, and have washed their robes, and made them white in the blood of the Lamb.

v.6 Yet have I set my (3 g) King upon my (h) holy hill of Zion.

(3 g) King
(3 g) Kingdom (O.T.):vv.1-9;Ps.16:9.
(Gen.1:26;Zech.12:8)
(h) holy hill
(h) Heb. godesh.
Sanctification (O.T.):v.6; Ps.20:6.(Gen.2:3; Zech.8:3)

Ps.2:1-9

v.1 WHY do the |nations| rage, and the peoples imagine a vain thing?
v.2 The kings of the earth set themselves, and the rulers take counsel together, against the LORD, and against his anointed, saying,
v.3 Let us break their bands asunder, and cast away their cords from us.
v.4 He who sitteth in the heavens shall laugh; the Lord shall have them in derision.
v.5 Then shall he speak unto them in his wrath, and (e) vex them in his (f) |great| displeasure.
v.6 Yet have I set my (3 g) king upon my (h) holy hill of Zion.
v.7 I will declare the decree: The LORD hath said unto me, (a) Thou art my Son; this day have I begotten thee.
v.8 Ask of me, and I shall give thee the (b) |nations| for thine inheritance, and the uttermost parts of the earth for thy possession.
v.9 (c) Thou shalt break them with a rod of iron; thou shalt (d) dash them in pieces like a potter's vessel.

Ps.16:9

v.9 Therefore my heart is glad, and my glory rejoiceth; my flesh also shall rest in hope.

Gen.1:26

v.26 And God said, Let us make man in our image, after our likeness; and let them have dominion over the fish of the sea, and over the fowls of the air, and over the cattle, and over all the earth, and over every creeping thing that creepeth upon the earth.

Zech.12:8

v.8 In that day shall the LORD defend the inhabitants of Jerusalem; and he that is feeble among them at that day shall be like David; and the house of David shall be like God, like the angel of the LORD before them.

See the above v.6

Ps.20:6

v.6 Now know I that the LORD saveth his anointed; he will hear him from his holy heaven with the saving strength of his right hand.

Gen.2:3

v.3 And God blessed the seventh day, and sanctified it, because that in it he had rested from all his work which God created and made.

Zech.8:3

v.3 Thus saith the LORD: I am returned unto Zion, and will dwell in the midst of Jerusalem; and Jerusalem shall be called a city of truth, and the mountain of the LORD of hosts, the holy mountain.

v.7 I will declare the decree: The Lord hath said unto me; (a) Thou art my Son; this day have I begotten thee.

(a) Thou art
(a) Acts 13:33;Heb.1:5;5:5

v.33 God hath fulfilled the same unto us their children, in that he hath raised up Jesus again as it is also written in the second psalms. Thou art my Son, this day have I begotten thee.

Heb.1:5

v.5 For unto which of the angels said he at any time, Thou art my Son, this day have I begotten thee? And again, I will be to him a Father, and he shall be to me a Son?

Heb.5:5

v.5 So also Christ glorified not himself to be made an high priest, but he that said unto him, Thou art my Son, today have I begotten thee.

v.8 Ask of me; and I shall give thee the (b) |nations| for thine inheritance, and the uttermost parts of the earth for thy possession.

(b) |nation|
(b) heathen

v.9 (c) Thou shalt break them with a rod of iron; thou shalt (d) dash them in pieces like a potter's vessel.

(c) Thou shalt
(c) Christ (second advent):vv.6-9
Ps.24:10(Dt.30:3;Acts1:11,note
(d) dash—Day (of the Lord)
See the above vv.6-9

Ps.24:10

v.10 Who is this King of glory? The LORD of hosts, he is the King of glory. Selah.

Dt.30:3

v.3 That then the LORD thy God will turn thy captivity, and have compassion upon thee, and will return and gather thee from all the nations where the LORD thy God hath scattered thee.

Acts1:11,note

v.11 Who also said, Ye men of Galilee, why stand ye gazing up into heaven? This same Jesus, who is taken up from you into heaven, shall so come in like manner as ye have seen him go into heaven.

Note: 1(1:11) The Two Advents, Summary:

(1) The O.T. for view of the coming Messiah is in two aspects—that of rejection and suffering (e.g. in Isa.53); and that of earthly glory and power (e.g. in Isa.11; Jer.23; Ezek.37).Often these two aspects blend in one passage (e.g. Ps.22). The prophets themselves were perplexed by this seeming contradiction (1 Pet.1:10-11). It was solved by partial fulfillment. In due time the Messiah, born of a virgin according to Isaiah's prophecy (7:14), appeared among men and began His ministry by announcing the predicted kingdom as "at hand" (Mt.4:17, note 4). The rejection of King and kingdom followed.

(2) There-upon the rejected king announced His approaching crucifixion, departure, and return (Mt.12:38-40; 16:1-4,21,27;24;25;Lk.12:35-46; 17:20-36; 18:31-34;19:12-27).

(3) He uttered predictions concerning the course of events between His departure and return (Mt.13:1-50; 16:18;24:4-26). And

(4) this promised return of Christ is a prominent theme in The Acts, Epistles, and The Revelation.

Taken together the N.T. teachings concerning the return of Jesus Christ may be summarized as follows:

(1) The return of Christ is an event, not a process, and is personal and corporeal (Mt.23:39;24:30;25;31; Mk.14:62;Lk.17:24; Jn.14:3; Acts1:11;Phil.3:20-21;1Th.4:14-17).

(2) His coming has a threefold relation: to the Church,

to Israel, and to the nations: (a) To the Church, the descent of the Lord into the air, to raise believers who have died and to change the living Christians, is a constant expectation and hope(1Cor.15:51-52;Phil.3:20;1 Th.1:10;4:13-17; 1Tim.6:14; Ti.2:13;Rev.22:20) (b) To Israel, the return of the Lord to the earth is to accomplish the yet unfulfilled prophecies Davidic Covenant (2 Sam.7:16,note cp. Acts15:14-17 with Zech.14:1-9).See Kingdom (O.T.), 2 Sam.7:8-17;Zech.12:8,note (N.T.) Lk.1:31-33; 1 cor.15:24,note. (c) To the Gentile nations, the return of Christ is to bring the destruction of the present political world system (Dan.2:34-35;Rev.19:11,note), and the judgment of Mt.25:31-46, followed by world wide Gentile conversion and participation in the blessings of the kingdom (Isa.2:2-4;11:10;60:3; Zech.8:3,20-23;14:16-21).

v.10 Be wise now, therefore, O ye kings; be instructed, ye judges of the earth.

v.11 Serve the Lord with (e) fear, and rejoice with trembling.

(e) fear
(e) Ps.19:9,note

v.9 The (2) fear of the LORD is clean, enduring forever; the |ordinances| of the LORD are true and righteous altogether.

Note: 2(19:9) "The fear of the LORD" is an O.T. expression meaning reverential trust, including the hatred of evil.

v.12 Kiss the Son, lest he be angry, and ye kindled but a little. Blessed are all they who (f) put their (1) trust in him.

(f) put their trust in him
(f) Faith:v.12;Ps.28:7.
(Gen.3:20;Heb.11:39,note)
See the above v.12

Ps.28:7

v.7 The LORD is my strength and my shield; my heart trusted in him, and I am helped. Therefore, my heart greatly rejoiceth, and with my song will I praise him.

Gen.3:20

v.20 And Adam called his wife's name Eve, because she was the mother of all living.

Heb.11:39,note

v.39 And these all, having |received witness| through faith, received not the promise, Note: 3 (11:39)Faih, Summary: the essence of faith consists in believing and receiving what God has revealed, and may be defined as that trust in the God of the Scriptures and in Jesus Christ whom He has sent, which receives Him as Lord and Savior and impels to loving obedience and good works (Jn.1:12; Jas.2:14-26). The particular uses of faith give rise to its secondary definitions:

(1) For salvation, faith personal trust, apart from meritorious works, in the Lord Jesus Christ as delivered because of our offenses and raised again because of our Justification (Rom.4:5,23-25;5:1).
(2) As used in prayer, faith is the "confidence that we have in him, that if we ask anything according to his will, he heareth us" (1Jn.5:14-15).
(3) As used in reference to unseen things of which Scripture speaks, faith gives "substance" to them so that we act upon the conviction of their reality (Heb.11:1-3). And
(4) as a working principal in life, the uses of faith are illustrated in this chapter.

1(2:12); Trust is the characteristic O.T. word for N.T. "faith" and "believe." It occurs 152 time in the O.T., and is the rending of Hebrew words signify to take refuge (e.g. Ruth 2:12); to lean on (e.g. Ps.56:3); to roll on (e.g.Ps.22:8); to wait for (e.g. Job 35:14).

CHRIST'S DEITY FULLY RECOGNIZED

PSALM 8

v.1 O Lord, our Lord, how excellent is thy name in all the earth, who hast set thy (a) glory above the heavens!

(a) glory
(a) Cp.Ps.19:1

v.1 THE heavens declare the glory of God, and the firmament showed his handiwork.

v.2 (b) Out of the mouth of babes and sucklings hast thou ordained strength because of thine enemies, that thou mightest still the enemy and the avenger.

(b) Out
(b) Mt. 21:16;cp. 1Cor.1:26-31

v.16 And said unto him, Hearest thou what these say? And Jesus saith unto them, **Yea; have ye never read, Out of the mouth of babes and sucklings thou hast perfected praise?**

1 Cor.1:26-31

v.26 For ye see your calling, brethren, how that not many wise men after the flesh, not many mighty, not many noble, are called;

v.27 But God hath chosen the foolish things of the world to confound the wise; and God hath chosen the weak things of the world to confound the things which are mighty;
v.28 And base things of the world, and things which are despised, hath God chosen, yea, and things which are not, to bring to |nothing| things that are,
v.29 That no flesh should glory in his presence.
v.30 But of him are ye in Christ Jesus, who of God is made unto us wisdom, and righteousness, and sanctification, and redemption;
v.31 That, according as it is written, He that glorieth, let him glory in the Lord.

v.3 When I consider thy heavens, the work of thy fingers, the moon and the stars, which thou hast ordained,
v.4 What is (c) man, that thou art mindful of him? And the Son of man, that thou (d) visitest him?

(c) man
(c) Job 7:17-18;Heb.2:6-8
(d) visitest;
(d) Job 10:12

Job 7:17-18

v.17 What is man, that thou shouldest magnify him, and that thou shouldest set thine heart upon him,
v.18 And that thou shouldest visit him every morning, and | test | him every moment?

Heb.2:6-8

v.6 But one in a certain place testified, saying, What is man, that thou art mindful of him? Or the son of man, that thou visitest him?
v.7 Thou madest him a little lower than the angel; thou crowneth him with glory and honor, and didst set him over the works of thy hands;

v.8 Thou hast put all things in subjection under his feet. For in that he put all in subjection under him, he left nothing that is not put under him. But now we see not yet all things put under him.

v.5 For thou hast made him a little lower than the (e) angels, and has crowned him with glory and honor.

(e) angels
(e) Heb.1:4,note See Ps.68 :17—Messianic Psalm

v.4 Being made so much better than the angels, as he hath by inheritance obtained a more excellent name than they.

v.6 Thou madest him to have have (f) dominion over the works of thy hands; thou hast put (g) all things under his feet:

(f) dominion
(f) Gen. 1:26
(g) all things
(g) 1 Cor.15:27

Gen.1:26

v.26 And God said, Let us make man in our image, after our likeness; and let them have dominion over the fish of the sea, and over the fowl of the air and over the cattle, and over all the earth, and over every creeping thing that creepeth upon the earth.

1 Cor.15:27

v.27 For he hath put all things under his feet. But when he saith all things are put under him, it is manifest that he is excepted who did put all things under him.

v.7 All sheep and oxen, yea, and the beasts of the field,

v.8 The fowl of the air, and the fish of the sea, and whatsoever passeth through the paths of the seas.
v.9 O LORD, our Lord, how excellent is thy name in all the earth!

In Ps.8, while His Deity is fully recognized (v.1; Ps.110 with Mt.22:41-46), He is seen as Son of man (vv.4-6) who, "made [for] a little [while] lower than the angels," is to have dominion over the redeemed creation (Heb.2:6-11). Thus this Psalm speaks primarily of what God bestowed upon the human race as represented in Adam (Gen.1:26,28).

PREDICTION OF THE RERSURRECTION OF THE KING

PSALM 16

v.1 (q) PRESERVE me, O God; for in thee do I put my (b) trust.

(q) PRESERVE me
(q) Ps. 17:8
(b) trust
(b) Ps. 2:12

Ps. 17:8

v.8 Keep me as the apple of the eye; hide me under the shadow of thy wings,

Ps. 2:12

Trust is the characteristic O.T. word for the N. T. "faith," and "believe" It occurs 152 times in the O. T., and is the rendering of Hebrew words signifying to take refuge (e. g. Ruth 2:12); to lean on (e. g. Ps. 56:3); to roll on (e.g. Ps. 22:8);to wait for (e.g. Job 35:14).

v.2 O my soul, thou hast said unto the Lord, Thou art my Lord; my goodness extended not to thee;
v.3 But to the saints who are in the earth, and to the excellent, in (r) whom is all my delight.

(r) whom is all my delight
(r) Ps. 119:63

v.63 I am a companion of all those who fear thee, and of those who keep thy precepts.

v.4 Their sorrows shall be multiplied, who haste after (1) another god; their drink offerings of (s) blood will I not offer, nor take up their names into my (t) lips.

(1) another god;
(1) 1 Cor.8:5-6
(s) blood;
(s) Ps. 106:37-38
(t) lips;
(t) Ex.23:13;Josh.23:7

1 Cor.8:5-6

v.5 For though there be that are called gods, whether in heaven or in earth (as there are many, and lords many),
v.6 But to us there is but one God, the Father, of whom are all things, and we in him; and one Lord Jesus Christ, by whom are all things, and we by him.

Ps. 106:37-38

v.37 Yea, they sacrificed their sons and their daughters unto |demons|,
v.38 And shed innocent blood, even the blood of their sons and their daughters, whom they sacrificed unto the idols of Canaan; and the land was polluted with blood.

Ex. 23 :13

v.13 And in all things that I have said unto you be circumspect: and make no mention of the name of other gods, neither let it be heard out of thy mouth.

Josh. 23:7

v.7 That ye come not among these nations, these that remain among you; neither make mention of the name of their gods, nor cause to swear by them, neither serve them, nor bow yourselves unto them.

v. 5 The Lord is the portion of mine inheritance and of my cup; thou maintainest my lot.
v.6. The lines are fallen unto me in pleasant places; yea, I have a goodly heritage.
v.7 I will bless the LORD, who hath given me counsel: my (u) |heart| also instructs me in the night seasons.

(u) |heart|
(u) KJV reins

v.8 (v) I have set the LORD always before me; because he is at my right hand, I shall not be moved.

(v) I have set the LORD always before me
(v) vv. 8-11; Acts 2:25-28

v.8 I have set the LORD always before me; because he is at my right hand, I shall not be moved.
v.9. (w) Therefore my heart is glad, and my glory rejoiceth; my flesh also shall rest in (x) hope.
v.10 For thou wilt not leave (a) soul in (b) |sheol|, neither wilt thou (c)| permit| thine Holy One to see corruption.
v.11 Thou wilt show me the path of life. In thy presence is fullness of joy; at thy right hand there are pleasures for evermore.

Acts 2:25-28

v.25 For David speaketh concerning him: I foresaw the Lord always before my face; for he is on my right hand, that I should not be moved.

v.26 Therefore did my heart rejoice, and my tongue was glad; moreover my flesh also shall rest in hope,
v.27 Because thou wilt not leave my soul in |hades|, neither wilt thou |allow| thine Holy One to see corruption.
v.28 Thou hast made known to me the ways of life; thou shalt make me full of joy with thy countenance.

v.9 (w) Therefore my heart is glad, and my glory rejoiceth; (2) my flesh also shall rest in (x) hope.

(w) therefore—everything that went before
(2) my flesh also shall rest in hope;
(2) prediction of the resurrection of the King.
David Covenant, 2 Sam. 2(7:16) Acts 2:25-31
(x) hope;
(x) Resurrection—Isa.26:19.(2 Ki.4:35;1 Cor.15:19;52

2 Sam. 2 (7:16)

v.16 And thine house and thy kingdom shall be established forever before thee; thy throne shall be established forever.

Acts 2:25-31

v.25 For David speaketh concerning him: I foresaw the Lord always before my face; for he is on my right hand, that I should not be moved.
v.26 Therefore did my heart rejoice, and my tongue was glad; moreover my flesh also shall rest in hope,
v.27 Because thou wilt not leave my soul in |hades|, nither wilt thou | allow| thine Holy One to see corruption.
v.28 Thou hast made known to me the ways of life; thou shalt make me full of joy with thy countenance.
v.29 Men and brethren, let me freely speak unto you of the patriarch, David, that he is both dead and buried, and his sepulcher is with us unto this day.

v.30 Therefore, being a prophet, and knowing that God had sworn with an oath to him, that of the fruit of his loins, according to the flesh, he would raise up Christ to sit on his throne;
v.31 He, seeing this before, spoke of the resurrection of Christ, that his soul was not left in |hades|, neither his flesh did see corruption.

Isa.26:19

v.19 Thy dead men shall live, together with my dead body shall they arise. Awake and sing, ye that dwell in dust; for thy dew is like the dew of herbs, and the earth shall cast out the dead.

2 Ki.4:35

v.35 Then he returned, and walked in the house to and fro, and went up, and stretched himself upon him; and the child sneezed seven times, and the child opened his eyes.

1 Cor.15 19:52

v.19 If in this life only we have hope in Christ, we are all of men most miserable.
v.52 In a moment, in the twinking of an eye, at the last trumpet; for the trumpet shall sound, and the dead shall be raised incorruptible, and we shall be changed.

v.10 For thou wilt not leave (a) my soul in (b)|sheol|, neither wilt thou (c) |permit| thine Holy One to see corruption.

(a) my soul in
(a) Christ (first advent):v.10;Ps.22:1
(Gen.3:15; Acts 1:11)
(b)|sheol|
(b) KJV hell. See Hab.2:5,note;cp. Lk.16:23
(c) KJV suffer Ps.49:15;Acts13:35
See the above v.10

Ps.22:1

v.1 MY God, my God, why hast thou forsaken me? Why art thou so far from helping me, and from the words of my roaring?

Gen.3:15

v.15 And I will put enmity between thee and the woman, and between thy seed and her seed; he shall bruise thy head, and thou shalt bruise his heel.

Acts 1:11

v.11 Who also said, ye men of Galilee, why stand ye gazing up into heaven? This same Jesus, who is taken up from you into heaven, shall so come in like manner as ye seen him go into heaven.

Hab.2:5,note

v.5 Yea, also, because he transgresseth by wine, he is a proud man, neither keepeth at home, who enlargeth his desire as |sheol|, and is as death, and cannot be satisfied, but gathereth unto himself all nations, and heapeth unto himself all peoples.

Note: 4(2:5) Sheol is, in the O.T., the place to which the dead go.

(1) Often, therefore, it is spoken of as the equivalent of the grave, where all human activities cease; the terminus toward which all human life moves (e.g. Gen.42:38; Job 14:13; Ps.88:3).

(2) To the man "under the sun," the natural man, who of necessity judges from appearances, sheol seems no more than the grave—the end and total cessation, not only of the activities of life, but also of life itself (Eccl.9:5,10). But

(3) Scripture reveals sheol as a place of sorrow (2 Sam.22:6;Ps.18:5;116:3), into which the wicked are

turned (Ps.9:17), and where they are fully conscious (Isa.14:9-17; Ezek.32:21). Compare Jon.2:2; what the belly of the great fish was to Jonah, sheol is to those who are therein. The sheol of the O.T. and hades of the N.T. are identical. See Lk.16:23,note.

Lk.16:23

v.23 **And in |hades| he lifted up his eyes, being in torments, and seeth Abraham afar off, and Lazarus in his bosom.**

Ps.49:15

v.15 But God will redeem my soul from the power of |sheol|; for he shall receive me. Selah.

Acts 13:35

v.35 Wherefore, he saith also in another psalm, Thou shalt not |allow| thine Holy One to see corruption.

v.11 Thou wilt show me the path of life. In thy presence is fulness of joy; at thy right hand there are pleasures for evermore. 1(16:4) Of course there is only one God (1 Cor.8:5-6). The pagan had, however, those whom they called "gods", e.g. in David's day, Dagon and Baal. Then and now, whatever preempts the place in one's heart that belongs to the true God may be said to be a god, e.g. self and the pleasures of this world (2 Tim.3:2,4). 2(16:9) The 16th Psalm is a prediction of the resurrection of the King. As a prophet, David declared that, not at His first advent but at some time subsequent to His death and resurrection, the Messiah would assume the Davidic throne. Cp. Acts 2:25-31 with Lk.1:32-33 and Acts15:13-17. See Davidic Covenant, 2 Sam.7:16, note kingdom (O.T.)., Zech.12:8,note.

CHRIST'S, SUFFERING THE– GOOD SHEPHERD

PSALM 22

v.1 1 My (a) God, (b) My God, why hast thou forsaken me? Why
art thou so far from helping (c) me, and from the words of
my roaring?

(a) God;
(a) Mt. 27:46
(b) My God;
(b) Sacrifice (prophetic): vv. 1-18; Isa.52:14.(Gen. 3:15; Heb.10;18)
(c) me;
(c) Christ (first advent):vv.1-18;Isa.7:14.
(Gen.3:15; Acts 1:11)

(a) Mt. 27:46

v. 46 And about the ninth hour Jesus cried with a loud voice, saying, **Eli, Eli, la / ma sabach /thani?** that is to say, My God, my God, why hast thou forsaken me?

(b) Sacrifice (prophetic):1-18

v.1 1MY (a) God, (b) my God, why hast thou forsaken me? Why art thou so far from helping me, and from the words of my roaring?
v.2 O my God, I cry in the daytime, but thou hearest not; and in the night season, and am not silent.
v.3 But thou art holy, O thou who inhabitest the praises of Israel.
v.4 Our fathers trusted in thee; they (d) trusted, and thou didst deliver them.
v.5 They cried unto thee, and were delivered; they trusted in thee, and were not confounded.
v.6 But I am a worm, and no man; a reproach of men, and (e) despised by the people.
v.7 2 All they who see me laugh me to scorn; they shoot out the lip, they shake the head, saying,
v.8 He (f) trusted on the LORD that he would deliver him; let him deliver him; seeing he delighted in him.
v.9 But thou are he who (g) took me out of the womb; thou (h) didst make me hope upon my mother's breasts.

v.10 I was cast upon thee from the womb; thou art my God from my mother's (i) |body|.
v.11 Be not far from me; for trouble is near; for there is none to help.
v.12 Many bulls have compassed me; strong bulls of (j) Bashan have beset me round.
v.13 They (k) gaped upon me with their mouths, like a ravening and a roaring lion.
v.14 I am poured out like water, and all my bones are out of joint: my heart is like wax; it is melted (l) |within me|.
v.15 My strength is dried up like a potsherd, and my tongue cleaveth to my jaws; and thou hast brought me into the dust of death.
v.16 For (m) dogs have compassed me; the assembly of the wicked have enclosed me; 3they (n) pierced my hands and my feet.
v.17 I may (o) | count | all my bones; they look and stare upon me.
v.18 They part my garments among them, and (p) cast lots upon my vesture.

Isa.52:14

v.14 As many were |astounded| at thee—his visage was so marred more than any man, and his form more than the sons of men-

Gen.3:15

v.15 And I will put enmity between thee and the woman, and between thy seed and her seed; he shall bruise thy head, and thou shalt bruise his heel.

Heb.10:18

v.18 Now where remission of these is, there is no more offering for sin.

See the above vv.1-18

Isa.7:14

v.14 Therefore the Lord himself shall give you a sign; Behold, | the | virgin shall conceive, and bear a son, and shall call his name Immanuel.

Gen.3:15

v.15 And I will put enmity between thee and the woman, and between thy seed and her seed; he shall bruise thy head, and thou shalt bruise his heel.

Acts 1:11

v.11 Who also said, Ye men of Galilee, why stand ye gazing up into heaven? This same Jesus, who is taken up from you into heaven, shall so come in like manner as ye have seen him go into heaven.

v.2 O my God, I cry in the daytime, but thou hearest not; and in the night season, and am not silent.
v.3 But thou art holy, O thou who inhabitest the praises of Israel.
v.4 Our fathers trusted in thee; they (d) trusted, and thou didst deliver them.

(d) trusted
(d) See Ps.2:12,note

v.12 Kiss the Son, lest he be angry, and ye perish from the way, when his wrath is kindled but a little. Blessed are all they who put their trust in him.
Note: 1(2:12) Trust is the charcteristic O.T. word for the N.T. "faith," and "believe." It occurs 152 times in the O.T., and is the rendering of Hebrew words signifying to take refuge (e.g. Ruth 2:12); to lean on (e.g. Ps.56:3); to roll on (e.g.Ps.22:8); to wait for (e.g. Job 35:14).

v.5 They cried unto thee, and were delivered; they trusted in thee, and were not confounded.
v.6 But I am a worm, and no man; a reproach of men, and despised by the people.
v.7 2 All they who see me laugh me to scorn; they shoot out the lips, they shake the head, saying,
v.8 He (f) trusted on the LORD that he would deliver him; let him deliver him, seeing he delighted in him.

(f) trusted on the LORD
(f) Lit. rolled. Cp. Mt.27:43; see Ps.2:12,note

Mt.27:43

v.43 He trusted in God; let him deliver him now, if he will have him; for he said, I am the Son of God.

Ps.2:12,note; See Messianic Psalm Ps.2:12,note

v.9 But thou art he who (g) took me out of the womb; thou (h) didst make me hope upon my mother's breasts.

(g) took me out
(g) Ps.71:6
(h) didst make me hope
(h) Lit. didst make me trust

Ps.71:6

v.6 By thee have I been held up from the womb; thou art he who took me out of my mother; my praise shall be continually of thee.
v.10 I will cast upon thee from the womb; thou art my God from my mother's (i) |body| .

(i) |body|
(i) KJV belly

v.11 Be not far from me; for trouble is near; for there is none to help.

v.12 Many bulls have compassed me; strong bulls of (j) Bashan have beset me round.

(j) Bashan
(j) Dt.32:14

v.14 Butter of |cows|, and milk of sheep, with fat of lambs, and rams of the breed of Bashan, and goats, with the fat of kidneys of wheat; and thou didst drink the pure blood of the grape.

v.13 They (k) gaped upon me with their mouths, like a ravening and a roaring lion.

(k) gaped upon me
(k) Job.16:10

v.10 They have gaped upon me with their mouth; they have smitten me upon the cheek reproachfully; they have gathered themselves together against me.

v.14 I am poured out like water, and all my bones are out of joint: my heart is like wax; it is melted (l) |within me|.

(l) |within me|
(l) KJV in the midst of my bowels.

v.15 My strength is dried up like a potsherd, and my tongue cleaveth to my jaws; and thou hast brought me into the dust of death.

v.16 For (m) dogs have compassed me; the assembly of the wicked have enclosed me; 3 they (n) pierced my hands and my feet.

(m) dogs have compassed me
(m) Cp. Rev.22:15
3 they
(n) pierced my hands and feet
(n) Isa.53:7;cp.Jn.20:20-25

Rev.22:15

v.15 For |outside| are dogs, and sorcerers, and |fornicators|, and murderers, and idolaters, and whosoever loveth and maketh a lie.

Isa.53:7

v.7 He was oppressed, and he was afflicted, yet he opened not his mouth; he is brought as a lamb to the slaughter, and a sheep before her shearers is dumb, so he openeth not his mouth.

Jn.20:20-25

v.20 And when he had so said, he showed unto them his hands and his side. Then were the disciples glad, when they saw the Lord.
v.21 Then said Jesus to them again, **Peace be unto you; as my Father hath sent me, even so send I you.**
v.22 And when he had said this, he breathed on them, and saith unto them, **Receive ye the Holy |Spirit|;**
v.23 **Whosoever's sins ye remit, they are remitted unto them; and whosever's sins ye retain, they are retained.**
v.24 But Thomas, one of the twelve, called Did'ymus, was not with them when Jesus came.
v.25 The other disciples, therefore, said unto him, We have seen the Lord. But he said unto them, Except I shall see in his hands the print of the nails, and put my finger into the print of the nail, and thrust my hand into his side, I will not believe.

v.17 I may (o)|count| all my bones; they look and share upon me.

(o) |count|
(o) KJV tell

v.18 They part my garments among them, and (p) cast lots upon my vesture.

(p) cast lots
(p) Mt.27:35

Mt. 27: 35

v.35 And they crucified him, and parted his garments, casting lots, that it might be fulfilled which was spoken by the prophet, They parted my garments among them, and upon my vesture did they cast lots.

v.19 But be not thou far from me, O LORD. O my strength, haste thee to help me.
v.20 Deliver my soul from the sword; my (q) |only one| from the power of the dog.

(q) |only one|
(q) KJV darling

v.21 Save me from the lion's mouth; for thou hast heard me from the horns of the (r) |wild oxen |

(r) |wild oxen|
(r) KJV unicorns

v.22 4 I will declare thy name unto my (s) brethren; in the midst of the congregation will I praise thee.

4 I will
(s) brethren
(s) Heb.2:12

v.12 Saying, I will declare thy name unto my brethren, in the midst of the church will I sing praise unto thee.

v.23 Ye who (t) fear the LORD, praise him; all ye, the seed of Jacob, glorify him; and fear him, all ye, the seed of Israel.

(t) fear the LORD
(t) See Ps.19:9,note

v.9 The fear of the LORD is clean, enduring forever; the |ordinances| of the LORD are true and righteous altogether.

Note: 1 (19:9) "The fear of the LORD" is an O.T. expression meaning reverential trust, including the hatred of evil.

v.24 For he hath not despised nor abhorred the affliction of the afflicted, neither hath he hidden his face from him; but when he cried unto him, he heard.
v.25 My praise shall be of thee in the great congregation; I will pay my vows before them that (t) fear him.

(t) fear him
(t) See Ps.19:9,note—Messianic Psalm 22:23

v.26 5 The (u) meek shall (v) eat and be satisfied; they shall praise the LORD that seek him; your heart shall live forever.

(u) meek
(u) Cp.Mt.5:5
(v) eat
(v) Jn.6:51-58; 1 Cor.11:26

Mt.5:5

v.5 **Blessed are the poor in spirit; for theirs is the kingdom of heaven.**

Jn.6:.51-58

v.51 **I am the living bread that came down from heaven; if any man eat of this bread, he shall live forever; and the bread that I will give is my flesh, which I will give for the life of the world.**

v.52 The Jews, therefore, strove among themselves, saying, How can this man give us his flesh to eat?

v.53 Then Jesus said unto them, **Verily, verily, I say unto you. Except ye eat the flesh of the Son of man, and drink his blood, ye have no life in you.**

v.54 **He who eateth my flesh, and drinketh my blood, hath eternal life; and I will raise him up at the last day.**

v.55 **For my flesh is |food| indeed, and my blood is drink indeed.**

v.56 **He that eateth my flesh, and drinketh my blood, dwelleth in me, and I in him.**

v.57 **As the living Father hath sent me, and I live by the Father, so he that eateth me, even he shall live by me.**

v.58 **This is that bread which came down from heaven, not as your fathers did eat manna, and are dead; he that eateth of this bread shall live forever.**

1 Cor.11:26

v.26 For as often as ye eat this bread, and drink this cup, ye do show the Lord's death till he come.

v.27 All the ends of the world shall remember and turn unto the Lord; and all the kindreds of the nations shall worship before thee.

v.28 For the kingdom is the LORD'S; and he is the governor among the nations.

v.29 All they that are fat upon earth shall eat and worship; all they that go down to the dust shall bow before him, and none can keep alive his own soul.

v.30 A (a) seed shall serve him; it shall be accounted to the Lord for a generation.

(a) seed shall serve him;
(a) Cp. Isa.53:10-11

v.10 Yet it pleased the LORD to bruise him; he hath put him to grief. When thou shalt make his soul an offering for sin, he shall see his seed, he shall prolong his days, and the pleasure of the LORD shall prosper in his hand.
v.11 He shall see of the travail of his soul, and shall be satisfied; by his knowledge shall my righteous servant justify many; for he shall bear their iniquities.

v.31 They shall come, and shall declare his rightousness unto a people that shall be born, that he hath done this.

CHRIST THE GREAT SHEPHERD

PSALM 23

v.1 THE LORD is my (b) shepherd; I shall (c) not want.

(b) shepherd;
(b) Isa.40:11;Ezek.34:11-12; Jon.10:11; 1 Pet.2:25
(c) not want
(c) Assurance-security vv.1-6;Ps.91:1.
(Ps.23:1;Jude 1);Phil. 4:19

Isa.40:11

v.11 He shall feed his flock like a shepherd; he shall gather the lambs with his arm, and carry them in his bosom, and shall gently lead those that are with young.

Ezek 34:11-12

v.11 For thus saith the Lord God: Behold, I, even I will both search my sheep, and seek them out.
v.12 As a shepherd seeketh out his flock in the day that he is among his sheep that are scattered, so will I seek out my sheep, and will deliver them out of all places where they have been scattered in the cloudy and dark day.

Jn.10:11

v.11 **I am the good sheperd; the good shepherd giveth his life for the sheep.**

1 Pet.2:25

v.25 For ye were as sheep going astray, but are now returned unto the Shepherd and Bishop of your souls.

vv.1:-6

v1 THE LORD is my (b) shepherd; I shall (c) not want.
v.2 He maketh me to lie down in green (d) pastures; he leadeth me beside the still waters.
v.3 He restoreth my soul; he (f) leadeth me in the paths of righteousness for his name's sake.
v.4 Yea, though I walk through the valley of the (g) shadow of death, I will (h) fear no evil; for thou art (i) with me; thy rod and thy staff they comfort me.
v.5 Thou (j) prepares a table before me in the presence of mine enemies; thou (k) anointest my head with oil; my cup runneth over.
v.6 Surely goodness and mercy shall follow me all the days of my life; and I will dwell in the house of the LORD forever.

Ps.91:1

v.1 HE who dwelleth in the secret place of the Most High shall abide under the shadow of the Almighty.

Ps. 23:1

v.1 THE LORD is my shepherd; I shall not want.

Jude 1

v.1 JUDE, the servant of Jesus Christ, and brother of James, to them that are sanctified by God, the Father, and preserved in Jesus Christ, and called:

Phil.4:19

v.19 But my God shall supply all your needs according to his riches in glory by Jesus Christ.

v.2 He maketh me to lie down in green (d) pastures; he leadeth me beside the (e) still waters.

(d) pasture ;
(d) Ezek. 34:14
(e) still waters
(e) Lit. waters of quietness. Cp. Rev.7:17

Ezek. 34:14

v.14 I will feed them in a good pasture, and upon the high mountains of Israel shall their fold be; there shall they lie in a good fold, and in a |rich| pasture shall they feed upon the mountains of Israel.

Rev.7:17

v.17 For the Lamb who is in the midst of the throne shall feed them, and shall lead them unto living fountains of waters; and God shall wipe away all tears from their eyes.

v.3 He restoreth my soul; he (f) leadeth me in the paths of righteousness for his name's sake.

(f) leadeth me
(f) Ps. 5:8; 31:3; Prov.8:20

Ps.5:8

v.8 Lead me, O Lord, in thy righteousness because of mine enemies; make thy way straight before my face.

Ps.31:3

v.3 For thou art my rock and my fortress; therefore, for thy name's sake lead me, and guide me.

Prov.8:20

v.20 I lead the way of righteousness, in the midst of the paths of thy |justice|,

v.4 Yea, though I walk through the valley of the (g) shadow of death, I will (h) fear no evil; for thou art (i) with me; thy rod and thy staff they comfort me.

(g) shadow of death,
(g) Job 3:5;10:21-22; 24:17;Ps.44:19;cp.Rev.1:18
(h) fear no evil;
(h) Ps.27:1
(i) with me;
(i) Isa.43:2

Job.3:5

v.5 Let darkness and the shadow of death stain it; let a cloud dwell upon it; let the blackness of the day terrify it.

Job 10:21-22

v.21 Who long for death, but it cometh not, and dig for it more than for hidden treasures;
v.22 Who rejoice exceedingly, and are glad, when they can find the grave?

Job24:17

v.17 For the morning is to them even as the shadow of death; if one know them, they are in the terrors of the shadow of death.

Ps.44:19

v.19 Though thou hast |severely| broken us in the place of |jackals|, and covered us with the shadow of death.

Rev.1:18

v.18 **I am he that liveth, and was dead; and behold, I am alive for evermore, Amen, and have the keys of |hades| and of death.**

Ps. 27:1

v.1 The LORD is my light and my salvation; whom shall I fear? The LORD is the strength of my life; of whom shall I be afraid?

Isa.43:2

v.2 When thou passest through the waters, I will be with thee; and through the rivers, they shall not overflow thee; when thou walkest through the fire, thou shalt not be burned, neither shall the flame kindle upon thee.

v.5 Thou (j) preparest a table before me in the presence of mine enemies; thou (k) anointest my head with oil; my cup runneth over.

(j) preparest
(j) Ps.104:15
(k) anointest
(k) Lit. makest fat. Ps. 92:10;Lk.7:46

Ps. 104:15

v.15 And wine that makest glad the heart of man, and oil to make his face to shine, and bread which strengthened man's heart.

Ps. 92:10

v. 10 But my horn shalt thou exalt like the horn of | a wild ox | ; I shall be anointed with fresh oil.

Lk.7:46

v.46 **And why call ye me, Lord, Lord, and do not the things which I say?**

v.6 Surely goodness and mercy shall follow me all the days of my life; and I will dwell in the house of the Lord forever.

Heb. 13: 20

v.20 Now the God of peace, that brought again from the dead our Lord Jesus, that great Shepherd of the sheep, through the blood of the everlasting covenant,

THE KING OF GLORY

PSALM 24

v. 1 THE (1) earth is the LORD'S, and the fullness thereof; the world, and they who dwell therein.

(l) earth is the LORD,
(l) 1 Cor.10:26,28

v.26 For the earth is the Lord's, and the fullness thereof.
v.28 But if any man say unto you This is offered in sacrifice unto idols, eat not for his sake that showed it, and for conscience sake; for the earth is the Lord's and the fullness thereof

v.2 For he hath (m) founded it upon the seas, and established it upon the (n) floods.

(m) founded
(m) Ps.89:11
(n) flood
(n) lit. rivers

Ps.89:11

v.11 The heavens are thine; the earth also is thine; as for the world and the fullness thereof, thou hast founded them.

lit. rivers

v.3 1 (0) Who shall ascend into the hill of the Lord? Or who shall stand in his holy place?

(o) who shall ascend
(o) Ps.15:1-5

v.1 Lord, who shall abide in thy tabernacle? Who shall dwell in thy holy hill?
v.2 He that walketh uprightly, and worketh righteousness, and speaketh the trust in his heart.
v.3 He that backbiteth not with his tongue, nor doeth evil to his neighbor, nor taketh up a reproach against his neighbor,
v.4 In whose eyes a vile person is |despised|, but he honoreth them who fear the Lord; he that sweareth to his own hurt, and changeth not;
v.5 He that putteth not out his money to | interest |, nor taketh reward against the innocent. He that doeth these things shall never be moved.

v 4 He who hath clean hands, and a (p) pure heart, who hath not lifted up his soul unto vanity, nor sworn deceitfully.

(p) pure heart,
(p) Mt. 5:8

Mt. 5:8

v. 8 **Blessed are the pure in heart; for they shall see God.**

v.5 He shall receive the blessing from the Lord, and righteousness from the God of his salvation.
v.6 This is the generation of them who seek him, who seek thy face, O Jacob. Selah.

[vv.3-6]—it is a question of worthiness, and no one is worthy but the Lamb [cp. Dan.7:13-14;Mt.25:31; Rev.5:1-10.

v.7 (q) Lift up your heads, O ye gates; and be ye lifted up, ye everlasting doors; and the (r) King of glory shall come in.

(q) Lift up
(q) Isa.26:2
(r) King of glory
(r) 1 Cor.2:8

Isa.26:2

v.2 Open ye the gates, that the righteous nation that keepeth the truth may enter in.

1 Cor.2:8

v.8 Which none of the princes of this | age | knew ; for had they known it, they would not have crucified the Lord of glory.

v. 8 Who is the King of glory? The Lord strong and mighty, the Lord mighty in (s) battle

(s) battle
(s) Rev.19:13-16

v.13 And he was clothed with a vesture dipped in blood; and his name is called The Word of God.
v.14 And the armies that were in heaven followed him upon white horses, clothed in fine linen, white and clean.
v.15 And out of his mouth goeth a sharp sword, that with it he should smite the nations, and he shall rule them with a rod of iron; and he treadeth the winepress of the fierceness and wrath of mighty God.
v.16 And he hath on his vesture and on his thigh a name written, KING OF KINGS, AND LORD OF LORDS.

v.9 Lift up your heads, O ye gates; even lift them up, ye everlasting doors; and the King of glory shall come in.

v.10 Who is the (t) King of glory? The LORD of hosts, he is the King of glory. Selah.

Summary: (1) Christ shall rule the earth [vv.1-2]
(2) Christ alone is worthy to rule the earth. [vv. 3-6]
(3) Worthy is the Lamb. Dan.7:13-14; Mt. 25:31; Rev.5:1-10 [vv. 7-10]

Dan.7:13-14

v.13 I saw in the night vision, and, behold, one like the Son of man came with the clouds of heaven, and came to the Ancient of days, and they brought him near before him.

v.14 And there was given him dominion, and glory, and a kingdom, that all people, nations, and languages should serve him; his dominion is an everlasting dominion, which shall not pass away, and his kingdom that which shall not be destroyed.

Mt. 25:31

v.31 **When the Son of man shall come in his glory, and all the holy angels with him, then shall he sit upon the throne of his glory.**

Rev.5: 1-10

v.1 And I saw in the right hand of him that sat on the throne a |scroll| written within and on the | back |, sealed with seven seals.

v.2 And I saw a strong angel proclaiming with a loud voice, Who is worthy to open the | scroll |, and to loose the seals?

v.3 And no man in heaven, nor in earth, neither under the earth, was able to open the | scroll |, neither to look on it.

v.4 And I wept much, because no man was found worthy to open and to read the scroll, neither to look on it.
v.5 And one of the elders saith unto me, Weep not; behold, the Lion of the tribe of Judah, the Root of David, hath prevailed to open the | scroll |, and loose its seven seals.
v.6 And I beheld and, lo, in the midst of the throne and of the four | living creatures |, stood a Lamb as though it had been slain, having seven horns and seven eyes, which are the seven spirits of God sent forth into all the earth.
v.7 And he came and took the | scroll | out of the right hand of him that sat upon the throne.
v.8 And when he had taken the | scroll |, the four | living creatures | and four and twenty elders fell down before the Lamb, having every one them harps, and golden | bowls | full of | incense |, which are the prayers of saints.
v.9 And they sang a new song, saying, Thou art worthy to take the | scroll |, and to open its seals; for thou wast slain, and hast redeemed us to God by thy blood out of every kindred, and tongue, and people, and nation;
v.10 And hast made us unto our God | a kingdom of | priests, and we shall reign on the earth.

v.10 Who is this King of glory? The Lord of hosts, he is the King of glory. Selah.

(t) King of glory
(t) Christ (second advent): vv. 7-10; Ps.50:3
(Dt.30:3; Acts1:11, note)

Ps. 50:3

v. 3 Our God shall come, and shall not keep silence; a fire shall devour before him, and it shall be very tempestuous round about him.

Dt.30 :1

v. 1 And it shall come to pass, when all these things are come upon thee, the blessing and the curse, which I have set before thee, and shalt call them to mind among all the nations, to which the Lord thy God hath driven thee,

Acts 1:11

v. 11 Who also said, ye men of Galilee, why stand ye gazing up into heaven? This same Jesus, who is taken up from you into heaven, shall come in like manner as ye have seen him go into heaven.

Note:

This promised return of Christ is a prominent theme in The Acts, Epistles, and The Revelation.

THE LORD'S SERVANT

JOY OF CHRIST IN RESSURECTION

PSALM 40

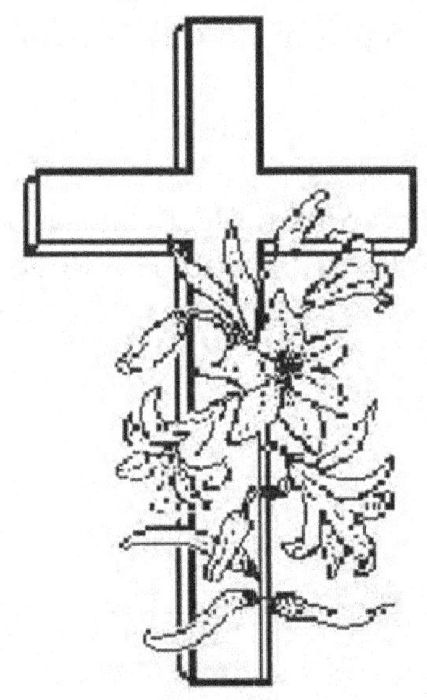

v.1 1I WAITED patiently for the LORD, and he inclined unto me,
and heard my cry.
v.2 He brought me up also out of (k) an horrible pit, out of the
miry clay, and set my feet upon a rock, and established my
goings.

(k) an horrible pit,
(k) lit. a pit of noise

v.3 And he hath put a new song in my mouth, even praise unto God; many shall see it, and (l) fear, and shall trust in the Lord.

(l) fear,
(l) Ps.19:9, note

Ps.19:9

v.9 The fear of the Lord is clean, enduring forever; the |ordinances| of the Lord are true and righteous altogether.

Note: 2 (19:9) "The fear of the Lord" is an O. T. expression meaning reverential trust, including the hatred of evil.

v.4 Blessed is that man who maketh the Lord his (m) trust, and respecteth not the proud, nor such as turn aside to lies.

(m) trust,
(m) Ps.2:12, note

v.12 Kiss the Son, lest with he be angry, and ye perish from the way, when his wrath is perish from the way, when his wrath is kindled but a little. Blessed are all they who put their trust in him.

Note: 1 (2:12) Trust is the characteristic O. T., word for the N. T. "faith," and "believe." It occurs 152 times in the O.T., and is the rendering of Hebrew words signifying to take refuge (e. g. Ruth 2:12); to lean on (e. g. Ps. 56:3); to roll on (e. g. Ps. 22:8); to wait for (e. g. Job. 35;14)

v.5 Many, O Lord, my God, are thy wonderful works which thou hast done, and thy thoughts which are (n) |toward us | ; they cannot be reckoned up in order unto thee. If I would declare and speak of them, they are more than can be numbered.

(n) | toward us | ;
(n) KJV to us-ward

Verses 3-5 are His resurrection testimony, "His new song."

v.6 (o) Sacrifice and offering thou didst not desire; mine ears hast thou (p) opened; burnt offering and sin offering hast thou not required.

(o) sacrifice
(o) vv. 6-8;Heb.10:5-9
(p) opened;
(p) cp.Ex.21:6

v.6 (o) Sacrifice and offering thou didst not desire; mine ears hast thou (p) opened; burnt offering and sin offering hast thou not required.
v.7 Then said I, Lo, I come; in the volume of the book it is written of me,
v.8 I delight to do thy (q) will, O my God; yea, (r) thy law is within my heart.

Heb. 10:5-9

v. 5 Wherefore, when he cometh into the world, he saith, Sacrifice and offering thou wouldest not, but a body hast thou prepared me;
v. 6 In burnt offerings and sacrifices for sin thou hast had no pleasure.
v.7 Then said I, Lo, I come (in the volume of the book it is written of me) to do thy will, O God.
v.8 Above, when he said, Sacrifice, and offering, and burnt offerings, and offering for sin thou wouldest not, neither hast pleasure in them, which are offered by the law,
v. 9 Then said he Lo, I come to do thy will, O God. He taketh away the first, that he may establish the second;

(p) opened; Ex.21:6

v.6 Then his master shall bring him unto the judges. He shall also bring him to the door, or unto the door post; and his master shall bore his ear through with an awl, and he shall serve him forever.

v.7 Then said I, Lo, I come; in the volume of the book it is written of me,
v.8 I delight to do thy (q) will O my God; yea, (r) thy law is within my heart.

(q) will
(q) Mt.26:39;Jn.4:34;6:38;Heb.10:7
(r) thy law is within my heart.
(r) Law (of Moses): v.8;Ps.78:10.(Ex.19:1Gal.3:24)

v.39 And he went a little further, and fell on his face, and prayed, saying, **O my Father, if it be possible, let this cup pass from me; nevertheless, not as I will, but as thou wilt.**

See the above v.8

Jn.4:34

v.34 Jesus saith unto them, **My | food | is to do the will of him that sent me, and to finish his work.**

Jn.6 :38

v.38 **For I came down from heaven, not do mine own will but the will of him who sent me.**

Heb. 10:7

v.7 Then said I, Lo I come (in volume of the book it is written of me) to do thy will, O God.

Ps. 78 :10

v.10 They kept not the covenant of God, and refused to walk in his law,

Ex.19 :1

v.1 In the third month, when the children of Israel were gone forth out of the land of Egypt, the same day came they into the wilderness of Sinai.

Gal. 3:24

v.24 Wherefore, the law was our schoolmaster to bring us unto Christ, that we might be justified by faith.

v.9 I have preached righteousness in the great congregation; lo, I have not (s) | restrained | my lips, O Lord, thou knowest.

(s) | restrained |
(s) | refrained KJV

v.10 I have not hidden thy righteousness within my heart; I have (t) declared thy faithfulness and thy salvation. I have not concealed thy loving-kindness and thy truth from the great congregation.

(t) declare thy faithfulness
(t) Acts 20:20,27

v. 20 And how I kept back nothing that was profitable unto you, but have shown you, and have taught you publicly, and from house to house,
v, 27 For I have not shunned to declare unto you all the counsel of God.

v.11 Withhold not thou thy tender mercies from me, O Lord; let thy loving—kindness and thy truth continually preserve me.

v.12 For innumerable evils have compassed me about. Mine iniquities have taken hold upon me, so that I am not able to look up. They are more than the hairs of mine head; therefore, my heart failed me.
v.13 (u) Be pleased, O Lord, to deliver me; O Lord, make haste to help me.

(u) Be pleased, O Lord, to deliver me
(u) vv.13-17;cp.Ps.70:1-5

v.13 (u) Be pleased, O Lord, to deliver me, O Lord, make haste to help me.
v.14 Let them be ashamed and confounded together who seek after my soul to destroy it; let them be driven backward and put to shame who wish me evil.
v.15 Let them be desolate for a reward of their shame, who say unto me, Aha, aha.
v.16 Let all those who seek thee rejoice and be glad in thee; let such as love thy salvation say continually, The Lord be magnified.
v.17 But I am poor and needy; (v) yet the Lord thinketh upon me. Thou art my help and my deliverer; (a) no tarrying, O my God.

Ps.70 :1-5

v.1 MAKE haste, O God, to deliver me; make haste to help me,
v.2 Let them be ashamed and confounded that seek my soul; let them be turned backward, and put to confusion, that desire my hurt.
v.3 Let them be turned back for a reward of their shame that say, Aha, aha.
v.4 Let all those who seek thee rejoice and be glad in thee ; and let such as love thy salvation say continually, Let God be magnified.
v.5 But I am poor and needy; make haste unto me, O God. Thou art my help and my deliverer; O Lord, make no tarring.

v.14 Let them be ashamed and confounded together who seek after my soul to destroy it; let them be driven backward and put to shame who wish me evil.
v.15 Let them be desolate for a reward of their shame, who say unto me, Aha, aha.
v.16 Let all those who seek thee rejoice and be glad in thee, let such as love thy salvation say continually, The LORD be magnified.
v.17 But I am poor and needy; (v) yet the Lord thinketh upon me. Thou art my deliverer; (a) make no tarrying, O my God.

(v) yet the Lord thinketh upon me
(v) 1 Pet.5:7
(a) make no tarrying
(a) Ps.70:5

1 Pet.5:7

v.7 Casting all your care upon him; for he careth for you.

Ps.70:5

v.5 But I am poor and needy; make haste unto me, O God. Thou art my help and my deliverer; O LORD, make no tarrying. 1(40:1) The 40th Psalm speaks of Messiah the LORD'S Servant obedient unto death. The Psalm begins with the joy of Christ in resurrection (vv. 1-2). He has been in the horrible pit of the grave but has been brought up. Verses 3-5 are His resurrection testimony, His "new song." Verses 6-8 are retrospective. When sacrifice and offering had become abominable because of the wickedness of the people (Isa.1:10-15), then the obedient Servant came to make the pure offering (vv.7-17;Heb.10:5-17).

BETRAYAL OF THE SON OF MAN

PSALM 41

v.1 BLESSED is he that considereth the (b) poor; the LORD will deliver him in time of trouble.

(b) poor
(b) lit. the weak or sick;Prov.14:21

Prov.14:21

v.21 He that despiseth his neighbor sinneth; but he that hath mercy on the poor, happy is he.

v.2 The Lord will preserve him, and keep him alive; and he shall be blessed upon the earth, and thou wilt not deliver him unto the will of his enemies.
v.3 The Lord will strengthen him upon the bed of languishing; thou wilt make all his bed in his sickness.
v.4 I said, LORD, be merciful unto me, (c) heal my soul; for I have sinned against thee.

(c) heal my soul
(c) Ps. 6:2; 147:3;2 Chr.30:20

Ps. 6:2

v.2 Have mercy upon me, O LORD; for I am weak. O LORD, heal me; for my bones are vexed.

Ps.147:3

v.3 He healeth the broken in heart, and bindeth up their wounds.

2 Chr.30:20

v.20 And the LORD hearkened to Hezekiah, and healed the people.

v.5 Mine enemies speak evil of me, When shall he die, and his name perish?
v.6 And if he come to see me, he speaketh vanity; his heart gathereth iniquity to itself; when he goeth abroad, he telleth it.
v.7 All who hate me whisper together against me; against me do they devise my hurt.
v.8 (d) An evil disease, say they, cleaveth (e) |closely to| him; and now that he lieth down, he shall rise up no more.

(d) An evil disease
(d) lit. A thing of Belial
(e) closely to
(e) KJV fast unto

v.9 1 Yea, (f) mine own familiar friend. in whom I (g) trusted, who did eat of my bread, hath lifted up his heel against me.

(f) mine own familiar friend
(f) Ps. 55:12-14; Mt. 26:14-16, 21-25,47-50;
Jn.13:18,-21-30;Acts 1:16-17
(g) trusted
(g) See Ps.2:12,note
See Messianic Psalm Ps.2:2,note

Ps. 55:12-14

v.12 For it was not an enemy that reproached me; then I could have borne it Neither was it he that hated me that did magnify himself against me; then I would have hidden myself from him;
v.13 But it was thou, a man mine equal, my guide, and |my familiar friend|.
v.14 We took sweet counsel together, and walked unto the house of God in company.

Mt. 26:14-16

v.14 Then one of the twelve, called Judas Iscariot, went unto the chief priests,
v.15 And said unto them, What will ye give me, and I will deliver him unto you? And they |bargained| with him for thirty pieces of silver.
v.16 And from that time he sought opportunity to betray him.
v.21 And as they did eat, he said, **Verily I say unto you that one of you shall betray me.**
v.22 And they were exceedingly sorrowful, and began every one of them to say unto him, Lord, is it I ?
v.23 And he answered and said, **He that dippeth his hand with me in the dish, the same shall betray me.**
v.24 **The Son of man goeth as it is written of him; but woe unto that man by whom the Son of man is betrayed ! It had been been good for that man if he had not been born.**
v.25 Then Judas, who betrayed him, answered and said, Master, is it I ? He said unto him, **Thou hast said.**
v.47 And while he yet spoke, lo, Judas, one of the twelve, came, and with him a great multitude with swords and |clubs|, from the chief priests and elders of the people.

v.48 Now he that betrayed him gave them a sign, saying, Whomsoever I shall kiss, that same is he; hold him fast.

v.49 And forthwith he came to Jesus, and said, Hail, master; and kissed him.

v.50 And Jesus said unto him, **Friend, why art thou come?** Then came they, and laid hands on Jesus, and took him.

Jn.13:18-21-30

v.18 **I speak not of you all (I know whom I have chosen), but that the scripture may be fulfilled, He that eateth bread with me hath lifted up his heel against me.**

v.21 When Jesus had thus said, he was troubled in spirit, and testified, and said, **Verily, verily, I say unto you that one of you shall betray me.**

v.22 Then the disciples looked one on another, doubting of whom he spoke.

v.23 Now there was leaning on Jesus' bosom one of his disciples, whom Jesus loved.

v.24 Simon Peter, therefore, beckoned to him, that he should ask who it should be of whom he spoke.

v.25 He, then, lying on Jesus' breast, saith unto him, Lord, who is it ?

v.26 Jesus answered, **He it is to whom I shall give a sop, when I have dipped it.** And when he had dipped the sop, he gave it to Judas Iscariot, the son of Simon.

v.27 And after the sop Satan entered into him. Then said Jesus unto him,

v.28 Now no man at the table knew for what intent he spoke this unto him.

v.29 For some of them thought, because Judas had the bag, that Jesus had said unto him, Buy those things that we have need of for the feast; or, that he should give something to the poor.

v.30 He, then, having received the sop, went immediately out; and it was night.

Acts 1:16-17

v.16 Men and brethren, this scripture must needs have been fulfilled, which the Holy | Spirit | , by the mouth of David, spoke before concerning Judas who was guide to them that took Jesus.
v.17 For he was numbered with us, and had obtained part in this ministry.

v.10 But thou, O LORD, be merciful unto me, and raise me up, that I may requite them.
v.11 By this I know that thou favorest me, because mine enemy doth not triumph over me.
v.12 And as for me, thou upholdest me in mine integrity, and (h) settest me before thy face forever.

(h) settest me before thy face;
(h) Job.36:7;Ps.21:6; 34:15

Job.36 :7

v.7 He withdraweth not his eyes from the righteous; but with kings are they on the throne; yea, he doth establish them forever, and they are exalted.

Ps.21:6

v.6 For thou hast made him most blessed forever; thou hast made him exceeding glad with thy countenance.

Ps.34:15

v.15 The eyes of the LORD are upon the righteous, and his ears are open unto their cry.

v.13 (i) Blessed be the Lord God of Israel from everlasting, and to everlasting. Amen, and Amen.

(i) Blessed be the Lord God;
(i) Cp.Ps.106:48

Ps. 106:48

v.48 Blessed be the Lord God of Israel from everlasting to everlasting; and let all the people say, Amen. Praise ye the Lord.

The experience is prophetic of the experience of our Lord Jesus who was forsaken by a close associate in (Jn.13:18-19).

Jn.13:18-19

v.18 **I speak not of you all (I know whom I have chosen), but that the scripture may be fulfilled, He that eateth bread with me hath lifted up his heel against me.**
v.19 **Now I tell you before it come, that, when it is come to pass; ye may believe that I am he.**

HIS ADVENT IN GLORY

PSALM 45

To the chief Musician upon (v) Sho-shan'nim, for the sons of Korah, Mas'chil, A Song of loves

(v) Sho-shan'nim
(v) Lillies

v.1 MY heart is (w) | overflowing with | a good matter; I speak of the things which I have made touching the king. MY tongue is the pen of a ready writer.

(w) | overflowing with |
(w) KJV inditing

v.2 Thou art fairer than the children of men; (x) grace is poured into thy lips; therefore God hath blessed thee forever

(x) grace is poured into thy lips
(x) Lk.4;22

Lk.4:22

v.22 And all bore him witness, and wondered at the gracious words which proceeded out of his mouth. And they said, Is not this Joseph's son?

v.3 Gird thy sword upon thy thigh, O most (a) mighty, with thy (g) glory and thy majesty.

(a) mighty
(a) Isa.9:6
(g) glory and thy majesty
(g) Jude 25

Isa.9:6

v.6 For unto us a child is born, unto us a son is given, and the government shall be upon his shoulder; and his name shall be called Wonderful, Counselor, The Mighty God, The Everlasting Father, The Prince of Peace.

Jude 25

v.25 To the only wise God, our Savior, be glory and majesty, dominion and power, both now and ever. Amen.

v.4 And in thy majesty ride prosperously because of trust and meekness and righteousness; and thy right hand shall teach thee (c) | awe-inspiring | things.

(c) | awe-inspiring |
(c) KJV terrible

v.5 Thine arrows are sharp in the heart of the king's enemies, whereby the people fall under thee.
v.6 (d) Thy throne, O God, is forever and ever; the (e) scepter of thy kingdom is a right scepter.

(d) thy throne,
(d) Ps.93:2; Heb.1:8
(e) scepter of thy kingdom
(e) Num.24:17

Ps.93:2

v.2 Thy throne is established of old; thou art from everlasting.

Heb. 1:8

v.8 But unto the Son he saith. Thy throne, O God, is forever and ever; a scepter of righteousness is the scepter of thy kingdom.

Num. 24:17

v.17 I shall see him, but not now: I shall behold him, but not |near|: there shall come a Star out of Jacob, and a Scepter shall rise out of Israel, and shall smite the corners of Moab, and destroy all the children of Sheth.

v.7 Thou lovest righteousness, and hatest wickedness; therefore God, thy God, hath (f) anointed thee with the oil of (g) gladness above thy fellows.

(f) anointed
(f) Ps.2:2
(g) gladness
(g) Ps. 21:6; Heb. 1:8-9

Ps.2:2

v.2 The kings of the earth set themselves, and the rulers take counsel together, against the LORD, and against his anointed, saying,

Ps.21:6

v.6 For thou hast made him most blessed forever; thou hast made him exceeding glad with thy countenance.

Heb. 1:8-9

v. 8 But unto the Son he saith, Thy throne, O God, is forever and ever; a scepter of righteousness is the scepter of thy kingdom.

v.9 Thou hast loved righteousness, and hated iniquity; therefore, God, even thy God, hath anointed thee with the oil of gladness above thy fellows.

v.8 All thy garments (h) smell of myrrh, and aloes, and cassia, out of the ivory palaces, whereby they have made thee glad.

(h) smell of myrrh
(h) Song 1:12-13

v.12 While the king sitteth at his table, my spikenard sendeth forth the |fragrance| thereof.

v.13 A bundle of myrrh is my well-beloved unto me; he shall lie all night |between| my breasts.

v.9 (i) Kings' daughters were among thy honorable women; upon thy (j) right hand did stand the queen in gold of O'phir.

(i) Kings' daughters
(i) Song 6:8
(j) right hand
(j) 1 Ki.2:19

v. 8 There threescore queens, and fourscore concubines, and virgins without number.

I Ki.2:19

v.19 Bath-sheba, therefore, went unto king Solomon, to speak unto him for Adoni'jah. And the king rose up to meet her, and bowed himself unto her, and sat down on the throne, and caused a seat to be set for the king's mother; and she sat on his right hand.

v.10 Hearken, O daughter, and consider, and incline thine ear; (k) forget also thine own people, and thy father's house;

(k) forget also thine own people
(k) Cp. Dt.21:13;Ruth 1:16

Dt.21:13

v.13 And she shall put the raiment of her captivity from off her, and shall remain in thine house and bewail her father and her mother a full month; and after that thou shalt go in unto her, and be her husband, and she shall be thy wife.

Ruth 1:16

v.16 And Ruth said, Entreat me not to leave thee, or to |turn away| from following after thee; for |where| thou goest, I will go; and where thou lodgest; I will lodge: thy people shall be my people, and thy God, my God.

v.11 So shall the king greatly desire thy beauty; (l) for he is thy Lord, and worship thou him.

(l) for he is thy Lord
(l) Ps.95:6; Isa.54:5

Ps. 95:6

v. 6 Oh, come, let us worship and bow down; let us kneel before the LORD our maker.

Isa.54:5

v.5 For thy Maker is thine husband; the LORD of hosts is his name; and thy Redeemer, the Holy One of Israel; The God of the whole earth shall he be called.

v.12 And the daughter of Tyre shall be there with a gift; even the rich among the people shall entreat thy favor.
v.13 The king's (m) daughter is all glorious within; her clothing is of wrought gold.

(m) The king's daughter-cp. Rev.19:7-8

Rev.19:7-8

v.7 Let us be glad and rejoice, and give honor to him; for the marriage of the Lamb is come, and his wife hath made herself ready.
v.8 And to her was granted that she should be arrayed in fine linen, clean and white; for the fine linen is the | righteousness | of saints.

v.14 (n) She shall be brought unto the king in raiment of needlework; the virgins, her companions who follow her, shall be brought unto thee.

(n) She shall be
(n) Song 1:4

(The Shulamite speaks)

v.4 Draw me after thee. The king hath brought me into his chambers.

v.15 With gladness and rejoicing shall they be brought; they shall enter into the king's palace.
v.16 Instead of thy fathers shall be thy children, whom thou mayest make princes in all the earth.
v.17 (o) I will make thy name to be remembered in all generations; therefore shall the people praise thee forever and ever.

(o) I will
(o) Mal.1:11

Mal. 1:11

v.11 For from the rising of the sun even unto the going down of the same, my name shall be great among the |nations|, and in every place incense shall be offered unto my name, and a pure offering; for my name shall be great among the |nations|, saith the LORD of hosts.

1(45:1) This great Psalms of the king, with Ps. 46-47, obviously looks forward to His advent in glory. The reference in Heb. 1:8-9 is not so much to the anointing as an event (Mt.3:16-17), as to the permanent state of the King (cp. Isa.11:1-2). The divisions are: (1) the supreme beauty of the King (vv. 1-2); (2) the coming of the King in glory (vv. 3-5; Rev.19 :11-21); (3) the Deity of the King and the character of His reign (vv.6-7; Isa.11:1-5; Heb.1:8-9); (4) as associated with Him in earthly rule, the queen is presented (vv.9-13); (5) the virgin companions of the queen, who would seem to be the Jewish remnant (see Rom.11;5, note; Rev.14:1-4), are next seen (vv. 14-15); and (6) the Psalm closes with a reference to the earthly fame of the King (vv. 16-17).

THE JOY OF ISRAEL IN THE KINGDOM

PSALM 68

v.1 1 Let God arise, let his enemies be scattered; let them also that hate him flee before him.

v.2 As smoke is driven away, so drive them away; (i) as wax melteth before the fire, so let the wicked perish at the presence of God.

(i) as wax melteth
(i) Ps. 97:5; Mic.1:4

Ps. 97:5

v.5 The hills melted like wax at the presence of the LORD, at the presence of the Lord of the whole earth.

Mic.1:4

v. 4 And the mountains shall be melted under him, and the valleys shall be cleft, like wax before the fire, and like the waters that are poured down a steep place.

v.3 But (j) let the righteous be glad; let them rejoice before God, yea, let them exceedingly rejoice.

(j) let the righteous be glad
(j) Ps.32:11;58:10; 64:10

Ps. 32:11

v. 11 Be glad in the LORD, and rejoice, ye righteous; and shout for joy, all ye that are upright in heart.

Ps. 58:10

v. 10 The righteous shall rejoice when he seeth the vengeance; he shall wash his feet in the blood of the wicked,

Ps. 64:10

v.10 The righteous shall be glad in the LORD, and shall trust in him; and all the upright in heart shall glory.

v.4 Sing unto God, sing praises to his name; (k) extol him who rideth upon the heavens (l) by his name, (m) | which is the LORD | , and rejoice before him.

(k) extol him who rideth upon the heavens;
(k) 68:33; Dt.33:26
(l) by his name;
(l) Ex.6:3
(m) which is the LORD;
(m) KJV JAH

Ps.68:33

v.33 To him who rideth upon the heavens of heavens, which were of old; lo, he doth send out his voice, and that a (h) mighty voice.

Dt.33:26

v.26 There is none like unto the God of Jeshu'run, who rideth upon the heaven in thy help, and in his excellency on the sky.

Ex.6:3

v. 3 And I appeared unto Abraham, unto Isaac, and Jacob, by the name of God Almighty, but by my name JEHOVAH was I not known to them.

v.5 A (n) father of the fatherless, and a judge of the widows, is God in his holy habitation.

(n) father of the fatherless
(n) Ps. 10:14,18;146:9

Ps.10:14,18

v. 14 Thou hast seen it; for thou beholdest mischief and spite, to requite it with thy hand. The poor committeth himself unto thee; thou art the helper of the fatherless.
v.18 To judge the fatherless and the oppressed, that the man of the earth may no more oppress.

Ps.146:9

v.9 The LORD preserveth the | sojourners | ; he relieveth the fatherless and widow, but the way of the wicked he turneth upside down.

v.6 (o) God setteth the solitary in families; (p) he bringeth out those who are bound with chains, but the rebellious dwell in a dry land.

(o) God setteth
(o) Ps. 113:9
(p) he bringeth out those
(p) Ps. 107:10, 14;146:7 Acts12:7

Ps.113:9

v.9 He maketh the barren woman to keep house, and to be a joyful mother of children. Praise ye the LORD.

Ps.107:10,14

v.10 Such as sit in darkness and in the shadow of death, being bound in affiction and iron,
v.14 He brought them out of darkness and the shadow of death, and broke their bands in sunder.

Ps. 146:7

v.7 Who executeth |justice| for the oppressed; who giveth food to the hungry. The LORD looseth the prisoners;

Acts 12:7

v.7 And, behold, |an| angel of the Lord came upon him, and a light |shone| in the prison; and he smote, Peter on the side, and raised him up, saying, Arise quickly. And his chains fell off from his hands.

v.7 O God, when thou wentest forth before thy people, when thou didst march through the wilderness, Selah,
v.8 The earth shook, the heavens also dropped at the presence of God; even Siani itself was moved at the presence of God, the God of Israel.
v.9 Thou, O God, didst send a plentiful rain, whereby thou didst confirm thine inheritance, when it was weary.
v.10 Thy congregation hath dwelt therein; (q) thou, O God, hast prepared of thy goodness for the poor.

(q) Thou, O God,
(q) Ps.74:19; Dt.26:5-9

Ps. 74:19

v.19 Oh, deliver not the soul of thy turtledove unto the multitude of the wicked; forget not the congregation of thy poor forever.

Dt.26:5-9

v.5 And thou shalt speak and say before the LORD thy God, A Syrian ready to perish was my father, and he went down into Egypt and sojourned there with a few, and became there a nation, great, mighty, and populous.

v.6 And the Egyptians |badly treated| us, and afflicted us, and laid upon us hard bondage;

v.7 And when we cried unto the LORD God of our fathers, the LORD heard our voice, and looked on our affliction, and our labor, and our oppression.

v. 8 And the LORD brought us forth out of Egypt with a mighty hand, and with an outstretched arm, and with |awe-inspiring terror|, and with signs, and with wonders;

v.9 And he hath brought us into this place, and hath given us this land, even a land that floweth with milk and honey.

v.11 The Lord gave the (r) word; great was the company of those who published it.

(r) word
(r) Inspiration:v.11; Isa.6:5 (Ex.4:15; 2 Tim.3:16)

Isa.6:5

v.5 Then said I, Woe is me! For I am undone, because I am a man of unclean lips, and I dwell in the midst of a people of unclean lips; for mine eyes have seen the king, the LORD of hosts.

Ex. 4:15

v.15 And thou shalt speak unto him, and put words in his mouth; and I will be with thy mouth, and with his mouth, and will teach you what ye shall do.

2 Tim. 3:16

v.16 But shun profane and vain babblings; for they will increase unto more ungodliness.

v.12 Kings of armies did flee apace; and she that tarried at home divided the spoil.
v.13 Though ye (s) |lie| among the (t) |sheepfolds|, yet shall ye be like the wings of a dove covered with silver, and her feathers with yellow gold.

(s) |lie|
(s) KJV have lien
(t) |sheepfolds|
(t) KJV pots

v.14 When the Almighty scattered kings therein, it was white like snow in Zalmon.
v.15 The hill of God is like the hill of Bashan, an high hill, like the hill of Bashan.
v.16 Why leap ye, ye high hills? This is the hill which God desireth to dwell in; yea, the LORD will dwell in it forever.
v.17 The chariots of God are twenty thousand, even thousands of (u) angels; the Lord is among them, as in Sinai, in the holy place.

(u) angels
(u) Heb.1:4, note

v.4 Being made so much better than the angels, as he hath by inheritance obtained a more excellent name than they.

Note 1(1:4) Angel, Summary:

Angel, i. e. "messenger," used of God, of men, and of order of created spiritual beings whose chief attributes are strength and wisdom (2 Sam.14:20; Ps.103:20; 104:4). In the O. T. the expression "the angel of the LORD" (sometimes "of God") usually implies the presence of Deity in angelic form (Gen. 16:1-13; 21: 17-19;22:11-16; 31:11-13; Ex.3:2-4; Jud. 2:1; 6:12-16; 13:3-22) See Jud. 2:1, note cp. Mal. 3:1, note. The word "angel" used of men in Lk.7:24, Gk.; Jas.2:25, Gk.; Rev. 1:20; 2:1, 8, 12,18; 3:1,7,14. In Rev.8:3-5 Christ is evidently meant. Sometimes "angel" is used of the spirit of man (Acts 12:15). Though angels are spirits (Ps.104:4; Heb. 1:14), power is given them to become visible in the semblance of human form (Gen.19:1, cp. v. 5; Ex.3:2; Num.22:22-31; Jud. 2:1; 6:11,22; 13:3,6; 1 Chr.21:6,20; Mt.1:20; Lk.1:26; Jn.20:12; Acts 7:30; 12:7-8,ect.). The word is always used in the masculine gender, though sex, in the human sense, is never ascribed to angels (Mt. 22:30; Mk.12:25). They are exceedingly numerous (Ps.68:17; Mt. 26:53;Heb. 12:22; Rev. 5:11;7:11). Their power is inconceivable (2 Ki.19:19:35). Their place is about the throne of God (Rev.5:11;7:11) Their relation to believers is that of "ministering spirits, sent forth to minister for them who shall be heirs of salvation," and this ministry has reference largely to the physical safety and well-being of children of God (1 ki.19:5; Ps. 34:7; 91:11; Dan. 6:22; Mt. 2:13,19;4:11; Lk.2:43; Acts 5:19;12:7-10).Comparing Heb. 1:14 with Mt. 18:10 and Ps.91:11, it appears that this care for the heirs of salvation begins in infancy and continues through life. The angels observe us. (Eccl. 5:6;1Cor.4:9; Eph.3:10), a fact which should influence conduct. Man is made "a little lower than the angels," and in incarnation Christ took "for a little [time]" this lower place (Ps. 8:4-5; Heb.2:7, marg.) that He might lift the Christian into His own sphere above angels (Heb.2:9-10). The angels are to accompany Christ in His second advent (Mt. 25:31). To them will be committed the preparation of the judgment of individual Gentiles among the nations (see Mt. 13:30,39,41-42;25:32, note). The Kingdom Age is not to be subject to angels, but to Christ and those for whom He was made a little lower than the angels (Heb.2:7)

An archangel, Michael, is mentioned as having a particular relation to Israel and to the resurrections (Dan.10:13,21;12:1-2 1 Th.4:16; Jude 9). The only other angel whose name is revealed, Gabriel, was employed in the most distinguished services (Dan. 8:16; 9:21; Lk.1:9,26). In regard to fallen angels, two classes are mentioned :

(1) "The angels who kept not their first estate [place], but left their own habitation" and are chained under darkness, awaiting judgment (Jude 6:2 Pet.2:4; cp. Jn.5:22; 1Cor. 6:3). See Gen. 6:4, note. And

(2) the angels who are not bound, but go about doing the will of Satan (see Rev. 20:10, note). They may be identical with the demons (see Mt. 7:22,note). Everlasting fire is prepared for Satan and his angels (Mt. 25:41;Rev.20:10).

v.18 Thou hast ascended on high, thou hast led captivity (v) captive. Thou hast received (w) gifts for men, yea, for the rebellious also, that the LORD God might dwell among them.

(v) captive
(v) Eph.4:8
(w) gifts for men
(w)Acts2:4,33; 10:44-46;1 Cor.12:4-11;Eph.4:7-12

Eph. 4:8

v.8 Wherefore, he "saith," When he ascended up on high, he led captivity captive, and gave gifts onto men.

Acts 2:4,33

v.4 And they were all filled with the Holy | Spirit |, and began to speak with other tongues, as the Spirit gave them utterance.

v.33 Therefore, being by the right hand of God exalted, and having received from the Father the promise of the Holy | Spirit |, he hath shed forth this, which ye now see and hear.

Acts 10:44-46

v.44 While Peter yet spoke these words, the Holy | Spirit | fell on all them who heard the word.

v.45 And they of the circumcision who believed were astonished, as many as came with Peter, because on the Gentiles also was poured out the gift of the Holy | Spirit |.

v.46 For they heard them speak with tongues, and magnify God. Then answered Peter,

1Cor.12:4-11

v.4 Now there are diversities of gifts, but the same Spirit.

v.5 And there are differences of administrations, but the same Lord.

v.6 And there are diversities of operations, but it is the same God who worketh all in all.

v.7 But the manifestation of the Spirit is given to every man to profit.

v.8 For to one is given, by the Spirit, the word of wisdom to another, the word of knowledge by the same Spirit;

v.9 To another, faith by the same Spirit; to another, the gifts of healing by the same Spirit;

v.10 To another, the working of miracles; to another, prophecy; to another, discerning of spirits; to another, various kinds of tongues; to another, the interpretation of tongues.
v.11 But all these worketh that one and the | very same | Spirit, dividing to every man severally as he will.

Eph.4:7-12

v.7 But unto every one of us is given grace according to the measure of the gift of Christ.
v.8 Wherefore, he saith, When he ascended up on high, he led captivity captive, and gave gifts unto men.
v.9 (Now that he ascended, what is it but that he also descended first into the lower parts of the earth?
v.10 He that descended is the same also that ascended up far above all heavens, that he might fill all things).
v.11 And he gave some, apostles; and some, prophets; and some, pastors and teachers;
v.12 For the perfecting of the saints for the work of the ministry for edifying of the body of Christ,

v.19 Blessed be the Lord, who daily loadeth us with benefits, even the God of our salvation. Selah.
v.20 He who is our God is the God of salvation; and unto God, the Lord, belong the issues from death.
v.21 But God shall wound the head of his enemies, and the hairy scalp of such an one as goeth on still in his trespasses.
v.22 The Lord said, I will bring (x) again from Bashan, I will bring my people again from the depths of the sea,

(x) again from Bashan
(x) Dt.30:1-9

v.1 And it shall come to pass, when all these things are come upon thee, the blessing and the curse, which I have set before thee, and thou shalt call them to mind among all the nations, to which the LORD thy God hath driven thee, v.2 And shalt return unto the LORD thy God, and shalt obey his voice according to all that I command thee this day, thou and thy children, with all thine heart, and with all thy soul,

v.3 That then the LORD thy God will turn thy captivity, and have compassion upon thee, and will return and gather thee from all the nations where the LORD thy God hath scattered thee.

v.4 If any of thine be driven out unto the outmost parts of heaven, from there will the LORD thy God gather thee, and from there will he fetch thee.

v.5 And the LORD thy God will bring thee unto the land which thy fathers possessed, and thou shalt possess it; and he will do good, and multiply thee above thy fathers.

v. 6 And the LORD thy God will circumcise thine heart, and the heart of the seed, to love the LORD thy God with all thine heart, and with all thy soul, that thou mayest live.

v. 7 And the LORD thy God will put all these curses upon thine enemies, and on them who hate thee, who persecuted thee.

v.8 And thou shalt return and obey the voice of the LORD, and do all his commandments which I command thee this day.

v 9 And the LORD thy God will make thee plenteous in every work of thine hand, in the fruit of thy body, and in the fruit of thy cattle, and in the fruit of thy land, for good; for the LORD will again rejoice over thee for good, as he rejoiced over thy fathers,

v.23 That thy foot may be dipped in the blood of thine enemies, and the tongue of thy dogs in the same.

v.24 They have been thy goings, O God, even the goings of my God, my King, in the sanctuary.

v.25 The singers went before, the players on instruments followed after; among them were the damsels playing with timbrels.

v.26 Bless ye God in the congregations, even the Lord, (a) from the fountain of Israel.

(a) from the fountain of Israel
(a) Or ye that are the fountain of Israel

v.27 There are (b) little Benjamin with their ruler, the princes of Judah and their council, the princes of Zebu,lun, and the princes of Naph'tali.

(b) little Benjamin with their ruler
(b) I Sam. 9:21

I Sam. 9:21

v.21 And Saul answered and said, Am not I a Benjamite, of the smallest of the tribes of Israel, and my family the least of all the families of the tribe of Benjamin? |Why|, then, speakest thou so to me?

v.28 Thy God hath commanded thy strength; strengthen, O God, that which thou hast (c) wrought for us.

(c) wrought for us
(c) Isa.26:12

Isa.26:12

v.12 LORD, thou wilt ordain peace for us; for thou also hast wrought all our works in us.

v.29 Because of thy temple at Jerusalem shall kings bring (d) presents unto thee.

(d) presents unto thee
(d) Ps. 45:12;72:10

Ps.45:12

v.12 And the daughter of Tyre shall be there with a gift; even the rich among the people shall entreat thy favor.

Ps.72:10

v.10 The kings of Tar' shish and of the isles shall bring presents; the kings of Sheba shall offer gifts.

v.30 Rebuke the company of spearmen, the multitude of the bulls, with the calves of the people, till every one submit himself with pieces of silver; scatter thou the people who delight in war.
v.31 Princes shall come out of (e) Egypt; (f) Ethiopia shall soon stretch out her hands unto God.

(e) Egypt
(e) Isa.19:19-23
(f) Ethiopia
(f) Heb. Cush.
Zeph.3:10

Isa.19:19-23

v.19 In that day shall there be an altar of LORD in the midst of the land of Egypt, and a pillar at the border of it to the LORD.
v.20 And it shall be for a sign and for a witness unto the LORD of hosts in the land of Egypt; for they shall cry unto the LORD because of the oppressors, and he shall send them a savior, and a great one, and he shall deliver them.
v.21 And the LORD shall be known to Egypt, and the Egyptians shall know the LORD in that day, and shall do sacrifice and oblation yea, they shall vow a vow unto the LORD, and perform it.

v.22 And the LORD shall smite Egypt; he shall smite and heal it: and they shall return even to the LORD, and he shall be entreated by them, and shall heal them.

v.23 In that day shall there be a highway out Egypt to Assyria, and the Assyrian shall come into Egypt, and Egyptians shall serve with the Assyrians.

Zeph.3:10

v.10 From beyond the rivers of Ethiopia my suppliants, even the daughter of my dispersed, shall bring mine offering.

v.32 Sing unto God, ye (g) kingdoms of the earth; oh, sing praises unto the Lord, Selah,

(g) kingdoms of the earth;
(g) Ps. 67:3

Ps. 67:3

v.3 Let the people praise thee, O God; let all the people praise thee.

v.33 To him who rideth upon the heavens of heavens, which were of old; lo, he doth send out his voice, and that a (h) mighty voice.

(h) mighty voice
(h) Ps.46:6; Isa.30:30

Ps.46:6

v.6 The | nations | raged, the kingdoms were moved; he uttered his voice, the earth melted.

Isa.30:30

v.30 And the Lord shall cause his glorious voice to be heard,
and shall show the lighting down of his arm, with the
indignation of his anger, and with flame of a devouring
fire, with scattering, and tempest, and hailstones.

v.34 Ascribe ye strength unto God; his excellency is over Israel,
and his strength is in the clouds.
v.35 O God, thou art (i) |awe-inspiring| out of thy holy places;
the God of Israel is he who giveth strength and power unto
his people. Blessed be God.

(i) |awe-inspiring |
(i) KJV terrible. Ps.65:5

Ps.65:5

v.5 By |awesome| things in righteousness wilt thou
answer us, O God of our salvation, who art the
confidence of all the ends of the earth, and those who
are afar upon the sea;

HIS HUMILIATION AND REJECTION

PSALM 69

v.1 1Save me, O God; for the waters are come in unto my soul.

1(69:1)

v.2 I sink in deep mire, where there is no standing: I am come into deep waters, where the floods overflow me.
v.3 I am weary of my crying. My throat is dried; mine eyes fail while I wait for my God.
v.4 (k) They that hate me without a cause are more than the hairs of mine head; they that would destroy me, being mine enemies wrongfully, are mighty. Then I restored that which I took not away.

(k) they that hate me without cause
(k) Ps.35:19;Jn.15:25

Ps. 35:19

v.19 Let not those who are mine enemies wrongfully rejoice over me; neither let them wink with the eye who hate me without a cause.

Jn.15:25

v.25 **But this cometh to pass, that the word might be fulfilled that is written in their law, They hated me without cause.**

v.5 O God, thou knowest my foolishness, and my sins are not hidden from thee.
v.6 Let not them who wait on thee, O Lord God of hosts, be ashamed for (l) my sake; let not those who seek thee be confounded for my sake, O God of Israel.

(l) my sake
(l) Cp. 2 Sam.12:14

2 Sam. 12:14

v.14 Howbeit, because by this deed thou hast given great occasion to the enemies of the LORD to blaspheme, the child also that is born unto thee shall surely die.

v.7 Because for thy sake I have borne reproach; shame hath covered my face.
v.8 (m) I am become a stranger unto my brethren, and an alien unto my mother's children.

(m) I am become a stranger
(m) Jn.7:3-5

v.3 His brethren, therefore, said unto him, Depart from here, and go into Judea, that thy disciples also may see the works that thou doest.
v.4 For there is no man that doeth anything in secret, and he himself seeketh to be known openly. If thou do these things, show thyself to the world.
v.5 For neither did his brethren believe in him.

v.9 (n) For the zeal of thine house hath eaten me up; and the (o) reproaches of those who reproached thee are fallen upon me.

(n) For the zeal of thine house
(n) Jn.2:17
(o) reproach of those;
(o) Rom.15:3

Jn.2:17

v.17 And his disciples remembered that it was written, The zeal of thine house hath eaten me up.

Rom.15:3

v.3 For even Christ pleased not himself; but, as it is written, The reproaches of them that reproached thee fell on me.

v.10 When I wept, and chastened my soul with fasting, that was to my reproach.
v.11 I made sackcloth also my garment; and I became a proverb to them.
v.12 They that sit in the gate speak against me, and I was the song of the (p) drunkards.

(p) drunkards
(p) Job.30:9

v.9 And now am I their song, yea, I am their byword.

v.13 But as for me, my prayer is unto thee, O LORD, in an (q) acceptable time; O God, in the multitude of thy mercy hear me, in the truth of thy salvation.

(q) acceptable time
(q) Isa.49:8; 2Cor.6:2

Isa.49:8

v.8 Thus saith the LORD: In an acceptable time have I heard thee, and in a day of salvation have I helped thee; and I will preserve thee, and give thee for a covenant of the people, to establish the earth, to cause to inherit the desolate heritages,

2Cor.6:2

v.2 (For he saith, I have heard thee in a time accepted, and in the day of salvation have I |helped| thee; behold, now is the accepted time; behold, now is the day of salvation),

v.14 Deliver me out of the mire, and let me not sink; let me be delivered from those who hate me, and out of the deep waters.
v.15 Let not the waterflood overflow me, neither let the deep swallow me up, and let not the pit shut her mouth upon me.
v.16 Hear me, O LORD; for thy loving-kindness is good. Turn unto me according to the multitude of thy tender mercies.
v.17 And hide not thy face from thy servant; for I am in trouble. Hear me speedily.
v.18 Draw (a) |near| unto my soul, and (b) redeem me because of mine enemies.

(a) |near|
(a) KJV nigh
(b) redeem me
(b) Redemption (Kinsman type):v.18
Ps.71:23.(Gen.48:16;Isa.59:20,note)
See the above v.18

Ps.71:23

v.23 My lips shall greatly rejoice when I sing unto thee; and my soul, which thou hast redeemed.

Gen.48:16

v.16 |An angel| who redeemed me from all evil, bless the lads; and let my name be named on them, and the name of my fathers, Abraham and Isaac; and let them grow into a multitude in the midst of the earth.

Isa.59:20,note

v.20 And the Redeemer shall come to Zion, and unto those who turn from transgression in Jacob, saith the LORD.

Note: 1(59:20) Redemption, kinsman type, Summary: The goel, or kinsman-redeemer, is a beautiful type of Christ:

(1) The kinsman redemption was of persons and an inheritance (Lev.25:25,48;Gal.4:5; Eph.1:7,11,14).
(2) The redeemer must be a kinsman (Lev.25:48-49; Ruth 3:12-13, see v.9, note; Gal.4:4; Heb. 2:14-15)
(3) The redeemer must be able to redeem (Ruth 4:4-6; Jer.50:34; Jn.10:11,18).
(4) Redemption is effected by the goel paying the just demand in full (Lev.25:27; Gal.3:13; 1 Pet.1:18-19). See notes at Ex.6:6 and Rom.3:24.

v.19 Thou hast known my reproach, and my shame, and my dishonor; mine adversaries are all before thee.
v.20 Reproach hath broken my heart, and I am full of heaviness; and I looked for some to take pity, but there was none; and for comforters, but I found none.
v.21 They gave me also gall for my (c) |food|, and in my (d) thirst they gave me vingar to drink.

(c) |food|
(c) KJV meat
(d) thirst
(d) Mt.27:34,48 ;Lk.23:36;

Mt.27:34,48

v.34 They gave him vinegar to drink, mingled with gall; and when he had tasted it, he would not drink.
v.48 And straightway one of them ran, and took a sponge, and filled it with vinegar, and put it on a reed, and gave him to drink.

Lk.23:36

v.36 And the soldiers also mocked him, coming to him, and offering him vinegar,

v.22 (e) Let their table become a snare before them; and that which should have been for their welfare, let it become a trap.

(e) Let their table become snare before them
(e) Rom. 11:9-10

Rom.11:9-10

v.9 And David saith, Let their table be made a snare, and a trap, and a stumbling block, and a recompense unto them;
v.10 Let their eyes be darkened that they may not see, and bow down their back always.

v.23 Let their eyes be darkened, that they see not; and make their loins continually to shake.
v.24 Pour out thine indignation upon them, and let thy wrathful anger take hold of them.
v.25 Let their habitation be (f) desolate, and let none dwell in their tents.

(f) desolate,
(f) Acts 1:20;cp.Mt.23:38;Lk.13:35

Acts 1:20

v.20 For it is written in the book of Psalms, Let his habitation be desolate, and let no man dwell therein; and bishopric let another take.

Mt.23:38

v.38 **Behold, your house is left unto you desolate.**

Lk.13:35

v.35 **Behold, your houses left unto you desolate; and verily I say unto Ye shall not see me, until the time come when ye shall say, Blessed is he that cometh in the name of the Lord.**

v.26 For they persecute him whom thou hast (g) smitten, and they talk to the grief of those whom thou hast wounded.

(g) smitten,
(g) Isa.53:4;1Pet 2:24

Isa.53:4

v.4 Surely he hath borne our griefs, and carried our sorrows; yet we did esteem him stricken, smitten of God, and afflicted.

1 Pet. 2:24

v.24 Who his own self bore our sins in his own body on the tree, that we, being dead to sins, should live unto righteousness; by whose stripes ye were healed.

v.27 Add (h) iniquity unto their iniquity, and let them not come into thy righteousness.

(h) iniquity,
(h) Neh.4:5; Rom.1:28

Neh.4:5

v.5 And cover not their iniquity, and let not their sin be blotted out from before thee; for they have provoked thee to anger before the builders.

Rom. 1:28

v.28 And even as they did not like to retain God in their knowledge, God gave them over to a reprobate mind, to do those things which are not |seemly|,

v.28 Let them be blotted out of the (i) book of the living, and not be (j) written with the righteous.

(i) book of the living,
(i) Ex.32:32;Phil.4:3;Rev.3:5;13:8
(j) written with the righteous.
(j) Lk.10:20;Heb.12:23

Ex.32:32

v.32 Yet now, if thou wilt forgive their sin—; and if not, blot me, I pray thee, out of thy book which thou hast written.

Phil.4:3

v.3 And I entreat thee also, true yokefellow, help those women who labored with me in the gospel, with Clement also, and with other my |fellow workers|, whose names are in the book of life.

Rev. 3:5

v.5 **He that overcometh, the same shall be clothed in white raiment; and I will not blot his name out of the book of life, but I will confess his name before my Father, and before his angles.**

Rev. 13:8

v.8 And all that dwell upon the earth shall worship him, whose names are not written in the book of life of the Lamb slain from the foundation of the world.

Lk.10:20

v.20 **Notwithstanding, in this rejoice not, that the spirit are subject unto you; but rather rejoice, because your names are written in heaven.**

Heb.12:23

v.23 To the general assembly and church of the first-born, who are written in heaven, and to God, the Judge of all, and to the spirits of just men made perfect,

v.29 But I am poor and sorrowful; let thy salvation, O God, set me up on high.
v.30 I will praise the name of God with a song, and will magnify him with thanksgiving.
v.31 (k) This also shall please the LORD better than an ox or bullock that hath horns and hoofs.

(k) this also shall please the LORD
(k) Ps. 50:13-14,23

Ps.50:13-14,23

v.13 Will I eat the flesh of bulls, or drink the blood of goats?
v.14 Offer unto God thanksgiving, and pay thy vows unto the Most High,
v.23 Whoso offereth praise glorifieth me; and to him that ordereth his |conduct| aright will I show the salvation of God.

v.32 (l) The humble shall see this, and be glad; and (m) your heart shall live that seek God.

(I) the humble shall see him,
(l) Ps.34:2
(m) your heart shall live that seek God.
(m) Ps. 22:26

Ps.34:2

v.2 My soul shall make her boast in the LORD; the humble shall hear of it, and be glad.

Ps.22:26

v.26 The meek shall eat and be satisfied; they shall praise the LORD that seek him; your heart shall live forever.

v.33 For the LORD heareth the poor, and despiseth not his (n) prisoners.

(n) prisoners
(n) Ps. 68:6

v. 6 God setteth the solitary in families; he bringeth out those who are bound with chains, but the rebellious dwell in a dry land.

v.34 Let the heaven and earth praise him, the seas, and everything that (o) moveth therein.

(o) moveth therein
(o) lit. creepeth

v.35 (p) For God will save Zion, and will build the cities of Judah, that they may dwell there, and have it in possession.

(p) For God will save Zion,
(p) Ps.51:18; Isa.44:26

Ps.51:18

v.18 Do good in thy good pleasure unto Zion; build thou the walls of Jerusalem.

Isa.44:26

v.26 Who confirmeth the word of his servant, and performeth the counsel of his messengers; who saith to Jerusalem, Thou shalt be inhabited; and to the cities of Judah, Ye shall be build, and I will raise up the decayed places thereof;

v.36 The seed also of his servants shall inherit it, and they who love his name shall dwell therein.

1(69:1) The N. T. quotations from, references to, this Psalm indicate in what it foreshadows Christ. It is the Psalm of His humiliation and rejection (vv.4,7-8,10-12). Verses 14-20 may well describe the exercises of His holy soul in Gethsemane (Mt. 26:36-45); whereas v. 21 is a direct reference to the cross (Mt.27:34,48; Jn.19:28-30).The imprecatory section (vv.22-28) is connected (Rom.11:9-10) with the present judical blindness of Israel, v.25 having special reference to Judas (Acts 1:20), who is thus made typical of his generation, which shared his guilt.

MESSIAH'S GLORIOUS KINGDOM

PSALM 72

v.1 1Give the (g) king thy judgments, O God, and thy righteousness unto the king's son.

1(72:1)
(g) king thy judgment
(g) Kingdom (O.T.):vv.1-20;Ps.89:4
(Gen.1:26;Zech. 12:8)

Ps. 89:4

v. 4 Thy seed will I establish forever, and build up thy throne to all generations. Selah.

Gen. 1:26

v.26 And God said, Let us make man in our image, after our likeness; and let them have dominion over the fish of the sea, and over the fowl of the air, and over the cattle, and over all the earth, and over every creeping thing that creepeth upon the earth.

Zech.12:8

v.8 In that day shall the LORD defend the inhabitants if Jerusalem; and he that is feeble among them at that day shall be like David; and the house of David shall be like God, like the angel of the LORD before them.

v.2 He shall judge thy people with righteousness, and thy poor with (h) |justice|.

(h) |justice|
(h) KJV judgment. Ps.25:9

Ps.25:9

v.9 The meek will he guide in |justice|; and the meek will he teach his way.

v.3 The mountains shall bring peace to the people, and the little hills, by righteousness.
v.4 He shall judge the poor of the people, he shall save the children of the needy, and shall break in pieces the oppressor.
v.5 They shall (i) fear thee as long as the sun and moon (j) endure, throughout all generations.

(i) fear thee as long
(i) Ps.19:9, note, See Messianic Psalm 22:3
(j) endure
(j) Ps.89:36

Ps.19:9

v.9 The fear of LORD is clean, enduring forever ; the |ordinances| of the LORD are true and righteous altogether.

Note 2 (19:9) "The fear of the LORD" is an O.T. expression meaning reverential trust, including the hatred of evil.

Ps.89:36

v.36 His seed shall endure forever, and his throne as the sun before me.

v.6 He shall come down like rain upon the mown grass, like showers that water the earth.

v.7 In his days shall the righteous flourish, and abundance of peace as long as the moon endureth.

v.8 He shall have dominion also from sea to sea, and from the (k) river unto the ends of the earth.

(k) river
(k) i. e. the Euphrates. Zech. 9:10

Zech. 9:10

v.10 And I will cut off the chariot from E'phraim, and the horse from Jerusalem, and the battle bow shall be cut off; and he shall speak peace unto the |nations|; and the dominion shall be from sea even to sea, and from the river even to the ends of the earth.

v.9 They that dwell in the wilderness shall bow before him, and his enemies shall (l) lick the dust.

(l) lick the dust;
(l) Isa.49:23

Isa.49:23

v.23 And kings shall be thy nursing fathers, and their queens, thy nursing mothers; they shall bow down to thee with their face toward the earth, and lick up the dust of thy feet, and thou shalt know that I am the LORD; for they shall not be ashamed who wait for me.

v.10 The kings of Tar' shish and of the (m) isles shall bring presents; the kings of Sheba and Seba shall offer gifts.

(m) isles shall bring presents;
(m) i.e. coasts

v.11 Yea, all kings shall fall down before him; all nations shall serve him.

v.12 For he shall deliver the needy when he crieth; the poor also, and him that hath no helper.
v.13 He shall spare the poor and needy, and shall save the souls of the needy.
v.14 He shall (f) redeem their soul from deceit and violence, and precious shall their blood be in his sight.

(f) redeem
(f) Redemption (kinsman type):v.23;72:14; Ps. 74:12.(Gen.48:16;Isa. 59:20, note)

Ps.72:14

v.14 He shall (f) redeem their soul from deceit and violence, and precious shall their blood be in his sight

Ps. 74:12

v.12 For God is my King of old, working salvation in the midst of the earth.

Gen. 48:16

v.16 | An angel | who redeemed me from all evil, bless the lads; and let my name be named on them, and the name of my fathers, Abraham and Isaac; and let them grow into a multitude in the midst of the earth.

Isa.59:20,note

v.20 And the Redeemer shall come to Zion, and unto those who turn from transgression in Jacob, saith the LORD.

Note: 1 (59:20) Redemption, kinsman type, Summary: The goel, or kinsman-redeemer, is a beautiful type of Christ:

(1) The kinsman redemption was of persons and an inheritance (Lev.25:25,48; Gal.4:5; Eph.1:7,11,14).
(2) The redeemer must be a kinsman (Lev.25:48-49;Ruth 3:12-13, see v.9, note; Gal.4:4;Heb.2:14-15).
(3) The redeemer must be able to redeem (Ruth 4:4-6; Jer.50:34; Jn.10:11,18).
(4) Redemption is effected by the goel paying the just demand in full (Lev.25:27; Gal.3:13; 1 Pet.1:18-19). See notes at Ex.6:6 and Rom.3:24.

2 (59:20) The time when the "Redeemer shall come to Zion" is fixed, relatively, by Rom.11:23-29, as following the completion of the Church. This is also the order of the great dispensational passage, Acts 15:14-17. In both, the return of the Lord to Zion follows the outcalling of the Church.

v.15 And he shall live, and to him shall be given of the gold of (n) Sheba; prayer also shall be made for him continually, and daily shall he be praised.

(n) Sheba;
(n) Isa.60:6

v.6 The multitude of camels shall cover thee, the dromedaries of Midian and E'phah; they all from Sheba shall come; they shall bring gold and incense, and they shall show forth the praises of the LORD.

v.16 There shall be an handful of (o) |grain| in the earth upon the top of the mountains; the fruit thereof shall shake like Lebanon, (p) and they of the city shall flourish like grass of the earth.

(o) |grain|
(o) KJV corn
(p) and they of the city shall flourish;
(p) Cp.1 Ki.4:20

v.20 Judah and Israel were many, as the sand which is by the sea in multitude, eating and drinking, and making merry.

v.17 His name (q) shall (j) endure forever; his name shall be continued as long as the sun, and men shall be blessed (r) in him. All nations shall call him blessed.

(q) shall
(q) Lit. shall be
(j) endure forever
(j) Ps.89:36
(r) in him
(r) Gen.12:3

v.36 His seed shall endure forever, and his throne as the sun before me.

Gen.12:3

v.3 And I will bless them that bless thee, and curse him that curseth thee: and in thee shall all families of the earth be blessed.

v.18 Blessed be the LORD God, the God of Israel, who only doeth wondrous things.
v.19 And blessed be his glorious name forever; and let the whole (s) earth be filled with his glory. Amen, and Amen.

(s) earth; (s) Num.14:21;Hab.2:14

Num.14:21

v.21 But as truly as I live, all the earth shall be filled with the glory of the LORD.

Hab.2:14

v.14 For the earth shall be filled with the knowledge of the glory of the LORD, as the waters cover the sea.

v.20 The prayers of David, the son of Jesse, are (a) ended.

(a) ended
(a) Cp.2 Sam.23:1-4

2 Sam.23:1-4

v.1 Now these are the last words of David. David, the son of Jesse, said, and the man who was raised up on high, the anointed of the God of Jacob, and the sweet psalmist of Israel, said,
v.2 The Spirit of the LORD spoke by me, and his word was in my tongue.
v.3 The God of Israel said, the Rock of Israel spoke to me, He who ruleth over men must be just, ruling in the fear of God.
v.4 And he shall be as the light of the morning, when the sun riseth, even a morning without clouds, as the tender grass springing out of the earth by clear shining after rain.

1(72:1) The 72nd Psalm forms a complete vision of Messiah's kingdom insofar as the O.T. revelation extended. David's prayers will find their fruition in the kingdom(2 Sam.23:1-4). Verse 1 refers to the investiture of the king's Son with the kingdom, the formal description of which is given in Dan. 7:13-14; Rev.5:5-10. Verses 2-7,12-14 give the character of the kingdom (cp. Isa.11:3-9). The emphatic word is "righteousness" Verses 8-19 speak of the universality of the kingdom. It is to be extended all over the earth. (Zech.18:13,20-23).

CONFIRMATION OF THE DAVIDIC KINGDOM

(d) Mas'chil of Ethan, the Ezrahite
(d) Instruction

PSALM 89

v.1 I will sing of the mercies of the LORD forever; with my mouth will I make known thy faithfulness to all generations.
v.2 For I have said, Mercy shall be built up forever; thy faithfulness shalt thou establish in the very heavens.
v.3 I have 1 made a covenant with my chosen, I have (e) sworn unto David, my servant:

(e) sworn unto David,
(e) 2 Sam.7:11;1Chr.17:10;cp.Jer.30:9 Ezek.34:23;Hos.3:5

2 Sam.7:11

v.11 And as since the time that I commanded judges to be over my people, Israel, and have caused thee to rest from all thine enemies. Also the LORD telleth thee that he will make thee an house.

1 Chr.17:10

v.10 And since the time that I commanded judges to be over my people, Israel. Moreover, I will subdue all thine enemies. Furthermore, I tell thee that the LORD will build thee an house.

Jer.30:9

v.9 But they shall serve the LORD, their God, and David, their king, whom I will raise up unto them.

Ezek.34:23

v.23 And I will set up one shepherd over them, and he shall feed them, even my servant, David; he shall feed them, and he shall be their shepherd.

Hos.3:5

v.5 Afterward shall the children of Israel return, and seek the LORD, their God, and David, their king, and shall fear the LORD and his goodness in the latter days.

v.4 Thy seed will I establish forever, and build up thy (f) throne (g) to all generation. Selah.

Verses 1-4 represents the comformation of the Davidic Covenant with his oath.

(f) throne
(f) Kingdom (O.T.)vv.3-4,19-21,36;
Isa.1:25.(Gen.1:26;Zech.12:8)
(g) to all his oath
(g) v.1;Lk.1:32-33

See the above vv.3-4

Ps.89,19-21,36

v.19 Then thou didst speak in vision to thy holy one, and saidst, I have laid help upon one who is mighty; I have exalted one chosen out of the people
v.20 I have found David, my servant; with my holy oil have I anointed him,
v.21 With whom my hand shall be established; mine arm also shall strengthen him.

v.36 His seed shall endure forever, and his throne as the sun before me.

Isa.1:25

v.25 And I will turn my hand upon thee, and |thoroughly| purge away dross, and take away all thy tin.

Gen.1:26

v.26 And God said, Let us make man in our image, after our likeness; and let them have dominion over the fish of the sea, and over the fowl of the air, and over the cattle, and over all the earth, and over every creeping thing that creepeth upon the earth.

Zech.12:8

v.8 In that day shall the LORD defend the inhabitants of Jerusalem; and he that is feeble among them at that day shall be like David; and the house of David shall be like God, like the angel of the LORD before them.

Ps.89:1

v.1 I will sing of the mercies of the LORD forever; with my mouth will I make known thy faithfulness to all generations.

Lk.1:32-33

v.32 He shall be great, and shall be called the Son of the Highest; and the Lord God shall give unto him the throne of his father, David.

v.33 And he shall reign over the house of Jacob forever; and of his kingdom there shall be no end.

v.5 And the heavens shall praise thy wonders, O LORD; thy faithfulness also in the congregation of the saints.

v.6 (h) For who in the heavens can be compared unto the LORD? Who among the sons of the mighty can be likened unto the LORD?

(h) For who in the heavens;
(h) Ps.40:5; 86:8;113:5

Ps.40:5

v.5 Many, O LORD, my God, are thy wonderful works which thou hast done, and thy thoughts which are |toward us|; they cannot be reckoned up in order unto thee. If I would declare and speak of them, they are more than can be numbered.

Ps.86:8

v.8 Among the gods there is none like unto thee, O Lord; neither are there any works like unto thy works.

Ps.113:5

v.5 Who is like unto the LORD, our God, who dwelleth on high,

v.7 God is greatly to be feared in the assembly of the saints, and to be had in reverence of all those who are about him.
v.8 O LORD God of hosts, who is a strong LORD (i) like unto thee? Or to thy faithfulness round about thee?

(i) like unto thee?
(i)Ex.15:11;1 Sam.2:2;Ps.35:10;71:19

Ex.15:11

v.11 Who is like unto thee, O LORD, among the gods? Who is like thee, glorious in holiness, fearful in praises, doing wonders?

1 Sam.2:2

v.2 There is none holy like the LORD; for there is none beside thee, neither is there any rock like our God.

Ps.35:10

v.10 All my bones shall say, LORD, who is like unto thee, who deliverest the poor from him that is too strong for him that spoileth him?

Ps.71:19

v.19 Thy righteousness also, O God, is very high, who hast done great things. O God, who is like thee?

v.9 Thou (j) rulest the raging of the sea; when the waves thereof arise, thou stillest them.

(j) rulest the raging of the sea;
(j) Ps.65:7;93:3-4;107:29

Ps.65:7

v.7 Who stilleth the noise of the seas, the noise of their waves, and the tumult of the people.

Ps.93:3-4

v.3 The floods have lifted up, O LORD, the floods lift up their voice; the floods lift up their waves.
v4 The LORD on high is mightier than the noise of many waters, yea, than the mighty waves of the sea.

Ps.107:29

v.29 He maketh the storm a calm, so that the waves thereof are still.

v10 Thou hast (k) broken (l) Rahab in pieces, as one that is slain; thou hast scattered thine enemies with thy strong arm.

(k) broken
(k) Ex.14:26-28
(l) Rahab in pieces,
(l) Or Egypt. Ps.87:4

Ex.14:26-28

v.26 And the LORD said unto Moses, Stretch out thine hand over the sea, that the waters may come again upon the Egyptians, upon their chariots, and upon their horsemen.
v.27 And Moses stretched forth his hand over the sea, and the sea returned to its strength when the morning appeared; and the Egyptians fled against it; and the LORD overthrew the Egyptians in the midst of the sea.
v.28 And the waters returned and covered the chariots, and the horsemen, and all the host of Phar'aoh that came into the sea after them; there remained not so much as one of them.

Ps. 87:4

v.4 I will make mention of Rahab and Babylon to them that know me; behold Philis'tia and Tyre, with Ethiopia: this man was born there.

v.11 The heavens are thine; the earth also is thine; as far the world and the fullness thereof, thou hast founded them.
v.12 The north and the south, thou hast created them; (m) Tabor and (n) Hermon shall rejoice in thy name.

(m) Tabor
(m) Josh.19:20
(n) Hermon shall rejoice in thy name
(n) Josh.12:1

Josh.19:22

v.22 And the |border| reacheth to Tabor, and Shahazum'mah, and Bethshe'mesh; and the lendl of their borders was at the Jordan sixteen cities with their villages

Josh.12:1

v.1 Now these are the kings of the land, whom the children of Israel smote and possessed their land on the other side of the Jordan toward the rising of the sun, from the river Arnon unto Mount Hermon, and all the |Ar'abah| on the east:

v.13 Thou hast a (o) mighty arm; strong is thy hand, and high is thy right hand.

(o) mighty arm;
(o) Lit. an arm with might

v.14 (p) |Righteousness and justice| are the inhabitation of thy throne; mercy and truth shall go before thy face.

(p) |Righteousness and justice|
(p) KJV Justice and judgment

v.15 Blessed are the people that know the joyful sound; they shall walk, O LORD, in the light of thy countenance.
v.16 In thy name shall they rejoice all the day, and in thy righteousness shall they be exalted.
v.17 For thou art the glory of their strength; and in thy favor our (q) horn shall be (r) exalted.

(q) horn
(q) see Dt.33:17, note
(r) exalted;
(r) v. 24;Ps.75:10;92:10;132:17

Dt.33:17,note

v.17 His glory is like the firstling of his bullock, and his horns are like the horns of | a wild ox | ; with them he shall push the people together to the ends of the earth; and they are the ten thousands of E'phraim, and they are the thousands of Manas'seh.

Note 2 (33:17) The words "horn" and "horns" (O. T., qeren; N.T. keras) are used in Scripture both literally and figuratively. In the latter sense at least three meanings appear: (1) strength in general (dt.33:17); (2) arrogant pride (Ps. 75:4-5); and (3) political and military power (Dan.8:20-21).

Ps.89:24

v.24 But my faithfulness and my mercy shall be with him; and in my name shall his horn be exalted.

Ps.75:10

v.10 All the horns of the wicked also will I cut off, but the horns of the righteous shall be exalted.

Ps.92:10

v.10 But my horn shalt thou exalt like the horn of | a wild ox | ; I shall be anointed with fresh oil.

Ps.132:17

v.17 There will I make the horn of David to bud; I have ordained a lamp for mine anointed.

v.18 For the LORD is our defense, and the Holy One of Israel is our King.

(2) The LORD is glorified for His power and goodness in connection with the covenant (vv.5-18).

v.19 Then thou didst speak in vision to thy holy one, and saidst, I have laid help upon one who is mighty; I have exalted one (s) chosen out of the people.

(s) chosen out of the people
(s) v.3;cp. 1 Ki.11:34

v.3 I have made a covenant with my chosen, I have sworn unto David, my servant:

1 Ki.11:34

v.34 Howbeit, I will not take the whole kingdom out of his hand, but I will make him prince all the days of his life, for David my servant's sake, whom I chose because he kept my commandments and my statutes.

v.20 (t) I have found David, my servant; with my holy (u) oil have I anointed him,

(t) I have fond David, my servant;
(t) Acts13:22
(u) oil have I anointed him,
(u) Sanctification (O.T.v:20;Jer.1:5.(Gen.2:3;Zech.8;3)

Acts 13:22

v.22 And when he had removed him, he raised up unto them David to be their king; to whom also he gave testimony, and said, I have found David, the son of Jesse, a man after mine own heart, who shall fulfill all my will.

See above Ps. 89:20

Jer.1:5

v. 5 Before I formed thee in the |womb|, I knew thee; and before thou camest forth out of the womb, I sanctified thee, and I ordained thee a prophet unto the nations.

Gen.2:3

v.3 And God blessed the seventh day, and sanctified it, because that in it he had rested from all his work which God created and made.

Zech.8:3

v.3 Thus saith the LORD: I am returned unto Zion, and will dwell in the midst of Jerusalem; and Jerusalem shall be called a city of truth, and the mountain of the LORD of hosts, the holy mountain.

v.21 With whom my hand shall be established; mine arm also shall strengthen
v.22 The enemy shall not (v) exact from him, nor the son of wickedness afflict him.

(v) exact from him,
(v) Or do violence, or outwit.

v.23 And I will beat down his foes before his face, and plague those who hate him.
v.24 But my faithfulness and my mercy shall be with him; and in my name shall his (q) horn be exalted.

(q) horn,
(q) see Dt.33:17, note

v.17 His glory is like the firstling of his bullock, and his horns are like the horns of |a wild ox|; with them he shall push the people together to the ends of the earth; and they are the ten thousands of E'phraim, and they are the thousands of Manas'seh.

Note: 2 (Dt.33:17) The words "horn" and "horns" (O.T., qeren; N.T. keras)) are used in Scripture both literally and figuratively. In the latter sense at least three meanings appear: (1) strength in general (Dt.33:17); (2) arrogant pride (Ps.75:4-5); and (3) political and military power (Dan.8:20-21).

v.25 I will (a) set his hand also in the sea, and his right hand in the rivers.

(a) set his hand also in the sea,
(a) Ps.72:8;cp.1Cor.15:27

Ps. 72:8

v.8 He shall have dominion also from sea to sea, and from the river unto the ends of the earth.

1Cor.15:27

v.27 For he hath put all things under his feet. But when he saith all things are put under him, it is manifest that he is excepted who did put all things under him.

v.26 He shall cry unto me, Thou art my (b) father, my God, and the rock of my salvation.

(b) father,
(b) 2 Sam.7:14; cp. Heb.1:5

2 Sam.7:14

v.14 I will be his father, and he shall be my son. If he commit iniquity, I will chasten him with the rod of men, and with the stripes of the children of men;

Heb.1:5

v.5 For unto which of the angels said he at any time, Thou art my Son, this day have I begotten thee? And again, I will be to him a Father, and he shall be to me a Son

v.27 Also I will make him my (c) firstborn, (d) higher than the kings of the earth.

(c) firstborn,
(c) Col.1:15; cp. Ex 4:22
(d) higher than the kings of the earth.
(d) Num.24:7;Ps.72:11; Rev.19:16

Col.1:15

v15 Who is the image of the invisible God, the first-born of | all creation | ;

Ex. 4:22

v.22 And thou shalt say unto Phar'-aoh, Thus saith the LORD, Israel is my son, even my first-born.

Num. 24:7

v.7 He shall pour the water out of his buckets, and his seed shall be in many waters, and his king shall be higher than Agag, and his kingdom shall be exalted.

Ps. 72:11

v.11 Yea, all kings shall fall down before him; all nations shall serve him.

Rev.19:16

v.16 And he hath on his vesture and on his thigh a name written, KING OF KINGS, AND LORD OF LORDS.

v.28 My mercy will I keep for him for evermore, and my covenant shall stand fast with him.
v.29 His seed also will I will make to endure forever, and his throne as the days of heaven.
v.30 If his children forsake my law, and walk not in mine (e) | ordinances | ;

(e) | ordinances | ;
(e) KJV judgments. Ezek.20:16

Ezek.20:16

v.16 Because they despised mine | ordinances |, and walked not in my statutes, but polluted by sabbaths; for their hearts went after their idols.

v.31 If they break my statutes, and keep not my commandments;
v.32 Then will I visit their transgression with the rod, and their iniquity with stripes.
v.33 (f) Nevertheless, my loving-kind-ness will I not utterly take from him, nor (g) | allow | my faithfulness to fail.

(f) Nevertheless,
(f) 2 Sam.7:14-15
(g) | allow | ;
(g) KJV suffer

2 Sam. 7:14-15

v.14 I will be his father, and he shall be my son. If he commit iniquity, I will chasten him with the rod of men, and with the stripes of the children of men;
v.15 But my mercy shall not depart away from him, as I took it from Saul, whom I put away before thee.

v.34 My covenant will I not break, nor will I (h) alter the thing that is gone out of my lips.

(h) alter
(h) Num. 23:19;Jer.33:20-22

Num. 23:19

v.19 God is not a man, that he should lie; neither the son of man, that he should repent. Hath he said, and shall he not do it ? Or hath he spoken, and shall he not make it good?

Jer.33:20-22

v. 20 Thus saith the LORD, If ye can break my covenant of the day, and my covenant of the night, and that there should not be day and night in their season,

v.21 Then may also my covenant be broken with David, my servant, that he should not have a son to reign upon his throne; and with the Levites, the priests, my ministers.

v.22 As the host of heaven cannot be numbered, neither the sand of the sea measured, so will I multiply the seed of David, my servant, and the Levites who minister unto me.

v.35 Once have I swore by my holiness that I will not (i) lie unto David.

(i) lie unto David
(i) 1 Sam.15:29;Ti.1:2

1 Sam.15:29

v.29 And also the Strength of Israel will not lie nor repent; for he is not a man, that he should repent.

Ti.1:2

v.2 In hope of eternal life, which God, who cannot lie, promised before the world began,

v.36 His seed shall endure forever, and his throne as the sun before me.

v.37 It shall be established forever like the moon, and as a faithful witness in heaven. Selah.

Verses 19-37. The LORD responds in two parts. (a) it confirms the covenant (vv.19-29) (b) warns that disobedience in the royal posterity of David will be punished with chastening (vv. 30-32).

v.38 Thou hast (j) cast off and abhorred, thou hast been (k) | angry | with thine anointed.

(j) cast off and abhorred,
(j) Ps.44:9;cp.77:7
(k) | angry | ;
(k) KJV wrath

Ps. 44:9

v.9 But thou hast cast off, and put us to shame, and goest not forth with our armies.

Ps.77:7

v.7 Will the Lord cast off forever? And will he be favorable no more?

v.39 Thou hast made void the covenant of thy servant; thou hast (l) profaned his (m) crown by casting it to the ground.

(l) profaned his
(l) Ps.74:7
(m) crown by casting it to the ground.
(m) cp. Lam. 5:16

Ps.74:7

v.7 They have cast fire into thy sanctuary; they have defiled by casting down the dwelling place of thy name to the ground.

Lam.5:16

v.16 The crown is fallen from our head; woe unto us, that we have sinned!

v.40 Thou hast broken down all his hedges; thou hast brought his strongholds to ruin.
v.41 All that pass by the way (n) spoil him; he is a reproach to his neighbors.

(n) spoil him;
(n) Ps.80:12

Ps.80:12

v.12 Why hast thou then broken down her hedges, so that all they who pass by the way do pluck her?

v.42 Thou hast set up the right hand of his adversaries; thou hast made all his enemies to rejoice.
v.43 Thou hast also turned the edge of his sword, and hast not made him to stand in the battle.
v.44 Thou hast made his glory to cease, and cast his throne down to the ground.
v.45 The days of his youth hast thou shortened; thou hast covered him with shame. Selah.
v.46 How long, LORD? Wilt thou hide thyself forever? Shall thy wrath burn like fire?
v.47 Remember how short my time (o) is ! (p) |Why| hast thou made all men in (q) vain?

(o) is!
(o) Ps.90:9;
(p) |why|
(p) KJV wherefore
(q) vain?
(q) Ps.62:9

Ps.90:9

v.9 For all our days are passed away in thy wrath; we spend our years as a tale that is told.

Ps. 62:9

v.9 Surely men of low degree are vanity, and men of high degree are a lie; to be laid in the balance, they are altogether lighter than vanity.

v.48 What man is he that liveth, and shall not see (r) death? Shall he deliver his soul from the (s) |power of sheol |? Selah.

(r) death?
(r) Eccl. 3:19; see Eccl. 9:10, Heb.9:27, note
(s) |power of sheol|
(s) KJV hand of the grave.
Hab.2:5,note; cp. Lk.16:23,note

Eccl. 3:19

v.19 For that which befalleth the sons of men befalleth beasts. Even one thing befalleth them: as the one dieth, so dieth the other; yea, they have all one breath, so that a man hath no pre-eminence above a beast; for all is vanity.

Eccl.9:10

v.10 Whatsoever thy hand findeth to do, do It with might; for there is no work, nor device, nor knowledge, nor wisdom in |sheol|, whither thou goest.

Heb. 9:27

v.27 And as it is appointed unto men once to die, but after this the judgment, 1(9:27) Death (physical), Summary:

(1) Physical death is a consequence of sin (Gen.3:19), and the universality of death proves the universality of sin (Rom.5:12-14).

(2) Physical death affects the body only, and is not cessation of existence or of consciousness (Hab.2:5, note; Lk.16:23,note; Rev. 6:9-10).
(3) All physical death ends in the resurrection of the body. See Resurrection, Job.19:25; 1Cor.15:52, note.
(4) Because physical death is a consequence of sin, it is not inevitable to the redeemed (Gen.5:24; 1Cor. 15:51-52; 1Th.4:15-17).
(5) Physical death has for the Christian a peculiar qualification. It. is called "sleep," because his body may be awakened at any moment (Phil. 3:20-21; 1 Th.4:14-18).
(6) The soul and spirit live, independently of the death of the body, which is described as a "tabernacle" (tent), in which the "I" dwells, and which may be put off (2Cor. 5:1-8; cp.1Cor.15:42-44; 2Pet.1:13-15).And
(7) at the Christian's death he is at once "with the Lord" and his body awaits resurrection at return of Christ (2Cor.5:1-8;Phil.1:23; 1Th.4:13-17).

Hab.2:5

v.5 Yea, also, because he transgresseth by wine, he is a proud man, neither keepeth at home, who enlargeth his desire as |sheol|, and is as death, and cannot be satisfied, but gathered into himself all nations, and heaped unto himself all peoples.

Note, 4(2;5) Sheol is, in the O.T., the place which the dead go.

(1) Often, therefore, it is spoken of as the equivalent of the grave, where all human activities cease; the terminus toward which all human life moves (e.g. Gen.42:38; Job14:13; Ps.88:3).
(2) To the man "under the sun," the natural man, who of necessity judges from appearances, sheol seems no more than the grave-

(3) Scripture reveals sheol as a place of sorrow (2 Sam.22:6; Ps.18:5;116:3), into which the wicked are turned (Ps. 9:17), and where they are fully conscious (Isa. 14:9-17; Ezek.32:21). Compare Jon.2:2; what the belly of the great fish was to Jonah, sheol is to those who are therein. The sheol of the O.T. and hades of the N.T. are identical.

Lk.16:23,note

v.23 **And in |hades| he lifted up his eyes, being in torments, and seeth Abraham afar off, and Lazarus in his bosom.**

Note: 2(16:23) The Greek word hades, like its Hebrew equivalent, sheol, is used in two ways:

(1) To indicate the condition of the unsaved between death and the great white throne judgement (Rev.20:13-15). Luke 16:23-24 shows that the lost in hades are conscious, possess full use of their faculties, memory, etc., and are in torment. This continues until the final judgment of the lost (2Pet.2:9, ASV), when all the unsaved, and hades itself, will be cast into the lake of fire (Rev.20:13-15).

(2) To indicate, in general, the condition of all departed human spirits between death and the resurrection. This usage is found occasionally in the O.T. but rarely, if ever, in the N.T. (cp.Gen.37:35; 42:38; 44:29,31). It should not lead anyone to think that there is a possibility of change from one state to the other after death, for v.23 shows that when the unsaved man who was in hades saw Abraham and Lazrus, they were "afar off," and v.26 states that between the two places there is a great gulf fixed, so that no one can pass from one to the other.

Some interpreters think that Eph.4:8-10 indicates that a change in the place of the departed believers occurred at the resurrection of Christ. It is certain that all who are saved go at once into the presence of Christ (2Cor.5:8; Phil.1:23). Jesus told the penitent thief: "Today shalt thou be with me in paradise" (Lk.23:43). Paul was "caught up to the third heaven . . . into paradise" (2Cor.12:1-4). Paradise is a place of great joy and bliss, but this bliss is not complete until the spirit is reunited with a glorified body at the resurrection of the just (1Cor.15:51-54; 1 Th. 4:16-17). Though both sheol and hades are sometimes translated "grave" (cp. Gen. 37:35; 1Cor.15:55), they never indicate a burial place but, rather, the state of the spirit after death.

v.49 Lord, where are thy former loving-kindnesses, which thou didst swear unto David in thy truth?
v.50 Remember, Lord, the reproach of thy servants; how I do bear in my bosom the reproach of all the mighty people,
v.51 Wherewith thine enemies have reproached, O LORD; wherewith they have reproached the footsteps of thine anointed.
v.52 (t) Blessed be the LORD for evermore. Amen, and Amen.

(t) Blessed be the LORD
(t) Ps.41:13; 72:19; 106:48

Ps.41:13

v.13 Blessed be the Lord God of Israel from everlasting to everlasting. Amen, and Amen.

Ps.72:19

v.19 And blessed be his glorious name forever; and let the whole earth be filled with his glory. Amen, and Amen.

Ps.106:48

v.48 Blessed be the LORD God of Israel from everlasting to everlasting; and let all the people say, Amen. Praise ye the LORD.

Verses (48-51). The third book of the psalms closes appropriately with a doxology (v. 52).

CHRIST, THE AFFLICTION OF HIS HOLY SOUL

PSALM 102

v.1 1 Hear my prayer, O LORD, and let my cry come unto thee. 1 (102:1)

v.2 (p) Hide not thy face from me in the day when I am in trouble; incline thine ear unto me; in the day when I call, answer me speedily.

(p) hide not thy face
(p) Ps.27:9;69:17

Ps.27:9

v.9 Hide not thy face far from me; put not thy servant away in anger. Thou hast been my help; leave me not, neither forsake me, O God of my salvation.

Ps. 69:17

v.17 And hide not thy face from thy servant; for I am in trouble. Hear me speedily.

v.3 For my days are (q) consumed like smoke, and my bones are burned like an hearth.

(q) consumed like smoke
(q) Jas. 4:14

v.14 Whereas ye know not what shall be on the |next day|. For what is your life? It is even a vapor that appeared for a little time, and then vanisheth away.

v.4 My heart is smitten, and withered like grass, so that I forget to eat my bread.
v.5 By reason of the voice of my groaning, my bones (j) |adhere| to my skin.

(j) |adhere|
(j) KJV cleave

v.6 I am like a pelican of the wilderness; I am like an owl of the desert.
v.7 I watch, and am like a sparrow alone upon the housetop.
v.8 Mine enemies reproach me all the day, and they that are mad against me are sworn against me.
v.9 For I have eaten ashes like bread, and mingled my drink with weeping,
v.10 Because of thine indignation and thy wrath; for thou hast lifted me up, and cast me down.
v.11 My days are like a shadow that declineth, and I am withered like grass.
v.12 But thou, O LORD, shalt endure forever, and thy remembrance unto all generations.
v.13 Thou shalt arise, and have mercy upon Zion; for the time to favor her, yea, the (r) set time, is come.

(r) set time,
(r) cp. Dan.8:19

v.19 And he said, Behold, I will make thee know what shall be in the last end of the indignation; for at the time appointed the end shall be.

v.14 For thy servants take pleasure in her stones, and favor the dust thereof.

v.15 So the (s) |nations| shall (t) fear the name of the LORD, and all the Kings of the earth thy glory.

(s) |nations|
(s) KJV heathen
(t) fear the name of the LORD,
(t) Ps.19:9, note

Ps.19:9,note

v.9 The fear of the LORD is clean, enduring forever; the |ordinances| of the LORD are true and righteous altogether.

Note: 2(19:9) "The fear of the LORD" is an O.T. expression reverential trust including the hatred of evil.

v.16 When the LORD shall build up Zion, he shall appear in his glory.
v.17 He will (a) regard the prayer of the destitute, and not despise their prayer.

(a) regard the prayer of the destitute,
(a) cp. Neh.1:6,11;2:8

v.6 Let thine ear now be attentive, and thine eyes open, that thou mayest hear the prayer of thy servant, which I pray before thee now, day and night, for the children of Israel, thy servants, and confess the sins of the children of Israel, which we have sinned against thee; both I and my father's house have sinned.
v.11 O Lord, I beseech thee, let now thine ear be attentive to the prayer of thy servant, and the prayer of thy servants, who |delight| to fear thy name; and prosper, I pray thee, thy servant this day, and grant him mercy in the sight of this man. For I was the king's cupbearer.

Neh.2:8

v.8 And a letter unto A'saph, the keeper of the king's forest, that he may give me timber to make beams for the gates of the palace which | is near | to the house, and for the wall of the city, And the king granted me, according to the good hand of my GOD, upon me.

v.18 This shall be written for the generation to come; and the
people who shall be created shall praise the LORD.
v.19 For he hath (b) looked down from the height of his
sanctuary; from heaven did the LORD behold the earth,

(b) looked down
(b) cp. Ex.3:7

v.7 And the LORD said, I have surely seen the affliction of my people who are in Egypt, and have heard their cry by reason of their taskmasters; for I know their sorrows;

v.20 To (c) hear the groaning of the prisoner; to loose (d) those
that are appointed to death;

(c) hear the groaning of the prisoner;
(c) Ps.79:11

v.11 Let the sighing of the prisoner come before thee; according to the greatness of thy power preserve thou those that are appointed to die;

(d) those that are appointed to die;
(d) lit. the children of death

v.21 To declare the name of the LORD in Zion, and his praise in
Jerusalem,
v.22 (e) When the people are gathered together, and the
kingdoms, to serve the LORD.

(e) When the people are gathered together,
(e) Isa.2:2-3;60:3

Isa.2:2-3

v.2 And it shall come to pass in the last days, that the mountain of the LORD's house shall be established in the top of the mountains, and shall be exalted above the hills; and all nations shall flow unto it.

v.3 And many people shall go and say, Come ye, and let us go up to the mountain of the LORD, To the house of the God of Jacob; and he will teach us of his ways, and we will walk in his paths; for out of Zion shall go forth the law, and the word of the LORD from Jerusalem.

Isa.60:3

v.3 And the |nations| shall come to thy light, and kings to the brightness of thy rising.

v.23 He weakened my strength in the way; he shortened my days.

v.24 I said, O my God, take me not away in the midst of my days; thy years are throughout all generations.

v.25 Of old hast thou laid the (f) foundation of the earth, and the heavens are the work of thy hands.

(f) foundation of the earth,
(f) vv. 25-27; Heb.1:10-12

v.25 Of old hast thou laid the (f) foundation of the earth, and the heavens are the work of thy hands.

v.26 They shall (g) perish, but thou shalt endure; yea, all of them shall (h) |become| old like a garment; like a vesture shalt thou change them, and they shall be changed.

v.27 But thou art the (i) same, and thy years shall have no end.

Heb.1:10-12

v 10 And, Thou, Lord, in the beginning hast laid the foundation of the earth; and the heavens are the work of thine hands.
v.11 They shall perish, but thou remainest; and they all shall |become| old as doth a garment,
v.12 And as a vesture shalt thou fold them up, and they shall be changed; but thou art the same, and thy years shall not fail.

v.26 They shall (g) perish, but thou shalt endure; yea, all of them shall (h)|become|old like a garment; like a vesture shalt thou change them, and they shall be changed.

(g) perish, but thou shalt endure;
(g)Isa.34:4; 51:6;Mt. 24:35;
2 Pet.3:7,10-12;Rev.20:11
(h)|become|
(h) KJV wax

Isa.34:4

v.4 And all the host of heaven shall be dissolved, and the heavens shall be rolled together like a scroll; and all their host shall fall down, as the leaf falleth off from the vine, and like a falling fig from the fig tree.

Isa.51:6

v.6 Lift up your eyes to the heavens, and look upon the earth beneath; for the heavens shall vanish away like smoke, and the earth shall |grow| old like a garment, and they that dwell therein shall die in like manner; but my salvation shall be forever, and my righteousness shall not be abolished.

Mt.24:35

v.35 **Heaven and the earth shall pass away, but my words shall not pass away.**

2 Pet 3:7;10-12

v.7 But the heavens and the earth which are now, by the same word are kept in store, reserved unto fire against the day of judgment and perdition of ungodly men.

2 Pet. 3:10-12

v.10 But the day of the Lord will come as a thief in the night, in which the heavens shall pass away with a great noise, and the elements shall melt with fervent heat; the earth also, and the works that are in it shall be burned up.
v.11 Seeing, then, that all these things shall be dissolved, what manner of persons ought ye to be in all holy |living| and godliness,
v.12 Looking for and hasting unto the coming of the day of God, in which the heavens, being on fire, shall be dissolved, and the elements shall melt with fervent heat?

Rev.20:11

v.11 And I saw a great white throne, and him that sat on it, from whose face the earth and the heaven fled away, and there was found no place for them.

v.27 But thou art the (i) same, and thy years shall have no end.

(i) same,
(i) Mal.3:6;Heb.13:8;Jas.1:17

Mal.3:6

v.6 For I am the LORD, I change not; therefore ye sons of Jacob are not consumed.

Heb.13:8

v.8 Jesus Christ, the same yesterday, and today, and forever.

Jas.1:17

v.17 Every good gift and every perfect gift is from above, and cometh down from the Father of lights, with whom is no variableness, neither shadow of turning.

v.28 The children of thy servants shall continue, and their seed shall be established before thee.

Finally, the remaining section heightens the contrast between frail man and unchanging God by bringing both theme together (vv.23-28).

1 (102:1) The reference of vv.25-27 to Christ (Heb.1:10-12). is assurance that, in the preceeding verses of this Psalm, there is shown, prophetically, the affliction of His holy soul in the days of His humiliation and rejection.

THE PSALM OF THE KING–PRIEST

PSALM 110

v.1 1THE (d) LORD said unto my (d) Lord, Sit thou at my right hand, (e) until I make thine enemies thy (f) footstool.

1 (110:1]
(d) LORD said unto my
(d) Lord, Sit thou at my right hand,
(d) Deity (names of):v.1;Mal.2:16.
(Gen.1:1;Mal.3:18)
(e) until I make thine enemies thy
(e) Christ (second advent):vv1-7;
Isa.9:7.(Dt.30:3;Acts1:11,note
(f) footstool
(f) 1Cor.15:25
See the above v.1

Mal.2:16

v.16 For the LORD, the God of Israel, saith that he hateth putting away; for one covereth violence with his garment, saith the LORD of hosts; therefore, take heed to your spirit, that ye deal not treacherously.

Gen.1:1

v.1 IN the beginning God created the heaven and the earth.

Isa.9:7

v.7 Of the increase of his government and peace there shall be no end, upon the throne of David, and upon his kingdom, to order it, and to establish it |with justice and with righteousness| from henceforth even forever. The zeal of the LORD of hosts will perform this.

Mal.3:18

v.18 Then shall ye return, and discern between the righteous and the wicked, between him that serveth God and him that serveth him not.

Ps.110:1-7

v.1 1THE (d) LORD said unto my (d) Lord, Sit thou at my right hand, (e) until I make thine enemies thy (f) footstool.

v.2 The LORD shall send the rod of thy strength (g) out of Zion; (h) rule thou in the midst of thine enemies.

v.3 Thy people shall be willing in the day of thy power; in the beauties of holiness from the womb of the morning, hast the dew of thy youth.

v.4 The LORD hast sworn, and will not (i) repent, Thou art a (j) priest forever after the order of (k) Melchiz'edek.

v.5 The Lord at thy right hand shall strike through kings in the day of his wrath.

v. 6 He shall judge among the (l) |nations|; he shall fill the places with the dead bodies; he shall wound the heads over many countries.

v.7 He shall drink of the brook in the way; therefore shall he lift up the head

Dt.30:3

v.3 That then the LORD thy God will turn thy captivity, and have compassion upon thee, and will return and gather thee from all the nations where the LORD thy God hath scattered thee.

Acts 1:11,note

v.11 Who also said, Ye men of Galilee, why stand ye gazing up into heaven? This same Jesus, who is taken up from you into heaven, shall so come in like manner as ye have seen him go into heaven.

1 (1:11) The Advents, Summary:

(1) The O.T. foreview of the coming Messiah is in two aspects—that of rejection and suffering (e.g. in Isa.53); and that of earthly glory and power (e.g. in Isa.11; Jer.23; Ezek.37). Often these two aspects blend in one passage (e.g. Ps. 22). The prophets themselves were perplexed by this seeming contradiction (Pet.1:10-11). It was solved by partial fulfillment. In due time the Messiah, born of a virgin according to Isaiah's prophecy (7:14), appeared among men and began His ministry by announcing the predicted kingdom as "at hand" (Mt.4:17,note 4). The rejection of king and kingdom followed.

(2) Thereupon the rejected king announced His approaching crucifixion, resurrection, departure, and return (Mt. 12:38-40; 16:1-4,21,27;24;25; Lk.12:35-46; 17:20-36; 18:31-34; 19:12-27).

(3) He uttered predictions concerning the course of events between His departure and return (Mt.13:1-50; 16:18; 24:4-26).

(4) this promised return of Christ is a prominent theme in The Acts, Epistle, and The Revelation.

1Cor.15:25

v.25 For he must reign, till he hath put all enemies under his feet.

v.2 The LORD shall send the rod of thy strength (g) out of Zion; (h) rule thou in the midst of thine enemies.

(g) out of Zion;
(g) Rom.11:26-27
(h) rule thou in the midst
(h) Ps.2:9;Dan.7:13-14

Rom.11:26-27

v.26 And so all Israel shall be saved; as it is written, Thereshall come out Zion the Deliverer, and shall turn away ungodliness from Jacob;
v.27 For this is my covenant unto them, when I shall take away their sins.

Ps.2:9

v.9 Thou shalt break them with a rod of iron; thou shalt dash them in pieces like a potter's vessel.

Dan.7:13-14

v.13 I saw in the night visions, and, behold, one like the Son of man came with the clouds of heaven, and came to the Ancient of days, and they brought him near before him.
v.14 And there was given him dominion, and glory, and a kingdom, that all people, nations, and languages should serve him; his dominion is an everlasting dominion, which shall not pass away, and his kingdom that which shall not be destroyed.

v.3 Thy people shall be willing in the day of thy power; in the beauties of holiness from the womb of the morning, thou hast the dew of thy youth.
v.4 The LORD hath sworn, and will not (i) repent, Thou art a (j) priest forever after the order of (k)Melchiz'edek.

(i) repent,
(i) See Zech.8:14,note

(j) priest
(j) Zech.6:13,Acts17:30
(k) Melchiz'edek
(k) Heb.5:6;6:20;7:21

Zech.8:14,note

v.14 For thus saith the LORD of hosts: As I thought to punish you, when your fathers provoked me to wrath, saith the LORD of hosts, and I repented not, Compare: 4(8:14), in the O.T. "repentance" mean to eased or comforted. It is used both of God and man. Acts.17:30, in the N.T., meaning a change of mind, in respect to sin, God, and self. For the Christians who fallen into sin, be proceeded by sorrow, leave the world and turn to Christ. As in the N.T., such change of mind is often accompanied by contrition and self-judgment. When applied to God the word is used phenomenally, according to O.T. custom.

Zech.6:13

v.13 Even he shall build the temple of the LORD; and he shall bear the glory, and shall sit and rule upon his throne; and he shall be a priest upon his throne; and the counsel of peace shall be between them both.

Heb.5:6

v.6 As he saith also in another place, Thou art a priest forever after the order of Melchiz'edek;

Heb.6:20

v.20 Where the forerunner is for us entered, even Jesus, made an high priest forever after the order of Melchiz'edek.

Heb.7:21

v.21 (For those priests were made without an oath, but this with an oath by him that said unto him, The Lord swore and will not repent, Thou art a priest forever after the order of Melchiz'edek),

v.5 The Lord at thy right hand shall strike through kings in the day of his wrath.

v.6 He shall judge among the (l) | nations | ; he shall fill the places with the dead bodies; he shall wound the heads over many countries.

(l) | nation |
(l) KJV heathen

v.7 He shall drink of the brook in the way; therefore shall he lift up the head.

1 (110:1) The importance of the 110th Psalm is attested by the remarkable prominence given to it in the N.T.

(1) It affirms the Deity of Jesus, thus answering those who deny the full divine meaning of His N.T. title of Lord (v.1; Mt.22:41-45;Mk.12:35-37;Lk.20:41-44; Acts2:34-35;Heb.1:13;10:12-13).
(2) It announces the eternal priesthood of Messiah—one of the most important statements of Scripture (v.4; Gen.14:18,note 4; Jn.14:6; 1 Tim. 2:5-6; Heb.5:6,note 7:1-28).
(3) Historically, Ps.110 begins with the ascension of Christ (v.1; Jn.20:17; Acts7:56; Rev.3:21). And
(4) prophetically, it looks forward (a) to the time when Christ will appear as the Rod of the LORD'S strenggth, the Deliverer out of Zion (Rom.11:25-27), and to the conversion of Israel (v.3; Joel 2:27; Zech.13:9; see Dt. 30:1-9, and note at v.3); and (b) to the judgement upon the Gentile powers which preceeds the setting up of the kingdom (vv.5-6;Joel 3:9-17; Zech.14:1-4;

Rev.19:11-21). See Armageddon (Rev.16:16; 19:17, note); Israel (Gen.12:2-3; Rom.11:26, note);Kingdom (Zech.12:8, and 1 Cor.15:24, notes).

CHRIST AS THE STONE OR ROCK

PSALM 118

v.1 OH, give thanks unto the LORD, for he is good; (p) because his mercy endureth forever.

> (p) because his mercy endureth forever.
> (p) Ps.136:1-26
>
> v.1 OH, give thanks unto the LORD, for he is good; for his mercy endureth forever.
> v.2 Oh, give thanks unto the God of gods; for his mercy endureth forever.

v.3 Oh, give thanks unto the Lord of lords; for his mercy endureth forever;
v.4 To him who alone doeth great wonders; for his mercy endureth forever;
v.5 To him who by wisdom made the heavens; for his mercy endureth forever;
v.6 To him who stretched out the earth above the waters; for his mercy endureth forever;
v.7 To him who made great lights; for his mercy endureth forever;
v.8 The sun to rule by day; for his mercy endureth forever;
v.9 The moon and stars to rule by night; for his mercy endureth forever;
v.10 To him who smote Egypt in their first-born; for his mercy endureth forever;
v.11 And brought out Israel from among them; for his mercy endureth forever;
v.12 With a strong hand, and with | an outstretched | arm; for his mercy endureth forever;
v.13 To him who divided the Red Sea into parts; for his mercy endureth forever;
v.14 And made Israel to pass through the midst of it; for his mercy endureth forever;
v.15 But overthrew Phar'aoh and his host in the Red Sea; for his mercy endureth forever;
v.16 To him who led his people through the wilderness; for his mercy endureth forever;
v.17 To him who smote great kings; for his mercy endureth forever;
v.18 And slew famous king's for his mercy endureth forever;
v.19 Sihon, king of the Amorites; for his mercy endureth forever;
v.20 And Og, the king of Bashan; for his mercy endureth forever;
v.21 And gave their land for an heritage; for his mercy endureth forever;

v.22 Even an heritage unto Israel, his servant; for his mercy endureth forever;
v.23 Who remembered us in our low estate; for his mercy endureth forever;
v.24 And hath redeemed us from our enemies; for his mercy endureth forever;
v.25 Who giveth food to all flesh; for his mercy endureth forever;
v.26 Oh, give thanks unto the God of heaven; for his mercy endureth forever;

v.2 Let Israel now say that his mercy endureth forever.
v.3 Let the house of Aaron now say that his mercy endureth forever;
v.4 Let them now who (b)fear the Lord say that his mercy endureth forever.

(b) fear
(b) Ps.19:9,note

v.9 The fear of the Lord is clean, enduring forever; the |ordinances| of the Lord are true and righteous altogether. 2(19:9) "The fear of the Lord" is an O.T. expression meaning reverential trust, including the hatred of evil.

v.5 I called upon the Lord in distress; the Lord answered me, and set me in a large place.
v.6 The (q) Lord is on my side; I will not fear. What can a man do unto me?

(q) Lord is on my side;
(q) Ps.56:9;Rom.8:31;Heb.13:6

Ps.56:9

v.9 When I cry unto thee, then shall mine enemies turn back: this I know; for God is for me.

Rom.8:31

v.31 What shall we then say to these things ? If God be for us, who can be against us?

Heb.13:6

v.6 So that we may boldly say, The Lord is my helper, and I will not fear what man shall do unto me.

v.7 The LORD taketh my part with those who help me; therefore shall I see my desire upon those who hate me.
v.8 It is better to trust in the LORD than to put confidence in (r) man.

(r) man
(r) Cp. 2Chr.32:7-8;Isa. 31:1-3

2Chr.32:7-8

v.7 Be strong and courageous, be not afraid nor for all the king of Assyria, nor for all the multitude who are with him; for there are more with us than with him.
v.8 With him is an arm of flesh; but with us is the LORD, our God, to help us, and to fight our battles. And the people rested themselves upon the words of Hezeki'ah, king of Judah.

Isa.31:1-3

v.1 Woe to those who go down to Egypt for help, and | rely | on horses, and trust in chariots, because they are many; and in horsemen, because they are very strong; but they look not unto the Holy One of Israel, neither seek the LORD!
v.2 Yet he also is wise, and will bring evil, and will not call back his words, but will arise against the house of the evildoers, and against the help of those who work iniquity.

v.3 Now the Egyptians are men, and not God; and their horses flesh, and not God; and their horses flesh, and not spirit. When the LORD shall stretch out his hand, both he that helpeth shall fall down, and he that is | helped | shall fall down, and they all shall fail together.

v.9 It is better to (a) trust in the LORD than to put trust confidence in princes.

(a) trust
(a)Ps.2:12,note

v.12 Kiss the Son, lest he be angry, and ye perish from the way, when his wrath is kindled but a little. Blessed are they who put their trust in him.

Note 1(2:12) Trust is the characteristic O.T. word the N.T. "faith," and "believe." It occur 152 times in the O.T., and is the rendering of Hebrew words signifying to take refuge (e.g. Ruth 2:12); to lean on (e.g. Ps.56:3); to roll on (e.g. Ps. 22:8); to wait for (e.g. Job.35:14).

v.10 All nations compassed me about, but in the name of the LORD will I destroy them.
v.11 (s) They compassed me about; yea, they compassed me about, but in the name of the LORD I will destroy them.

(s) They compassed me about;
(s) Ps.88:17

v.17 They came round about me daily like water; they compassed me about together.

v.12 They compassed me about like (t) bees; they are quenched (u) like the fire of thorns, for in the name of the LORD I will destroy them.

(t) bees;
(t) cp. Dt.1:44
(u) like the fire of thorns;
(u) cp.Nah.1:10

Dt.1:44

v.44 And the Amorites, who dwelt in that mountain, came out against you, and chased you as bees do, and destroyed you in Seir, even unto Hormah.

Nah.1:10

v.10 For while they are |entangled| together like thorns, and while they are drunk like drunkards, they shall be devoured like stubble fully dry.

v.13 Thou hast thrust (v)|hard| at me that I might fall, but the LORD helped me.

(v) |hard|
(v) KJV sore

v.14 The (a) LORD is my strength and song, and is become my salvation.

(a) LORD
(a) Ex.15:2; Isa.12:2

Ex.15:2

v.2 The Lord is my strength and song, and he is become my salvation; he is my God, and I will prepare him an habitation; my father's God, and I will exalt him.

Isa.12:2

v.2 Behold, God is my salvation; I will trust, and not be afraid; for the LORD, even |the LORD|, is my strength and my song; he also is become my salvation.

v.15 The voice of rejoicing and salvation is in the tabernacles of the righteous; the right hand of the LORD doeth valiantly.
v.16 The right hand of the LORD is exalted; the right hand of the LORD doeth valiantly.

v.17 I shall (b) not die, but live, and declare the works of the LORD.

(b) not die,
(b) Ps.116:8-9;cp.Ps.6:5;Hab.1:12

Ps.116:8-9

v.8 For thou hast delivered my soul from death, mine eyes from tears, and my feet from falling.
v.9 I will walk before the LORD in the land of the living.

Ps.6:5

v.5 For in death there is no remembrance of thee; in |sheol| who shall give thee thanks?

Hab.1:12

v.12 Art thou not from everlasting, O LORD, my God, mine Holy One? We shall not die. O LORD, thou hast ordained them for judgment; and, O Mighty God, thou hast established them for correction.

v.18 The LORD (c) hath chastened me (d)|very much|, but he hath not given me over unto death.

(c) hath chastened me
(c) 2Cor.6:9
(d) |very much;
(d) KJV sore

2Cor.6:9

v.9 As unknown, and yet always well known; as dying, and, behold, we live; as chastened, and not killed;

(d) |very much|
(d) KJV sore

v.19 (e) Open to me the gates of righteousness; I will go into them, and I will praise the LORD,

(e) Open
(e) Isa.26:2;cp. Ps.24:7

Isa.26:2

v.2 Open ye gates, that the righteous nation that keepeth the truth may enter in.

Ps.24:7

v.7 Lift up your heads, O ye gates; and be ye lifted up, ye everlasting doors; and the King of glory shall come in.

v.20 This gate of the LORD, (f) into which the righteous shall enter.

(f) into which the righteous shall enter.
(f) Isa.35:8;Rev.21:27;22:14-15

Isa.35:8

v.8 And an highway shall be there, and a way, and it shall be called The way of holiness; the unclean shall not pass over it, but it shall be for those; the wayfaring men, though fools, shall not err therein.

Rev.21:27

v.27 And there shall in no |way| enter into it anything that defileth, neither he that worketh abomination, or maketh a lie, but they who are written in the Lamb's book of life.

Rev.22:14-15

v.14 Blessed are they that |wash their robes|, that they may have right to the tree of life, and may enter in through the gates into the city.

v.15 For |outside| are dogs, and sorcerers, and |fornicators|, and murderers and idolaters and whosoever loveth and maketh a lie.

v.21 I will praise thee; for thou hast heard me, and art become my salvation.
v.22 The 1(g) stone which the builders refused is become the head of the corner.

1(g) stone which the builders refused
(g) 1(118:22) Christ (Stone):v.22;
Isa.8:14.(Gen.49:24;1Pet.2:8).

Ps. 118 looks beyond the rejection of the Stone (Christ) to His final exaltation in the kingdom, See above,v.22

Isa.8:14

v.14 And he shall be for a sanctuary; but for a stone of stumbling and for a rock of offense to both the houses of Israel, for a |trap| and for a snare to the inhabitants of Jerusalem.

Gen.49:24

v.24 But his bow abode strength, and the arms of his hands were made strong by the hands of the mighty God of Jacob (from there is the shepherd, the stone of Israel),

1 Pet.2:8

v.8 And a stone of stumbling, and a rock of defense, even to them who stumble at the word, being disobedient; whereunto also they were appointed.

v.23 (h) This is the Lord's doing; it is marvelous in our eyes.

(h) This is the LORD's doing;
(h) lit. This is from the LORD

v.24 This is the day which the LORD hath made; we will rejoice and be glad in it.
v.25 Save now, I beseech thee, O LORD! O LORD, I beseech thee, send now prosperity!
v.26 (i) Blessed is he that cometh in the name of the LORD; we have blessed you out of the house of the LORD.

(i) Blessed is he that cometh
(i) Mt.21:9;23:39;Mk.11:9; Lk.13:35;19:38;Jn.12:13

Mt. 21:9

v.9 And the multitudes that went before, and that followed, cried, saying, Hosanna to the Son of David! Blessed is he that cometh in the name of the Lord! Hosanna in the highest!

Mt.23:39

v.39 **For I say unto you, Ye shall not see me henceforth, till ye shall say, Blessed is he that cometh in the name of the Lord.**

Mk.11:9

v.9 And they that before, and they that followed, cried, saying, Hosanna! Blessed is he that cometh in the name of the Lord.

Lk.13:35

v.35 **Behold, your house is left unto you desolate; and verily I say unto you, Ye shall not see me, until the time come when ye shall say, Blessed is he that cometh in the name of the Lord.**

Lk.19:38

v.38 Saying, Blessed be the king who cometh in the name of the Lord; peace in heaven, and glory in the highest.

Jn.12:13

v.13 Took branches of palm trees, and went forth to meet him, and cried, Hosanna! Blessed is the King of Israel, cometh in the name of the Lord.

v.27 God is the LORD, who hath shown us light; bind the sacrifice with cords, even unto the horns of the altar.
v.28 Thou art my God, and I will praise thee; thou art my God, I will exalt thee.
v.29 2 Oh, give thanks unto the LORD, for he is good; for his mercy endureth forever.

2(118:29) The Messianic Psalms: Summary. That the Psalms contain a testimony to Christ, our Lord Himself affirmed (Lk.24:44,etc.), and the N.T. quotations from the Psalter point unerringly to those Psalms which have the Messianic character. A similar spiritual and prophetic character identifies others. See Ps.2:1,note.

(1) Christ is seen in the Psalms in two general attitudes: as suffering (e.g. Ps.22), and as entering into His kingdom glory (e.g.Ps.2 and 24. Cp.Lk.24:25-27).
(2) Christ is seen in His Person as (a) Son of God (Ps.2:7), and very God (Ps.45:6-7;102:25;110:1); (b) Son of man (Ps.8:4-6); and (c) Son of David (Ps.89:3-4,27,29).
(3) Christ is seen in His offices as (a) Prophet (Ps.22:22,25;40:9-10);(b) Priest (Ps.110:4);and (c) King (e.g.Ps.2 and 24).
(4) Christ is seen in His varied work, As Priest He offers Himself in sacrifice (Ps.22;40:6-8,with Heb.10:5-12), and, in resurrection, as the Priest—Shepherd, ever living to make intercession (Ps.23,

with Heb.7:21-25; 13:20). As Prophet He proclaims the name of the LORD as Father (Ps.22:22, with Jn.20:17). As King He fulfills the Davidic Covenant (Ps.89) and restore alike the dominion of man over creation (Ps.8:4-8;Rom.8:17-21) and the Father over all (1Cor.15:25-28).

(5) The Messianic Psalms give also the inner thoughts, the exercises of soul, of Christ in His earthly experiences (e.g. Ps.16:8-11;22:1-21;40:1-17).

118—Messianic Psalm—Scofield
Hallelujah (Hallel)—Scofield
Thanksgiving—King James Study Bible (Nelson)

Reflections

II
PENITENTIAL PSALMS

PLEA FOR MERCY

PSALM 6

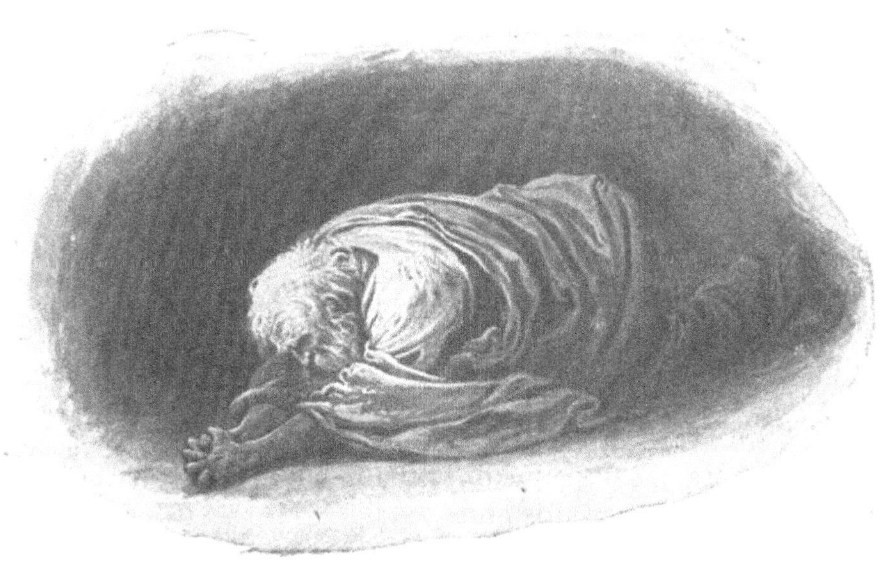

v.1 O LORD, (k) rebuke me not in thine anger, neither chasten me in thy hot displeasure.

(k) rebuke me not in thine anger,
(k)Ps.38:1;Jer.10:24

Ps.38:1

v.1 O LORD, rebuke me not in thy wrath; neither chasten me in thy hot displeasure.

Jer.10:24

v.24 O LORD, correct me, but with |justice|; not in thine anger, lest thou bring me to nothing.

v.2 Have mercy upon me, O LORD, for I am weak. O LORD, heal me; for my bones are vexed.
v.3 My soul is also (l) |very| (m) vexed; but thou, O LORD, how long?

(l) |very|
(l) KJV sore
(m) vexed;
(m)Ps.88:3;cp.Jn.12:27

Ps.88:3

v.3 For my soul is full of troubles, and my life draweth |near| unto |sheol|.

Jn.12:27

v.27 **Now is my soul troubled; and what shall I say? Father, save me from this hour. But for this cause came I unto this hour.**

v.4 Return, O LORD, deliver my soul: oh, save me from thy mercies' sake.
v.5 For in death there is (n) no remembrance of thee; in (o)|sheol| who shall give thee thanks?

(n) no remembrance of thee;
(n) Ps.30:9;88:9-11;115:17; Eccl.9:10
(o)|sheol|;
(o) KJV the grave.
See Hab.2:5,note; Lk.16:23,note

Ps.30:9

v.9 What profit is there in my blood, when I go down to

the pit? Shall the dust praise thee? Shall it declare thy truth?

Ps.88:9-11

v.9 Mine eye mourned by reason of affliction. LORD, I have called daily upon thee, I have stretched out my hands unto thee.
v.10 Thou hast broken Rahab in pieces, as one that is slain; thou hast scattered thine enemies with thy strong arm.
v.11 The heavens are thine; the earth also is thine; as for the world and the fullness thereof, thou hast founded them.

Ps.115:17

v.17 The dead praise not the LORD, neither any that go down into silence.

Eccl. 9:10

v.10 Whatsoever thy hand findeth to do, do it with thy might; for there is no work, nor device, nor knowledge, nor wisdom in |sheol|, whither thou goest.

Hab.2:5, note

v.5 Yea, also, because he transgresseth by wine, he is a proud man, neither keepeth at home, who enlargeth his desire as |sheol|, and is as death, and cannot be satisfied, but gathered unto himself all nations, and heapeth unto himself all peoples.

4(2:5) Sheol is in the O.T., the place to which the dead go. (1) Often, there, it is spoken of as the equivalent of the grave, where all human activities cease; the terminus toward which all human life moves (e.g. Gen.42:38; Job.14:13;Ps.88:3). (2) To the man "under the sun" the natural man, who of necessity judges from appearances, sheol seems no more than the grave—the end and total cessation, not only of the activities of life, but also of life itself (Eccl.9:5,10). But (3)Scripture reveals sheol as a place of sorrow(2Sam.22:6;Ps.18:5;116:3), into which the wicked are turned (Ps.9:17), and where they are fully conscious (Isa.14:9-17; Ezek.32:21).cp. Jon.2:2; what the belly of the great fish was to Jonah, sheol is to those who are therein. The sheol of the O.T. and hades of the N.T. are identical.

Lk.16:23,note

v.23 **And in |hades| he lifted up his eyes, being in torments, and seeth Abraham afar off, and Lazarus in his bosom.**

1 (16:23) The Greek word hades, like its Hebrew equivalent, sheol, is used in two ways;

(1) To indicate the condition of the unsaved between death and the great white throne judgment (Rev.20:11-15). Luke 16:23-24 shows that the lost in hades are conscious, possess full use of their faculties, memory, etc., and are in torment. This continues until the final judgment of the lost (2 pet.2:9, ASV), when all the unsaved, and hades itself, will be cast into the lake of fire (Rev.20:13-15).

(2) To indicate, in general, the condition of all departed human spirits between death and the resurrection. This usage is found occasionally in the O.T. but rarely, if ever, in the N.T. (cp.Gen.37:35;42:38; 44:29,31).It should not lead anyone to think that there is a possibility of change from one state to the other after death, for v.23 shows that when the unsaved man who was in hades saw Abraham and Lazarus, they were "afar off," and v.26 states that between the two places there is a great gulf fixed, so that no one can pass from one to the other.

Some interpreters think that Eph.4:8-10 indicates that a change in the place of the departed believers occurred at the resurrection of Christ. It is certain that all who saved go at once into the presence of Christ (2 Cor.5:8; Phil.1:23). Jesus told the penitent thief: "Today shalt thou be with me in paradise" (Lk.23:43). Paul was "caught up to the third heaven . . . into paradise" (2 Cor.12:1-4). Paradise is a place of great joy and bliss, but this bliss is not complete until the spirit is reunited with a glorified body at the resurection of the just (1 Cor.15:51-54; 1Th.4:16-17). Though both sheol and hades are sometimes translated "grave" (cp. Gen.37:35; 1Cor.15:55), they never indicate a burial place but, rather, the state of the spirit after death.

v.6 I am weary with my groaning; all the night make I my bed to swim; I water my couch with my tears.
v.7 Mine eye is consumed because of grief; it (p) | groweth | old because of all mine enemies.

(p) | groweth |
(p) KJV waxeth

v.8 Depart from me, all ye workers of (q) iniquity; for the LORD hath heard the voice of my weeping.

(q) iniquity;
(q) cp. Mt.7:23

Mt.7:23

v.23 **And then will I profess unto them, I never knew you; depart from me, that work iniquity.**

v.9 The LORD hath heard my supplication; the LORD will receive my prayer.
v.10 Let all mine enemies be ashamed and (l) | very | vexed; let them return and be ashamed suddenly.

(l) | very |
(l) KJV sore

THE BLESSEDNESS OF FORGIVENESS

PSALM 32

v.1 BLESSED is he whose transgression is forgiven, whose sin is covered.
v.2 Blessed is the man unto whom the LORD (o) imputeth not
(p) iniquity, and in whose spirit there is (q) no guile.

(o) imputeth not
(o) Imputation:
vv.1-2;see above
Rom.4:3(Gen.15:6;Jas.2:23)
(p) iniquity;
(p) Rom.4:7-8
(q) no guile
(q) Jn.1:47

Rom.4:3

v.3 For what saith the scripture? Abraham believed God,
and it was counted unto him for righteousness.

Gen.15:6

v.6 And he believed in the LORD; and he counted it to
him for righteousness.

Jas.2:23

v. 23 And the scripture was fulfilled which saith, Abraham

believed God, and it was imputed unto him for righteousness; and he was called the friend of God.

Rom.4:7-8

v.7 Saying, Blessed are they whose iniquities are forgiven, and whose sins are covered.
v.8 Blessed is the man to whom the Lord will not impute sin.

Jn.1:47

v.47 Jesus saw Nathanael coming to him, and saith of him, **Behold an Israelite indeed, in whom is no guile!**

v.3 When I kept silence, my bones (r) |became| old through my roaring all the day long.

(r) my bones |became| old
(r) KJV waxed

v.4 For day and night thy hand was heavy upon me; my moisture is turned into the drought of summer. Selah.
v.5 I acknowledged my sin unto thee, and mine iniquity have I not hidden. I said, I will (s) confess my transgressions unto the LORD, and thou (t) forgavest the iniquity of my sin. Selah.

(s) confess my transgressions
(s) 2 Sam.12:13;Ps.38:18;Prov.28:13;1 Jn.1:9
(t) forgavest the iniquity of my sin;
(t) Forgiveness v.5;Ps.99:8.
Lev.4:20;Mt.26:28, note)

2 Sam.12:13

v.13 And David said unto Nathan, I have sinned against the LORD And Nathan said unto David, The LORD also hath put away thy sin; thou shalt not die.

Ps.38:18

v.18 For I will declare mine iniquity; I will be sorry for my sin.

Prov.28:13

v.13 He that covereth his sins shall not prosper, but whoso confesseth and forsaketh them shall have mercy.

1 Jn.1:9

v.9 If we confess our sins, he is faithful and just to forgive us our sins, and to cleanse us from all unrighteousness.

Ps.32:5.

v.5 I acknowledged my sin unto thee, and mine iniquity have I not hidden. I said, I will confess my transgressions unto the Lord, and thou forgavest the iniquity of my sin. Selah.

Ps.99:8

v.8 Thou answeredst them, O Lord our God: thou wast a God who forgavest them though thou hast taken vengeance on their |misdeeds|.

Lev.4:20

v.20 And he shall do with the bullock as he did with the bullock for a sin offering, so shall he do with this: and the priest shall make an atonement for them, and it shall be forgiven them.

Mt.26:28

v.28 **For this is my blood of the new testament, which is shed for many for the remission of sins.**

v.6 For this shall every one that is godly pray unto thee in a time when thou mayest be found; surely, in the floods of great waters, they shall not come (u) | near | unto him.

(u) | near |
(u) nigh

v.7 Thou art my hiding place; thou shalt preserve me from trouble; thou shalt compass me about with songs of deliverance. Selah.
v.8 I will instruct thee and teach thee in the way which thou shalt go; I will guide thee with mine eyes.
v.9 Be ye not like the (a) horse, or like the mule, that have no understanding, whose mouth must be held in with bit and bridle, lest they come near unto thee.

(a) horse,
(a) Prov.26:3

Prov.26:3

v.3 A whip for the horse, a bridle for the ass, and a rod for the fool's back.

v.10 Many sorrows shall be to the wicked; but he that (b) trusteth in the LORD, mercy shall compass him about.

(b) trustest in
(b)Faith:v.10;Ps.37:3.
(Gen.3:20);Heb.11:39,note)
v.10;See the above

Ps.37:3

v.3 Trust in the LORD, and do good; so shalt thou dwell in the land, and verily thou shalt be fed.

Gen.3:20

v.20 And Adam called his wife's name Eve, because she was the mother of all living.

Heb.11:39

v.39 And these all, having |received witness| through faith, received not the promise,

v.11 Be glad in the Lord, and rejoice, ye that are upright in heart. This Psalm describes the blessedness of forgiveness as no other does.

GODLY SORROW FOR SIN

PSALM 38

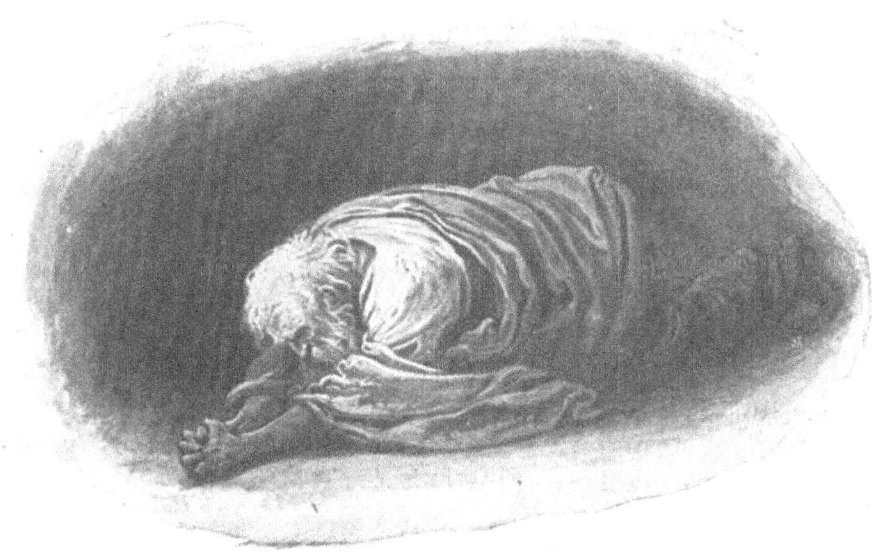

v.1 O LORD, (f) rebuke me not in thy wrath; neither chasten me in thy hot displeasure.

(f) rebuke me not in thy wrath;
(f) Ps.6:1

Ps.6:1

v.1 O LORD, rebuke me not in thine angry, neither chasten me in thy hot displeasure.

v.2 For thine arrows stick fast in me, and thy hand presseth me (g) | greatly | .

(g) | greatly |
(g) KJV sore

v.3 There is no soundness in my flesh because of thine anger; neither is there any (h) rest in my bones because of my sin.

(h) rest
(h) Lit. peace or health

v.4 For mine iniquities are gone over mine head; like an heavy burden they are too heavy for me.
v.5 My wounds (i) | are repulsive and | corrupt because of my foolishness.

(i) My wounds | are repulsive and |
(i) KJV stink and are

v.6 I am troubled; I am bowed down greatly; I go mourning all the day long.
v.7 For my loins are filled with a loathsome disease, and there is no soundness in my flesh.
v.8 I am feeble and (g) | very | broken; I have roared by reason of the disquietness of my heart.

(g) | very | broken;
(g) KJV sore

v.9 Lord, all my desire is before thee, and my groaning is not hidden from thee.
v.10 My heart panteth, my strength faileth me; as for the light of mine eyes, it also is gone from me.
v.11 My lovers and my friends (j) stand aloof from my sore, and my kinsmen stand afar off.

(j) stand aloof from my sore,
(j) Ps. 31:11;cp.Lk.23:49

Ps.31:11

v.11 I was a reproach among all mine enemies, but especially among my neighbors, and a fear to my acquaintance; they that did see me without fled from me.

Lk.23:49

v.49 And all his acquaintances, and the woman that followed him from Galilee, stood afar off, beholding these things.

v.12 They also who seek after my life lay snares for me and they who seek my hurt (k)speak mischievous things, and imagine deceits all the day long.

(k) speak mischievous things,
(k) cp.2 Sam.16:7-8

2 Sam.16:7-8

v.7 And thus said Shim'ei when he cursed, Come out, come out, thou bloody man, and thou |worthless fellow|;
v.8 The LORD hath returned upon thee all the blood of the house of Saul, whose stead thou hast reigned; and the LORD hath delivered the kingdom into the hand of Absalom, thy son; and behold, thou art taken in thy mischief, because thou art a bloody man.

v.13 But I, like a deaf man, heard not; and I was like a dumb man who openeth not his mouth.
v.14 Thus I was like a man who heareth not, and in whose mouth are no reproofs.
v.15 For in thee, O LORD, do I hope; thou wilt (l)hear, O LORD, my God.

(l) hear, O Lord, my God.
(l) Or answer

v.16 For I said, Hear me, lest otherwise they should rejoice over me: when my foot slippeth, they magnify themselves against me.
v.17 (m) For I am ready to halt, and my sorrow is continually before me.

(m) For I am ready to halt
(m) Ps.51:3

Ps.51:3

v.3 For I acknowledge my transgressions, and my sin is ever before me.

v.18 For I will (n) declare mine iniquity; I will be (o) sorry for my sin.

(n) declare mine iniquity;
(n) Ps.32:5
(o) sorry for my sin.
(o) 2 Cor.7:9-10

Ps.32:5

v.5 I acknowledge my sin unto thee, and mine iniquity have I not hidden. I said, I confess my transgressions unto the Lord, thou forgavest the iniquity of my sin. Selah.

2 Cor.7:9-10

v.9 Now I rejoice, not that ye were made sorry but that ye sorrowed to repentance; for ye were made sorry after a godly manner, that ye might receive damage by us in nothing.

v.10 For godly sorrow worketh repentance to salvation not to be repented of; but the sorrow of the world worketh death.

v.19 But mine enemies are lively, and they are strong; and they that hate me wrongfully are multiplied.
v.20 They also that render evil for good are mine adversaries; (p) because I follow the thing that is good.

(p) because I follow the things that is good.
(p) cp. lPet.3:14;Jn.3:12

1 Pet.3:14

v.14 But and if ye suffer for righteousness' sake, happy are ye; and be not afraid of their terror, neither be troubled,

Jn.3:12

v.12 **If I have told you earthly things, and ye believe not, how shall ye believe, if I tell you heavenly things?**

v.21 Forsake me not, O LORD; O my God, (q) be not far from me.

(q) be not far from me.
(q) Ps.35:22

Ps.35:22

v.22 This thou hast seen, O LORD; keep not silence. O Lord, be not far from me.

v.22 Make haste to help me, O Lord, my salvation.

A PSALM OF PENITENCE

PSALM 51

(t) Bath-sheba 2 Sam.11:1-12:13

v.1 And it came to pass, after the year was |ended|, at
the time when kings go forth to battle, that David

sent Joab, and his servants with him, and all Israel, and they destroyed the children of Ammon, and besieged Rabbah. But David tarried still at Jerusalem.

v.2 And it came to pass at eventide, that David arose from his bed, and walked upon the roof of the king's house. And from the roof he saw a woman washing herself, and the woman was very beautiful to look upon.

v.3 And David sent and inquired about the woman. And one said, Is not this Bath-sheba, the daughter of Eli'am, the wife of Uri'ah, the Hittite?

v.4 And David sent messengers, and took her. And she came in unto him, and he lay with her; for she was purified from her uncleanness. And she returned unto her house.

v.5 And the woman conceived, and sent and told David, and said, I am with child.

v.6 And David sent to Joab, saying, Send me Uri'ah, the Hittite. And Joab sent Uriah to David.

v.7 And when Uri'ah was come unto him, David demanded of him how Joab did, and how the people did, and how the war prospered.

v.8 And David said to Uri'ah, Go down to thy house, and wash thy feet, And Uriah departed out of the king's house, and there followed him a |present| from the king.

v.9 But Uri'ah slept at the door of the king's house with all the servants of his lord, and went not down to his house.

v.10 And when they had told David, saying, Uri'ah went not down unto his house, David said unto Uriah, Camest thou, not from thy journey? Why then, didst thou not go down unto thine house?

v.11 And Uri'ah said unto David, The ark, and Israel, and Judah abide in tents; and my lord, Joab, and the servants of the lord, are encamped in the open fields. Shall I, then, go into mine house, to eat and drink, and to lie with my wife? As thy soul liveth, I will not do this thing.

v.12 And David said to Uriah, Tarry here today also, and tomorrow I will let thee depart. So Uriah adode in Jerusalem that day, and the |next|.

v.13 And David said unto Nathan, I have sinned against the LORD. And Nathan said unto David, The LORD also hath put away thy sin; thou shalt not die.

v.1 1 HAVE (u) mercy upon me, O God, according to thy loving—kind-ness; according unto the multitude of thy tender mercies blot out my transgressions.

1(51:1)
(u) Have mercy upon me,
(u) Bible prayers (O.T.):vv.1-19;
Isa.37:15. (Gen.15:2;Hab.3:1)
See vv.1-19

Isa.37:15

v.15 And Hezeki'ah prayed unto the LORD, saying ff.,

Gen.15:2

v.2 And Abram said, Lord God, what wilt thou give me, seeing I go childless, and the |heir| of my house is this Elie'zer of Damascus?

Hab.3:1

v.1 A PRAYER of Habak'kuk, the prophet, upon Shigio'noth.

v.2 Wash me (v) |thoroughly| from mine iniquity, and cleanse me from my sin.

(v) |thoroughly|
(v) KJV thoroughly

v.3 For I acknowledge my transgressions, and my sin is ever before me.

v.4 Against thee, thee only, have I sinned, and done this evil in thy sight, that thou mightest be (w) justified when you speakest, and be clear when thou judgest.

(w) justified when you speakest,
(w) Rom.3:4

Rom.3:4

v.4 God forbid: yea, let God be true, but every man a liar; as it is written, That thou mightest be justified in thy sayings, and mightest overcome when thou art judged.

v.5 (x) Behold, I was shaped in iniquity, and in sin did my mother conceive me.

(x) Behold,
(x) Job.14:4;Ps.58:3; Jn.3:6; Rom.5:12;Eph.2:3

Job.14:4

v.4 Who can bring a clean thing out of an unclean? Not one.

Ps.58:3

v.3 The wicked are estranged from the womb: they go astray as soon as they be born, speaking lies.

Jn.3:6

v.6 **That which is born of the flesh is flesh; and that which is born of the Spirit is spirit.**

Rom.5:12

v.12 Wherefore, as by one man sin entered into the world, and death by sin; and so death passed upon all men, for that all have sinned:*

Eph.2:3

v.3 Among whom also we all had our conversation in times past in the lusts of the flesh, fulfilling the desires of the flesh and of the mind; and were by nature the children of wrath, even as others.

v.6 Behold, thou desirest truth in the inward parts, and in the hidden part thou shalt make me know wisdom.
v.7 (y) Purge me with 2 hyssop, and I shall be clean: wash me, and I shall be (a) whiter than snow.

(y) Purge me
(y) Heb.9:19;Lev.14:1-7
(a) whiter than snow.
(a) Isa.1:18

Heb.9:19

v.19 For when Moses had spoken every precept to all the people according to the law, he took the blood of calves and of goats, with water, and scarlet wool, and hyssop, and sprinkled both the book, and all the people,

Lev.14:1-7

v.1 And the LORD spoke unto Moses, saying,
v.2 This shall be the law of the leper in the day of his cleansing:
v.3 And the priest shall go forth out of the camp; and the priest shall look, and behold, if the plague of the leprosy be healed in the leper;
v.4 Then shall the priest command to take for him that is to be cleansed two birds alive and clean, and cedar wood, and scarlet, and hyssop:
v.5 And the priest shall command that one of the birds be killed in an earthen vessel over running water:
v.6 As for the living bird, he shall take it, and the cedar wood, and the scarlet, and the hyssop, and shall dip

them and the living bird in the blood of the bird that was killed over the running water:

v.7 And he shall sprinkle upon him that is to be cleansed from the leprosy seven times, and shall let the living bird loose into the open field.

Isa.1:18

v.18 Come now, and let us reason together, saith the LORD: though your sins be as scarlet, they shall be as white as snow; though they be red like crimson, they shall be as wool.

v.8 Make me hear joy and gladness, that the (b) bones which thou hast broken may rejoice.

(b) bones
(b) cp.Ps.35:9-10

Ps.35:9-10

v.9 And my soul shall be joyful in the LORD, it shall rejoice in his salvation.

v.10 All my bones shall say, LORD, who is like unto thee, which deliverest the poor from him that is too strong for him, yea, the poor and the needy from him that spoileth him?

v.9 Hide thy face from my sins, and blot all mine iniquities.

v.10 (c) Create in me a clean heart, O God; and renew a right spirit within me.

(c) create in me a clean heart,
(c) Acts 15:9;Ezek.18:31;Eph.2:10

Acts 15:9

v.9 And put no difference between us and them, purifying their hearts by faith.

Ezek.18:31

v.31 Cast away from you all your transgressions, whereby ye have transgressed; and make you a new heart and a new spirit; for why will ye die, O house of Israel?

Eph.2:10

v.10 For we are his workmanship, created in Christ Jesus unto good works, which God hath before ordained that we should walk in them.

v.11 Cast me not away from thy presence; and take not thy holy (d) Spirit from me.

(d) Spirit from me.
(d) Holy Spirit (OT.) vv.11-12; Ps.104:30
(Gen.1:2;Zech.12:10)
See vv.11-12

Ps. 104:30

v.30 Thou sendest forth thy spirit, they are created: and thou renewest the face of the earth.

Gen.1:2

v.2 And the earth was without form, and void; and darkness was upon the face of the deep. And the Spirit of God moved upon the face of the water.

Zech.12:10

v.10 And I will pour upon the house of David, and upon the inhabitants of Jerusalem, the Spirit of grace and of supplications; and they shall look upon me whom they have pierced, and they shall mourn for him, as one mourned for his only son, and shall be in bitterness for him, as one that is in bitterness for his first-born.

v.12 Restore unto me the joy of thy salvation; and uphold me with thy (e) free (1) spirit.

(e) KJV free
(e)2Cor.3:17;
(1) spirit; generous

2Cor.3:17

v.17 Now the Lord is that Spirit: and where the Spirit of the Lord is, there is liberty.

v.13 Then will I (f) teach transgressors thy ways; and sinners shall be converted unto thee.

(f) teach transgressors thy ways;
(f) Cp.Ps.19:7-8;Prov.11:30;Acts2:38-41

Ps.19:7-8

v.7 The law of the LORD is perfect, converting the soul; the testimony of the LORD is sure, making wise the simple.
v.8 The statutes of the LORD are right, rejoicing the heart; the commandment of the LORD is pure, enlightening the eyes.

Prov.11:30

v.30 The fruit of the righteous is a tree of life; and he that winneth souls is wise.

Acts2:38-41

v.38 Then Peter said unto them, Repent, and be baptized, every one of you, in the name of Jesus Christ for the receive the gift of the Holy |Spirit|.
v.39 For the promise is unto you, and to your children, and to all that are afar off, even as many as the Lord, our God, shall call.

v.40 And with many other words did he testify and exhort, saying, Save yourself from this | crooked | generation.
v.41 Then they that gladly received his word were baptized; and the same day there were added unto them about three thousand souls.

v.14 Deliver me from blood guiltiness, O God, thou God of my salvation: and my tongue shall sing aloud of thy righteousness.
v.15 O Lord, open thou my lips; and my mouth shall show forth thy praise.
v.16 For (g) thou desirest not sacrifice; else would I give it: thou delightest not in burnt offering.

(g) thou desirest not sacrifice;
(g) 1 Sam.15:22;Ps.50:8-14;Mic.6:6-8

1 Sam.15:22

v.22 And Samuel said, Hath the LORD as great delight in burnt offerings and sacrifices, as in obeying the voice of the LORD? Behold, to obey is better than sacrifice, and to hearken than the fat of rams.

Ps.50:8-14

v.8 I will not reprove thee for thy sacrifices or thy burnt offerings, to have been continually before me.
v.9 I will take no bullock out of thy house, nor he—goats out of thy folds:
v.10 For every beast of the forest is mine, and the cattle upon a thousand hills.
v.11 I know all the fowls of the mountains; and the wild beasts of the field are mine.
v.12 If I were hungry, I would not tell thee: for the world is mine, and the fullness thereof.
v.13 Will I eat the flesh of bulls, or drink the blood of goats?
v.14 Offer unto God thanksgiving, and pay thy vows unto the Most High:

Mic.6:6-8

v.6 |With what| shall I come before the LORD, and bow myself before the High God? Shall I come before him with burnt offerings, with calves of a year old?
v.7 Will the LORD be pleased with thousands of rams, or with ten thousands of rivers of oil? Shall I give my first-born for my transgression, the fruit of my body for the sin of my soul?
v.8 He hath showed thee, O man, what is good; and what doth the LORD require of thee, but to do justly, and to love mercy, and to walk humbly with thy God?

v.17 (h) The sacrifices of God are a broken spirit: a broken and a contrite heart, O God, thou wilt not despise.

(h) the sacrifices of God;
(h) Ps.34:18;Isa.57:15;66:2

Ps.34:18

v.18 The LORD is nigh unto them that are of a broken heart; and saveth such as be of a contrite spirit.

Isa.57:15

v.15 For thus saith the high and lofty One that inhabiteth eternity, whose name is Holy; I dwell in the high and holy place, with him also who is of a contrite and humble spirit, to revive the spirit of the humble, and to revive the heart of the contrite ones.

Isa.66:2

v.2 For all those things hath mine hand made, and all those things have been, saith the LORD: but to this man will I look, even to him that is poor and of a contrite spirit, and trembleth at my word.

v.18 Do good in thy good pleasure unto Zion: build thou the walls of Jerusalem.

v.19 Then shalt thou be pleased with the (i) sacrifices of righteousness, with burnt offering: and whose burnt offering: then shall they offer bullocks upon thine altar.

(i) sacrifices of righteousness,
(i) Ps.4:5;Mal.3:3

Ps.4:5

v.5 Offer the sacrifices of righteousness, and put your trust in the LORD.

Mal.3:3

v.3 And he shall sit as a refiner and purifier of silver: and he shall purify the sons of Levi, and purge them as gold and silver, that they may offer unto the LORD an offering in righteousness.

1(51:1) This Psalm is the confession of David's sin with Bathsheba the Psalm gives expression to why David was "a man after God's own heart" 1 Jn.1:9: If we confess our sins, he is faithful and just to forgive us our sins, and to cleanse us from all unrighteousness.

CHRIST, THE AFFLICTION OF HIS HOLY SOUL

PSALM 102

v.1 1 Hear my prayer, O LORD, and let my cry come unto thee. 1 (102:1)

v.2 (p) Hide not thy face from me in the day when I am in trouble; incline thine ear unto me; in the day when I call, answer me speedily.

(p) Hide not thy face
(p) Ps.27:9;69:17

Ps.27:9

v.9 Hide not thy face from me; put not thy servant away angry. Thou hast been my help; leave me not, neither forsake me, O God of my salvation.

Ps. 69:17

v.17 And hide not thy face from thy servant; for I am in trouble. Hear me speedily.

v.3 For my days are (q) consumed like smoke, and my bones are burned like an hearth.

(q) consumed like smoke,
(q) Jas. 4:14

v.14 Whereas ye know not what shall be on the |next day|. For what is your life? It is even a vapor that appeared for a little time, and then vanisheth away.

v.4 My heart is smitten, and withered like grass, so that I forget to eat my bread.
v.5 By reason of the voice of my groaning, my bones (j)|adhere| to my skin.

(j) |adhere|
(j) KJV cleave

v.6 I am like a pelican of the wilderness; I am like an owl of the desert.
v.7 I watch, and am like a sparrow alone upon the housetop.
v.8 Mine enemies reproach me all the day, and they that are mad against me are sworn against me.
v.9 For I have eaten ashes like bread, and mingled my drink with weeping,
v.10 Because of thine indignation and thy wrath; for thou hast lifted me up, and cast me down.
v.11 My days are like a shadow that declineth, and I am withered like grass.

v.12 But thou, O LORD, shalt endure forever, and thy remembrance unto all generations.

v.13 Thou shalt arise, and have mercy upon Zion; for the time to favor her, yea, the (r) set time, is come.

(r) set time, is come.
(r) cp. Dan.8:19

v.19 And he said, Behold, I will make thee know what shall be in the last end of the indignation; for at the time appointed the end shall be.

v.14 For thy servants take pleasure in her stones, and favor the dust thereof.

v.15 So the (s) |nations| shall (t) fear the name of the LORD, and all the Kings of the earth thy glory.

(s) |nations|
(s) KJV heathen
(t) fear the name of the LORD;
(t) Ps.19:9, note

Ps.19:9,note

v.9 The fear of the LORD is clean, enduring forever; the |ordinances| of the LORD are true and righteous altogether.

Note: 2(19:9) "The fear of the LORD" is an O.T. expression reverential trust including the hatred of evil.

v.16 When the LORD shall build up Zion, he shall appear in his glory.

v.17 He will (a) regard the prayer of the destitute, and not despise their prayer

(a) regard the prayer of the destitute,
(a) cp. Neh.1:6,11;2:8

v.6 Let thine ear now be attentive, and thine eyes open, that thou mayest hear the prayer of thy servant, which I pray before thee now, day and night, for the children of Israel, thy servants, and confess the sins of the children of Israel, which we have sinned against thee; both I and my father's house have sinned.

v.11 O Lord, I beseech thee, let now thine ear be attentive to the prayer of thy servant, and the prayer of thy servants, who |delight| to fear thy name; and prosper, I pray thee, thy servant this day, and grant him mercy in the sight of this man. For I was the king's cupbearer.

Neh.2:8

v.8 And a letter unto A'saph, the keeper of the king's forest, that he may give me timber to make beams for the gates of the palace which |is near| to the house, and for the wall of the city, and for the house that I shall enter into. And the king granted me, according to the good hand of my GOD, upon me.

v.18 This shall be written for the generation to come; and the people who shall be created shall praise the LORD.
v.19 For he hath (b) looked down from the height of his sanctuary; from heaven did the LORD behold the earth,

(b) looked down
(b) cp. Ex.3:7

v.7 And the LORD said, I have surely seen the affliction of my people who are in Egypt, and have heard their cry by reason of their taskmasters; for I know their sorrows;

v.20 To (c) hear the groaning of the prisoner; to loose (d) those that are appointed to death;

(c) hear the groaning of the prisoner;
(c) Ps.79:11

v.11 Let the sighing of the prisoner come before thee; according to the greatness of thy power preserve thou those that are appointed to die;

(d) those that are appointed to die;
(d) lit. the children of death

v.21 To declare the name of the LORD in Zion, and his praise in Jerusalem,
v.22 (e) When the people are gathered together, and the kingdoms, to serve the LORD.

(e) When the people are gathered together,
(e) Isa.2:2-3;60:3

Isa.2:2-3

v.2 And it shall come to pass in the last days, that the mountain of the LORD's house shall be established in the top of the mountains, and shall be exalted above the hills; and all nations shall flow unto it.
v.3 And many people shall go and say, Come ye, and let us go up to the mountain of the LORD, To the house of the God of Jacob; and he will teach us of his ways, and we will walk in his paths; for out of Zion shall go forth the law, and the word of the LORD from Jerusalem.

Isa.60:3

v.3 And the |nations| shall come to thy light, and kings to the brightness of thy rising.

v.23 He weakened my strength in the way; he shortened my days.
v.24 I said, O my God, take me not away in the midst of my days; thy years are throughout all generations.
v.25 Of old hast thou laid the (f) foundation of the earth, and the heavens are the work of thy hands.

(f) foundation of the earth,
(f) vv. 25-27; Heb.1:10-12

v.25 Of old hast thou laid the (f) foundation of the earth, and the heavens are the work of thy hands.
v.26 They shall (g) perish, but thou shalt endure; yea, all of them shall (h) |become| old like a garment; like a vesture shalt thou change them, and they shall be changed.
v.27 But thou art the (i) same, and thy years shall have no end.

Heb.1:10-12

v 10 And, Thou, Lord, in the beginning hast laid the foundation of the earth; and the heavens are the work of thine hands.
v.11 They shall perish, but thou remainest; and they all shall |become| old as doth a garment,
v.12 And as a vesture shalt thou fold them up, and they shall be changed; but thou art the same, and thy years shall not fail.

v.26 They shall (g) perish, but thou shalt endure; yea, all of them shall (h) |become| old like a garment; like a vesture shalt thou change them, and they shall be changed.

(g) perish, but thou shalt endure;
(g) Isa.34:4; 51:6;Mt. 24:35;
2 Pet.3:7,10-12;Rev.20:11
(h) |become|
(h) KJV wax

Isa.34:4

v.4 And all the host of heaven shall be dissolved, and the heavens shall be rolled together like a scroll; and all their host shall fall down, as the leaf falleth off from the vine, and like a falling fig from the fig tree.

Isa.51:6

v.6 Lift up your eyes to the heavens, and look upon the earth beneath; for the heavens shall vanish away like smoke, and the earth shall |grow| old like a garment, and they that dwell therein shall die in like manner; but my salvation shall be forever, and my righteousness shall not be abolished.

Mt.24:35

v.35 **Heaven and the earth shall pass away, but my words shall not pass away.**

2 Pet 3:7;10-12

v.7 But the heavens and the earth which are now, by the same word are kept in store, reserved unto fire against the day of judgment and perdition of ungodly men.

2 Pet. 3:10-12

v.10 But the day of the Lord will come as a thief in the night,
in which the heavens shall pass away with a great noise,
and the elements shall melt with fervent heat; the earth
also, and the works that are in it shall be burned up.
v.11 Seeing, then, that all these things shall be dissolved,
what manner of persons ought ye to be in all holy
|living| and godliness,
v.12 Looking for and hasting unto the coming of the day of
God, in which the heavens, being on fire, shall be
dissolved, and the elements shall melt with fervent heat?

Rev.20:11

v.11 And I saw a great white throne, and him that sat on it, from whose face the earth and the heaven fled away, and there was found no place for them.

v.27 But thou art the (i) same, and thy years shall have no end.

(i) same,
(i) Mal.3:6;Heb.13:8;Jas.1:17

Mal.3:6

v.6 For I am the LORD, I change not; therefore ye sons of Jacob are not consumed.

Heb.13:8

v.8 Jesus Christ, the same yesterday, and today, and forever.

Jas.1:17

v.17 Every good gift and every perfect gift is from above, and cometh down from the Father of lights, with whom is no variableness, neither shadow of turning

v.28 The children of thy servants shall continue, and their seed shall be established before thee.

Finally, the remaining section heightens the contrast between frail man and unchanging God by bringing both theme together (vv.23-28).

1 (102:1) The reference of vv.25-27 to Christ (Heb.1:10-12). is assurance that, in the preceeding verses of this Psalm, there is shown, prophetically, the affliction of His holy soul in the days of His humiliation and rejection.

WAITING FOR THE MORNING

PSALM 130

v.1 Out of the depths have I cried unto thee, O LORD.
v.2 Lord, hear my voice; let thine ears be attentive to the voice of my supplications.
v.3 If thou LORD, shouldest mark iniquities, O Lord, who shall (e) stand?

(e) who shall stand?
(e) Nah.1:6

Nah.1:6

v.6 Who can stand before his indignation? And who can abide in the fireceness of his anger?His fury is poured out like fire, and the rocks are thrown down by him.

v.4 But there is forgiveness with thee, that thou mayest be feared?

(f) that thou mayest be feared?
(f) Ki.8:39-40;see Ps.19:9,note;Messianic Ps.16)

IKi.8:39-40

v.8 Then hear thou in heaven, thy dwelling place, and forgive, and do, and give to every man according to his ways, whose heart thou knowest (for thou, even thou only, knowest the hearts of all the children of men), v.40 That they may fear thee all the days that they live in the land which thou gavest unto our fathers.

v.5 I wait for the Lord, my soul doth wait, and in his word do I hope.
v.6 (g) My soul waited for the Lord more than they that watch for the morning; I say, more than they that watch for the morning.

(g) My soul waited for the Lord
(g) Ps.33:20;40:1;Isa.8:17

Ps.33:20

v.20 Our soul waited for the Lord; he is our help and our shield.

Ps.40:1

v.1 I waited patiently for the Lord, and he inclined unto me, and heard my cry.

Isa.8:17

v.17 And I will wait upon the Lord, who hideth his face from the house of Jacob, and I will look for him.

v.7 Let Israel (h)hope in the Lord; for with the Lord (i) there is mercy, and with him is plenteous (j) redemption.

(h) hope in the Lord;
(h) Ps. 131:3
(i) there is mercy;
(i) Ps.86:5,15;Isa.55:7
(j) with him is plenteous redemption.
(j) Redemption (kinsman type) :vv.7-8; Prov.23:11.(Gen.48:16;Isa.59:20, note)

Ps.131:3

v.3 Let Israel hope in the LORD from henceforth and forever.

Ps.86:5,15

v.5 For thou, Lord, art good, and ready to forgive, and plenteous in mercy unto all those who call upon thee.
v.15 But thou, O Lord, art a God full of compassion, and gracious, long-suffering, and plenteous in mercy and truth.

Isa.55:7

v.7 Let the wicked forsake his way, and the unrighteous man his thoughts, and let him return unto the LORD, and he will have mercy upon him; and to our God; for he will abundantly pardon.
v.7 Let Israel (h) hope in the LORD; for with the LORD (i) there is mercy, and with him is plenteous (j) redemption.
v.8 And he shall redeem Israel from all his iniquities.

Prov.23:11

v.11 For their redeemer is mighty; he shall plead their cause with thee.

Gen.48:16

v.16 |An angel| who redeemed me from all evil, bless the lads; and let my name be named on them, and the name of my fathers, Abraham and Isaac; and let them grow into a multitude in the midst of the earth.

Isa.59:20,note (see note in Messianic Ps.72)

v.20 And the Redeemer shall come to Zion, and unto those who turn from transgression in Jacob, saith the LORD.

v.8 And he shall redeem Israel from all his iniquities.

AN URGENT APPEAL FOR HELP

PSALM 143

v.1 HEAR my prayer, O LORD, give ear to my supplications; in thy faithfulness answer me, and in thy righteousness.
v.2 And enter not into judgment with thy servant; (h) for in thy sight shall no man living be justified.

(h) for in thy sight
(h) Ex.34:7;Job 4:17;9:2;15:14;25:4;
Ps.130:3;Eccl.7:20;Rom.3:20;Gal.2:16

Ex.34:7

v.7 Keeping mercy for thousands, forgiving iniquity and transgression and sin, and who will by no means clear the guilty, visiting the iniquity of the fathers upon the children, and upon the children's children, unto the third and to the fourth generation.

Job 4:17

v.17 Shall mortal man be more just than God? Shall a man be more pure than his maker?

Job 9:2

v.2 I know it is so of a truth; but how should man be just before God?

Job 15:14

v.14 What is man, that he should be clean? And he who is born of a woman, that he should be righteous?

Job 25:4

v.4 How then can a man be justified with God? Or how can he be clean that is born of a woman?

Ps.130:3

v.3 If thou, LORD, shouldest mark iniquities, O Lord, who shall stand?

Eccl.7:20

v.20 For there is not a just man upon earth, that doeth good and sinneth not.

Rom.3:20

v.20 Therefore, by the deeds of the law there shall no flesh be justified in his sight; for by the law is the knowledge of sin.

Gal.2:16

v.16 Knowing that a man is not justified by the works of the law, but by the faith of Jesus Christ, even we have believed in Jesus Christ, that we might be justified by faith of Christ, and not by the works of the law; for by works of the law shall no flesh be justified.

v.3 For the enemy hath persecuted my soul; he hath smitten my life down to the ground; he hath made me to dwell in darkness, as those who have been long dead.
v.4 Therefore is my spirit (c) overwhelmed within me; my heart within me is desolate.

(c) overwhelmed within me;
(c) Ps.77:3

Ps.77:3

v.3 I remembered God, and was troubled; I complained, and my spirit was overwhelmed. Selah.

v.5 (i) I remember the days of old; I meditate on all thy works; I muse on the work of thy hands.

(i) I remember the days of old;
(i) Ps.77:5,10-11

Ps.77:5

v.5 I have considered the days of old, the years of ancient times.
v.10 And I said, This is my infirmity; but I will remember the years of the right hand of the Most High.
v.11 I will remember the works of the LORD; surely I will remember thy wonders of old.

v.6 I stretch forth my hands unto thee; my soul thirsteth after thee; like a thirsty land. Selah.

v.7 Hear me speedily, O LORD; my spirit faileth. Hide not thy face from me, lest I be like unto them that go down into the pit.
v.8 Cause me to hear thy loving—kindness in the morning; for in thee do I trust. (j) Cause me to know the way wherein I should walk; for I lift up my soul unto thee.

(j) Cause me to know the way;
(j)Ps.5:8

Ps.5:8

v.5 Lead me, O LORD. in thy righteousness because of mine enemies; make thy way straight before my face.

v.9 Deliver me, O LORD, from mine enemies; I flee unto thee to hide me.
v.10 Teach me to do thy will; for thou art my God. Thy (k) Spirit is good; lead me into the land of righteousness.

(k) Thy Spirit is good;
(k) Holy Spirit
(O.T.):v.10;Isa.11:2.
(Gen.1:2;Zech.12:10)
(k) Holy Spirit
See the above v.10

Isa.11:2

v.2 And the Spirit of the LORD shall rest upon him, the spirit of wisdom and understanding, the spirit of counsel and might, the spirit of knowledge and of the fear of the LORD,

Gen.1:2

v.2 And the earth was without form, and void; and darkness was upon the face of the deep. And the Spirit of God moved upon the face of the waters.

Zech.12:10

v.10 And I will pour upon the house of David, and upon the inhabitants of Jerusalem, the Spirit of grace and of supplications; and they shall look upon me whom they have pierced, and they shall mourn for him, as one mourneth for his only son, and shall be in bitterness for him, as one that is in bitterness for his first-born.

v.11 (l) | Revive | me, O Lord, for thy name's sake; for thy righteousness' sake bring my soul out of trouble.

(l) | Revive | me,
(l) KJV Quicken. Ps.138:7

v.7 Though I walk in the midst of trouble, thou wilt revive me; thou shalt stretch forth thine hand against the wrath of mine enemies, and thy right hand shall save me.

v.12 And of thy mercy cut off mine enemies, and destroy all them that afflict my soul; for I am thy servant.

III

IMPRECATORY PSALMS

CRIES TO GOD TO AVENGE

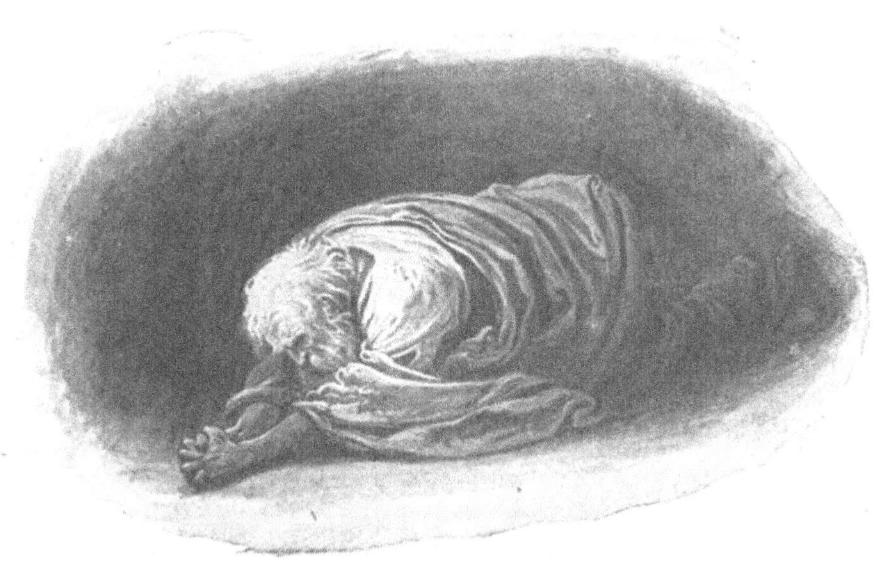

DAVID'S PRAYER AGAINST HIS ENEMIES

PSALM 35

v.1 PLEAD my cause, O LORD, with those who strive with me; (f) fight against those who fight against me.

> (f) fight against those who fight against me.
> (f) Cp. Ex.14:25

> v.25 And the LORD took off their chariot wheels, that they drove them heavily; so that the Egyptians said, Let us flee from the face of Israel; for the LORD fighteth for them against the Egyptians.

v.2 (g) Take hold of shield and buckler, and stand up for mine help.

> (g) Take hold of my shield and buckler,
> (g) Cp.Ps.44:26;91:4

Ps.44:26

> v.26 Arise for our help, and redeem us for thy mercies' sake.

Ps.91:4

> v.4 He shall cover thee with his feathers, and under his wings shalt thou trust; his truth shall be thy shield and buckler.

v.3 Draw out also the spear, and stop the way against those who persecute me. Say unto my soul, I am thy salvation.
v.4 (h) Let them be confounded and put to shame who seek after my soul; let them be (i) turned back and brought to confusion who devise my hurt.

(h) Let them be confounded
(h)v.26;Ps.40:14,15
(i) turned back and brought to confusion
(i) Ps. 129:5

Ps.35:26

v.26 Let them be ashamed and brought to confusion together who rejoice at mine hurt; let them be clothed with shame and dishonor who magnify themselves against me.

Ps. 40:14,15

v.14 Let them be ashamed and confounded together who seek after my soul to destroy it; let them be driven backward and put to shame who wish me evil.
v.15 Let them be desolate for a reward of their shame, who say unto me, Aha, aha.

Ps.129:5

v.5 Let them all be confounded and turned back that hate Zion.

v.5 Let them be as chaff before the wind; and let the (j) angel of the LORD chase them.

(j) angel of the LORD chase them.
(j) Angel of the LORD:
vv.5,6;Isa.37:36.(Gen.16:7;Jud.2:1,note)

v.5 Let them be as chaff before the wind: and let the (j) angel of the LORD chase them.

v.6 Let their way be dark and slippery, and let the (j) angel of the LORD persecute them.

Isa.37:36

v.36 Then the angel of the LORD went forth, and smote in the champ of the Assyrians a hundred and fourscore and five thousand; and when |men| arose early in the morning, behold, |these were dead|.

Gen.16:7

v.7 And the angel of the LORD found her by a fountain of water in the wilderness, by the fountain in the way to Shur.

Jud.2:1

v.1 And an angel of the LORD came up from Gilgal to Bo'chim, and said, I made you go up out of Egypt, and have brought you unto the land which I swore to give unto your fathers; and I said, I will never break my covenant with you.

1(2:1) This particular angel, as distinguished in Scripture from all others, is often referred to in the O.T. (cp.Gen.16:9; 22:11;48:16;Ex.3:2;14:19; Num.22:22;Jud.2:4; 6:11;13:3; 2Ki.19:35;Isa.63:9; Zech.1:12;12:8).

(1) He is named "the angel of the LORD [Jehovah]" (Gen.16:7), "the angel of God" (Gen.21:17), "the angel of his [God's] presence" (Isa.63:9), and probably "the messenger [angel] of the covenant" (Mal.3:1).
(2) He is clearly identified with the LORD Himself in His self-manifestation to men. In Gen.31:11-13 the angel said to Jacob, "I am the God of Bethel." In Ex.3:2-6 the same angel said to Moses, "I am the God of thy father, the God of Abraham."

v.6 Let their way be dark and slippery, and let the (j) angel of the LORD persecute them.
v.7 For without cause have they hidden for me their net in a pit, which without cause they have digged for my soul.
v.8 Let (k) destruction come upon him unawares, and let his net that he hath hidden catch himself; into that very destruction let him fall.

(k) destruction
(k) 1Th.5:3

v.3 For when they shall say, Peace and safety, then sudden destruction cometh upon them, as travail upon a woman with child, and they shall not escape.

v.9 And my soul shall be joyful in the LORD; it shall rejoice in his salvation.
v.10 (l) All my bones shall say, LORD, (m) who is like unto thee, who deliverest the poor from him that is too strong for him, yea, the poor and the needy from him that spoileth him?

(l) All my bones shall say LORD,
(l)Ps.51:8
(m) who is like unto thee;
(m)Ex.15:11;Ps.71:19; 86:8; Mic.7:18

Ps. 51:8

v.8 Make me hear joy and gladness, that the bones which thou hast broken may rejoice.

Ex.15:11

v.11 Who is like unto thee, O LORD, among the gods? Who is like thee, glorious in holiness, fearful in praises, doing wonders?

Ps.71:19

v.19 Thy righteousness also, O God, is very high, who hast done great things. O God, who is like thee?

Ps. 86:8

v.8 Among the gods there is none like unto thee, O Lord; neither are there any works like unto thy works,

Mic.7:18

v.18 Who is a God like unto thee, who pardoned iniquity, and passeth by the transgression of the remnant of his heritage? He retained not his anger forever, because he delighted in mercy.

v.11 (n) False witnesses did rise up; they laid to my charge things that I knew not.

(n) False witnesses did rise up;
(n) Lit. Witnesses of wrong

v.12 They rewarded me evil for good to the spoiling of my soul.
v.13 But as for me, (o) when they were sick, my clothing was sackcloth; I humbled my soul with fasting, and my prayer (p) returned into mine own bosom.

(o) when they were sick,
(o) cp. Job 30:25;Ps.69:10-11
(p) returned into mine own bosom;
(p) cp. Mt.10:13;Lk.10:6

Job 30:25

v.25 Did not I weep for him that was in trouble? Was not my soul grieved for the poor?

Ps.69:10-11

v.10 When I wept, and chastened my soul with fasting, that was to my reproach.
v.11 I made sackcloth also my garment; and I became a proverb to them.

Mt.10:13

v.13 **And if the house be worthy, let your peace come upon it; but if it be not worthy, let your peace return to you.**

Lk.10:6

v.6 **And if the son of peace be there, your peace shall rest upon it; if not, it shall turn to you again.**

v.14 I (q) behaved myself as though he had been my friend or brother; I bowed down heavily, as one who mourned for his mother.

(q) behave myself
(q) Lit. walked

v.15 But in mine adversity they rejoiced, and gathered themselves together; yea, the (r) | godless | gathered themselves together against me, and I knew it not; they did tear me, and ceased not.

(r) | godless | gathered themselves together
(r) KJV abjects. Cp. Job 30:1

Job 30:1

v.1 But now they that are younger than I | hold | me in derision, to have set with the dogs of my flock.

v.16 With hypocritical 1 mockers in feasts, they gnashed upon me with their teeth.

1 mockers in feasts,

1 (35:16) These were paid jesters who were hired to amuse the guests at a banquet.

v.17 Lord, how long wilt thou (s) look on? Rescue my soul from their destructions, mine (t) |only one| from the lions.

(s) how long wilt thou look on? Rescue my soul
(s) Hab.1:13
(t) |only one|
(t) KJV darling. Ps.22:20

Hab.1:13

v.13 Thou art of purer eyes than to behold evil, and canst not look on iniquity; |why| lookest thou upon them that deal treacherously, and holdest thy tongue when the wicked devoured the man that is more righteous than he?

Ps.22:20

v.20 Deliver my soul from the sword; my |only one| from the power of the dog.

v.18 I will give thee thanks in the great congregation; I will praise thee among (u) |many| people.

(u) |many| people
(u) KJV much

v.19 (v) Let not those who are mine enemies wrongfully rejoice over me; neither let them (w) wink with the eye who hate me without a cause.

(v) Let not those who are mine enemies
(v) Ps.69:4;109:3;Lam.3:52;cp.Jn.15:25
(w) wink;
(w) cp. Prov.6:13;10:10

Ps.69:4

v.4 They that hate me without a cause are more than the hairs of mine head; they that would destroy me, being mine enemies wrongfully, are mighty. Then I restored that which I took not away.

Ps.109:3

v.3 They compassed me about also with words of hatred, and fought against me without a cause.

Lam.3:52

v.52 Mine enemies chased me |hard|, like a bird, without cause.

Jn.15:25

v.25 **But this cometh to pass, that the word might be fulfilled that is written in their law, They hated me without a cause.**

Prov.6:13

v.13 He winketh with his eyes, he speaketh with his feet, he teaches with his fingers;

Prov.10:10

v.10 He that winketh with the eye causeth sorrow, but a prating fool shall fall.

v.20 For they speak not peace, but they devise deceitful matters against those who are quite in the land.
v.21 Yea, they opened their mouth wide against me, and said, Aha, aha, our eye hath seen it.
v.22 This thou hast seen, O LORD; keep not silence. O Lord, be not far from me.
v.23 Stir up thyself, and awake to my (x) | right | , even unto my cause, my God and my Lord.

(x) awake to my | right | ,
(x) KJV judgment;Ps.97:2

v.2 Clouds and darkness are around about him; righteousness and | justice | are the habitation of his throne.

v.24 Judge me, O LORD my God, according to thy righteousness, and let them not rejoice over me.
v.25 Let them not say in their hearts, Ah, so would we have it; let them not say We have swallowed him up.
v.26 Let them be ashamed and brought to confusion together who rejoice at mine hurt; let them be clothed with shame and dishonor who magnify themselves against me.
v.27 (y) Let them shout for joy, and be glad, who favor my righteous cause. Yea, let them say continually, Let the LORD be magnified, who hath pleasure in the prosperity of his servant.

(y) Let them shout for joy,
(y) cp.Rev.18:20

v.20 Rejoice over her, thou heaven, and ye holy apostles and prophets; for God hath avenged you on her.

v.28 And my tongue shall speak of thy righteousness and thy praise all the day long.

JUDGMENT ON THE DECEITFUL

PSALM 52

(j) Mas'chil
(j) Instruction
(k) Ahim'elech
(k) I Sam.22:9

v.9 Then answered Do'eg, the Edomite, who was set over the servants of Saul, and said, I saw the son of Jesse coming to Nob, to Ahim'elech, the son of Ahi'tub.

v.1 WHY boastest thou thyself in mischief, O mighty man? The goodness of God endureth continually.
v.2 Thy tongue deviseth mischiefs, like a sharp razor, working deceitfully.
v.3 Thou lovest evil more than good, and lying rather than to speak righteousness. Selah.
v.4 Thou lovest all devouring words, O thou deceitful tongue.
v.5 God shall likewise (l) destroy thee forever; he shall take thee away, and pluck thee out of thy dwelling place, and root thee out of the land of the living. Selah.

(l) destroy thee forever;
(l) Lit. beat thee down.

v.6 The righteous also shall see, and fear, and shall laugh at him:

v.7 Lo, this is the man who made not God his strength, but (m) trusted in the abundance of his riches, and strengthened himself in his wickedness.

(m) trusted in the abundance of his riches,
(m) See Ps.2:12,note
(m) See Ps. 40;4 Messianic Psalms

v.8 But I am like a green olive in the house of God; I trust in the mercy of God forever and ever.

v.9 I will praise thee forever, because thou hast done it; and I will wait on thy name; for it is good before thy saints.

A COMPLAINT CONCERNING FALSE FRIENDS

PSALMS 55

(a) Negi'noth,
(a) Stringed instrument
(b) Mas'chil, A Psalm of David
(b) Instruction

v.1 Give ear to my prayer, O God, and hide not thyself from my supplication.
v.2 Attend unto me, and hear me; I mourn in my complaint, and make a noise,

v.3 Because of the oppression of the wicked; for they cast iniquity upon me, and in wrath they hate me.
v.4 My heart is (e) very pained within me, and the terrors of death are fallen upon me.

(e) very pained within me,
(e) KJV sore

v.5 Fearfulness and trembling are come upon me, and horror hath (f) overwhelmed me.

(f) overwhelmed me;
(f) Lit. covered me

v.6 And I said, Oh, that I had wings like a dove! For then would I fly away, and be at rest.
v.7 Lo, then would I wander far off, and remain in the wilderness, Selah.
v.8 I would hasten my escape from the windy storm and tempest.
v.9 Destroy, O Lord, and (g) | confuse | their tongues; for I have seen violence and strife in the city.

(g) | confuse | their tongues;
(g) KJV divide

v.10 Day and night they go about it upon the walls; mischief also and sorrow are in the midst of it.
v.11 Wickedness is in the midst thereof; deceit and guile depart not from her streets.
v.12 For it was not an enemy that reproached me; then I could have borne it. Neither was it he that hated me that did (h) magnify himself against me; then I would have hidden myself from him;

(h) magnify himself against me;
(h) Ps.35:26;38:16

Ps.35:26

v.26 Let them be ashamed and brought to confusion together who rejoice at mine hurt; let them be clothed with shame and dishonor who magnify themselves against me.

Ps.38:16

v.16 For I said, Hear me, lest otherwise they should rejoice over me. When my foot slippeth, they magnify themselves against me.

v.13 But it was thou, a man mine equal, my guide, and (i) | my familiar friend | .

(i) | my familiar friend | .
(i) KJV mine acquaintance.Ps.41:9

v.9 Yea, mine own familiar friend, in whom I trusted, who did eat of my bread, hath lifted up his heel against me.

v.14 We took sweet counsel together, and walked unto the house of God in company.
v.15 Let death seize upon them, and let them go down (j) | alive | into (k) | sheol | ; for wickedness is in their dwellings and among them.

(j) | alive | into
(j) KJV Num.16:30-33
(k) | sheol | ;
(k) KJV hell.
See:Hab.2:5,note;cp.Lk.16:23
II Penitential Ps.6:5

Num. 16:30-33

v.30 But if the LORD make a new thing, and the earth open her mouth and swallow them up, with all that appertains unto them, and they go down |alive| into |sheol|; then ye shall understand that these men have provoked the LORD.
v.31 And it came to pass, as he had |finished| speaking all these words, that the ground |split open| that was under them;
v.32 And the earth opened its mouth, and swallowed them up, and their houses, and all the men that appertained unto Korah, and all their goods.
v.33 They, and all that appertained to them, went down alive into |sheol|, and the earth closed upon them; and they perished from among the congregation.

(k) | sheol |KJV; hell.
See Hab.2:5, note; cp Lk.16:23
See: II Penitential Ps.6 :5

v.16 As for me I will call upon God, and the LORD shall save me.
v.17 Evening, and morning, and at (l) noon, will I pray, and cry aloud, and he shall hear my voice.

(l) noon, will I pray, and cry aloud,
(l) Dan.6:10

v.10 Now when Daniel knew that the writing was signed, he went into his house; and his windows being open in his chamber toward Jerusalem, he kneeled upon his knees three times a day, and prayed, and gave thanks before his God, as he did |previously|.

v.18 He hath delivered my soul in peace from the battle that was against me; (m) for there was many with me.

(m) for there was many with me.
(m) 2Chr.32:7-8

v.7 Be strong and courageous, be not afraid nor dismayed for the king of Assyria, nor for all the multitude who are with him; for there are more with us than with him.

v.8 With him is an arm of flesh; but with us is the LORD, our God, to help us, and to fight our battles. And the people rested themselves upon the words of Hezeki'ah, king of Judah, and unto all Judah who were at Jerusalem, saying.

v.19 God shall hear, and afflict them, (n) even he who abideth of old. Selah. Because they (o) | do not change | , therefore they fear not God.

(n) even he who abideth of old.
(n) Dt.33:27
(o) | do not change | ,
(o) KJV have no change

Dt.33:27

v.27 The eternal God is thy refuge, and underneath are the everlasting arms; and he shall thrust out the enemy from before thee, and shall say, Destroy them.

v.20 (p) He hath put forth his hands against such as (q) are at peace with him; (r) he hath broken his covenant.

(p) He hath put forth his hands against
(p) cp.Acts12:1
(q) such as are at peace with him;
(q) Ps.7:4
(r) he hath broken his covenant.
(r) Lit. he hath profaned.

Acts.12:1

v.1 Now about that time Herod, the king, stretched forth his hands to vex certain of the church.

Ps.7:4

v.4 If I have rewarded evil unto him who was at peace with me (yea, I have delivered him who without cause is mine enemy),

v.21 (s) The words of his mouth were smoother than butter, but war was in his heart; his words were softer than oil, yet were they drawn swords.

(s) The words of his mouth
(s) Ps.28:3;57:4;62:4:64:3;Prov.5:3-4;12:18

Ps. 28:3

v.3 Draw me not away with the wicked, and with the workers of iniquity, who speak peace to their neighbors, but mischief is in their heart.

Ps.57:4

v.4 My soul is among lions, and I lie even among them that are set on fire, even the sons of men, whose teeth are spears and arrows, and their tongues a sharp sword.

Ps.62:4

v.4 They only consult to cast him down from his excellency; they delight in lies; they bless with their mouth, but they curse inwardly. Selah.

Ps.64:3

v.3 Who whet their tongue like a sword, and bend their bows to shoot their arrows, even bitter words,

Prov.5:3-4

v.3 For the lips of a strange woman drop as an honeycomb, and her mouth is smoother than oil,
v.4 But her end is bitter as wormwood, sharp as a two-edged sword.

Prov.12:18

v.18 There is he that speaketh like the piercing of a sword, but the tongue of the wise is health.

v.22 (t) Cast thy burden upon the LORD, and he shall sustain thee; (u) he shall never suffer the righteous to be moved.

(t) Cast thy burden upon the LORD,
(t) Ps.37:5;Mt.6:25;Lk.12:22;1Pet.5:7
(u) he shall never suffer the righteous
(u) Ps.37:24

Ps.37:5

v.5 Commit thy way unto the LORD, trust also in him, and he shall bring it to pass.

Mt.6:25

v.25 **Therefore, I say unto you, |Be not anxious| for your life, what ye shall eat, or what ye shall drink; nor yet for your body, what ye shall put on. Is not the life more than |food| and the body than raiment?**

Lk.12:22

v.22 And he said unto his disciples, **Therefore, I say unto you, |Be not anxious| for your life, what ye shall eat; neither for the body, what ye shall put on.**

1Pet.5:7

v.7 Casting all your care upon him; for he careth for you.

Ps.37:24

v.24 Though he fall, he shall not be utterly cast down; for the LORD upholdeth him with his hand.

v.23 But thou, O God, shalt bring them down into the pit of destruction. Bloody and deceitful men shall not live out half their days; but I will trust in thee.

A CRY FOR GOD'S VENGEANCE

PSALM 58

(h) Al-tash'heth
(h) Destroy not

v.1 Do ye indeed speak righteousness O congregation? O ye sons of men?
v.2 Yea, in heart ye work wickedness; ye weigh the violence of your hands in the earth.
v.3 The wicked are estranged from the womb; they go (m) astray as soon as they are born, speaking lies.

(m) they go astray
(m) Ps.53:3

v.3 Every one of them is gone back; they are altogether become filthy, There is none that doeth good, no not one.

v.4 Their poison is like the poison of a serpent; they are like the deaf adder that stoppeth her ear,
v.5 Which will not (n) hearken to the voice of charmers, charming never so (o) wisely.

(n) hearken to the voice
(n)Jer.8:17
(o) wisely
(o) cp. Mt.11;16-19

Jer.8:17

v.17 Seest thou not what they do in the cities of Judah and in the streets of Jerusalem?

Mt.11:16-19

v.16 **But whereunto shall I liken this generation? It is like unto children sitting in the |market places|, and called unto their fellow,**
v.17 **And saying, We have piped unto you, and ye have not danced; we have mourned unto you, and ye have not lamented.**
v.18 **For John came neither eating nor drinking, and they say, He hath a |demon|.**
v.19 **The Sons of man came eating and drinking, and they say, Behold a man gluttonous, and a winebibber, a friend of |tax collectors| and sinners. But wisdom is justified by her children.**

v.6 Break their teeth, O God, in their mouth; break out the great teeth of the young lions, O LORD.
v.7 (p) Let them melt away like waters which run continually. When he bendeth his bow to shoot his arrows, let them be as cut in pieces.

(p) Let them melt away like waters
(p) Josh. 7:5;Ps.112;10

Josh.7:5

v.5 And the men of A i smote of them about thirty and six men; for they chased them from before the gate even unto Sheb'arim, and smote them in the going down; wherefore the hearts of the people melted, and became as water.

Ps.112:10

v.10 The wicked shall see it, and be grieved; he shall gnash with his teeth, and melt away. The desire of the wicked shall perish.

v.8 Like a snail which melteth, let every one of them pass away; like the untimely birth of a woman, that they may not see the sun.
v.9 Before your (q) pots can feel the burning thorns, he shall take them away as with a whirlwind, both living, and in his wrath.

(q) pots can feel the burning thorns,
(q) Ps.118:12;Eccl.7:6

Ps.118:12

v.12 They compassed me about like bees; they are quenched like the fire of thorns, for in the name of the LORD I will destroy them.

Eccl.7:6

v.6 For as the cracking of thorns under a pot, so is the laughter of the fool; this also is vanity.

v.10 The righteous shall (r) rejoice when he seeth the (s) vengeance; (t) he shall wash his feet in the blood of the (u) wicked,

(r) rejoice
(r) Cp.Rev.19:1-5
(s) vengeance;
(s) Cp.Rev.19:1-5
(t) he shall wash
(t) Dt.32:43;Jer.11:20
(u) wicked;
(u) Ps.68:23

Rev.19:1-5

v.1 And after these things I heard a great voice of |many| people in heaven, saying, |Hallelujah|! Salvation, and glory, and honor, and power, unto the Lord, our God;

v.2 For true and righteous are his judgments; for he hath judged the great |harlot|, who did corrupt the earth with her fornication, and hath avenged the blood of his servants at her hand.

v.3 And again they said, |Hallelujah|! And her smoke rose up forever and ever.

v.4 And the four and twenty elders and the four| living creatures| fell down and worshiped God that sat on the throne, saying, Amen. |Hallelujah|!

v.5 And a voice came out of the throne, saying, Praise our God, all ye his servants, and ye that fear him, both small and great.

Dt.32:43

v.43 Rejoice, O ye nations, with his peoples; for he will avenge the blood of his servants, and will render vengeance to his adversaries, and will be merciful unto his land, and to his people.

Jer.11:20

v.20 But, O LORD of hosts, who judgest righteously, who |testest| |the heart and the mind|, let me see thy vengeance on them; for unto thee have I revealed my cause.

Ps.68:23

v.23 That thy foot may be dipped in the blood of thine enemies, and the tongue of thy dogs in the same.

v.11 So that a man shall say, Verily, there is a (v) reward for the righteous; verily he is a God that (w) judgeth in the earth.

(v) reward for the righteous;
(v) Prov.11:18;2Cor.5:10
(w) judgeth in the earth
(w) Ps.50:6;75:7

Prov.11:18

v.18 The wicked worketh a deceitful work, but to him that soweth righteousness shall be a sure reward.

2Cor.5:10

v.10 For we must all appear before the judgment seat of Christ, that everyone may receive the things done in his body, according to that he hath done, whether it be good or bad.

Ps.50:6

v.6 And the heavens shall declare his righteousness; for God is judge himself. Selah.

Ps.75:7

v.7 But God is the judge; he putteth down one, and setteth up another.

THE HELP OF THE HELPLESS

PSALM 59

(a) Al-tash,heth;
(a) destroy not
(b) him;
(b) 1 Sam.19:11

v.11 Saul also sent messengers unto David's house, to watch him, and to slay him in the morning; and Mi'chal, David's wife, told him, saying If thou save not thy life tonight, tomorrow thou shalt be slain.

v.1 Deliver me from mine enemies, O my God; defend me from those who rise up against me.
v.2 Deliver me from the workers of iniquity, and save me from bloody men.
v.3 For, lo, they lie in wait for my soul; the mighty are gathered against me, not for my transgression, nor for sin, O LORD.
v.4 They run and prepare themselves ©|apart from any fault of mine|; awake to help me, and behold.

(c) |apart from any fault of mine|;
(c) KJV without my fault

v.5 Thou therefore, O LORD God of hosts, the God of Israel, awake to visit all the (d)|nations|; be not merciful to any wicked transgressors. Selah.

(d) |nations|;
(d) KJV heathen

v.6 They return at evening; they make a noise like a dog, and go round about the city.
v.7 Behold, they belch out with their mouth. Swords are in their lips; for who, say they, doth (e) hear?

(e) for who, say they, doth hear?
(e) Ps.10:11;64:5;73:11

Ps.10:11

v.11 He hath said in his heart, God hath forgotten; he hideth his face; he will never see it.

Ps.64:5

v.5 They encourage themselves in an evil matter; they |speak| of laying snares |secretly|; they say, Who shall see them?

Ps.73:11

v.11 And they say, How doth God know? And is there knowledge in the Most High?

v.8 But thou, O LORD, shalt laugh at them; thou shalt have all the |nations| in derision.
v.9 Because of his strength will I wait upon thee; for God is (f)my defense.

(f) for God is my defense.
(f) Lit. my high place

v.10 The God of my mercy shall (g)|meet|me; God shall let (h)me see my desire upon mine enemies.

(g)|meet|me;
(g) KJV prevent
(h) me see;
(h)Ps.54:7;92:11;112:8

Ps.54:7

v.7 Lo, then would I wander far off, and remain in the wilderness. Selah.

Ps.92:11

v.11 Mine eye also shall see my desire on mine enemies, and mine ears shall hear my desire of the wicked that rise up against me.

Ps.112:8

v.8 His heart is established; he shall not be afraid, until he see his desire upon his enemies.

v.11 Slay them not, lest my people forget; scatter them by thy power, and bring them down, O Lord, our shield.
v.12 For the sin of their mouth and the words of their lips, let them even be taken in their pride; and for cursing and lying which they speak.
v.13 (i) Consume them in wrath, consume them, that they may not be; and (j) let them know that God ruleth in Jacob unto the ends of the earth. Selah.

(i) Consume
(i)Ps.104:35
(j) let them know that God ruleth
(j)Ps.83:18

Ps.104:35

v.35 Let the sinners be consumed out of the earth, and let the wicked be no more. Bless thou the LORD, O my soul. Praise ye the LORD.

Ps.83:18

v.18 That men may know that thou, whose name alone is | the LORD |, art the Most High over all the earth.

v.14 And at evening let them return, and let them make a noise
like a dog, and go round about the city.
v.15 Let them wander up and down for (k) | food | , and (l) | keep
on looking all night | if they are not satisfied.

(k) | food |
(k) KJV meat
(l) | keep on looking all night |
(l) KJV grudge

v.16 But I will sing of thy power; yea, I will sing aloud of thy
mercy in the morning; for thou hast been my defense and
refuge in the day of my trouble.
v.17 Unto thee, O my strength, will I sing; for God is my defense,
and the God of my mercy.

PRAYER FOR GOD'S JUDGMENT

PSALM 79

v.1 O God, the (j) | nations | are come into thine inheritance; thy holy temple have they defiled; (k) they have laid Jerusalem on heaps.

(j) | nations |
(j) KJV heathen
(k) they have;
(k) 2 Ki.25:9-10;2Chr.36:19;Mic.3:12

2 Ki.25:9-10

v.9 And he burned the house of the LORD, and the king's house, and all the houses of Jerusalem, and every great man's house burned he with fire.
v.10 And all the army of the Chalde'ans, who were with the captain of the guard, broke down the walls of Jerusalem round about.

2 Chr.36:19

v.19 And they burned the house of God, and broke down the wall of Jerusalem, and burned all it's palaces with fire, and destroyed all its | precious | vessels.

Mic.3:12

v.12 Therefore shall Zion for your sake be plowed as a field, and Jerusalem shall become heaps, and the mountain of the house as the high places of the forest.

v.2 The dead bodies of thy servants have they given to be (l) | food | unto the fowls of the heavens, the flesh of thy saints unto the beasts of the earth.

(l) | food |
(l) KJV meat

v.3 Their blood have they shed like water round about Jerusalem, and there was none to bury them.
v.4 We are become a reproach to our (m) neighbors, a scorn and derision to them that are round about us.

(m) neighbors,
(m) Ps.44:13

v.13 Thou makest us a reproach to our neighbors, a scorn and a derision to them that are round about us.

v.5 How long, LORD? Wilt thou be angry forever? Shall thy jealousy burn like fire?
v.6 Pour out thy wrath upon the (j) | nations | that have (n) not known thee, and upon the kingdoms that have not called upon thy name.

(j) | nations |
(j) KJV heathen
(n) not known thee,
(n) Isa.45:4-5;2Th.1:8

Isa.45:4-5

v.4 For Jacob, my servant's sake, and Israel mine elect, I have even called thee by thy name; I have surnamed thee, though thou hast not known me.
v.5 I AM the LORD, and there is none else, there is no God beside me; I girded thee, though thou hast not known me,

2 Th.1:8

v.8 In flaming fire taking vengeance on them that know not God, and that obey not the gospel of our Lord Jesus Christ;

v.7 For they have devoured Jacob, and laid waste his dwelling place.
v.8 Oh, remember not against us former iniquities; let thy tender mercies speedily (o) |meet| us; for we are brought very low.

(o) |meet| us;
(o) KJV prevent

v.9 Help us, O God of our salvation, for the glory of thy name; and deliver us, and purge away our sins, (p) for thy name's sake.

(p) for thy name's sake
(p) Jer.14:7,21

v.7 O LORD, though our iniquities testify against us, do it for thy name's sake; for our backslidings are many; we have sinned against thee.
v.21 Do not abhor us; for thy name's sake, do not disgrace the throne of thy glory; remember, break not thy covenant with us.

v.10 (q) |Why| should the (j) |nations| say, Where is their God? Let him be known among the (j) |nations| in our sight by the revenging of the blood of thy servants which is shed.

(q) |Why|
(q) KJV Wherefore
(j) |nations|
(j) KJV heathen

v.11 Let the sighing of the prisoner come before thee; according to the greatness of thy power preserve thou those that are appointed to die;

v.12 And render unto our neighbors sevenfold into their bosom their reproach, wherewith they have reproached thee, O Lord.

v.13 So (r) we, thy people and sheep of thy pasture, will give thee thanks forever; we will show forth thy praise to all generations.

(r) we
(r) Ps.74:1;95:7;100:3

Ps.74:1

v.1 O God, why hast thou cast us off forever? Why doth thine anger smoke against the sheep of thy pasture?

Ps.95:7

v.7 For he is our God, and we are the people of his pasture, and the sheep of his hand. Today if ye will hear his voice,

Ps.100:3

v.3 Know ye that the Lord, he is God; it is he who hath made us, and not we ourselves; we are his people, and the sheep of his pasture.

THE CAPTIVES CRY FOR VENGEANCE

PSALM 137

v.1 BY the rivers of Babylon, there we sat down, yea, we wept,
when we remembered Zion.
v.2 We (g) | hung | our harps upon the willows in the midst
thereof.

(g) | hung |
(g) KJV hanged

v.3 For there they that carried us away captive required of us a
(h) song; and they that wasted us required of us mirth, saying,
Sing us one of the songs of Zion.

(h) song;
(h) Lit. the words of a song

v.4 How shall we sing the LORD'S song in a (i) | foreign | land?

(i) | foreign |
(i) KJV strange

v.5 If I forget thee, O Jerusalem, let my right hand forget her
cunning.
v.6 If I do not remember thee, let my (j) tongue cleave to the roof
of my mouth, if I prefer not Jerusalem above my chief joy.

(j) tongue cleave
(j) Ezek.3:26;Job 29:10

Ezek.3:26

v.26 It is good that a man should both hope and quietly wait for the salvation of the LORD.

Job29:10

v.10 The noble held their peace, and their tongue cleaved to the roof of their mouth.

V.7 Remember, O LORD, the children of (k) Edom in the day of Jerusalem, who said, (l) |Raze| it, (m)|raze| it even to the foundation thereof.

(k) Edom in the day of Jerusalem,
(k) Jer.49:7;Lam.4:22;Ezek.25:12-14
Obad.10-14; see Gen.36:1,note
(l)|Raze| it, KJV Rase
(m)|raze| it, KJV rase

Jer.49:7

v.7 Concerning Edom, thus saith the LORD of hosts: Is wisdom no more in Teman? Is counsel perished from the prudent? Is their wisdom vanished?

Lam.4:22

v.22 The punishment of thine iniquity is accomplished, O daughter of Zion; he will no more carry thee away into captivity. He will |punish| thine iniquity, O daughter of Edom; he will |uncover| thy sins.

Ezek.25:12-14

v.12 Thus saith the Lord God: Because Edom hath dealt against the house of Judah by taking vengeance, and hath greatly offended, and revenged himself upon them,

v.13 Therefore thus saith the Lord God; I will also stretch out mine hand upon Edom, and will cut off man and beast from it; and Teman; and they of Dedan shall fall by the sword.
v.14 And I will lay vengeance upon Edom by the hand of my people Israel: and they shall do in Edom according to mine anger and according to mine fury; and they shall know my vengeance, saith the Lord God.

Obad.10-14

v.10 For thy violence against thy brother, Jacob, shame shall cover thee, and thou shalt be cut off forever.*
v.11 In the day that thou stoodest on the other side, in the day that the strangers carried away captive his forces, and foreigners entered into his gates, and cast lots upon Jerusalem, even thou wast as one of them.
v.12 But thou shouldest not have looked on the day that he became a stranger; neither shouldest thou have rejoiced over the children of Judah in the day of their destruction; neither shouldest thou have spoken proudly in the day of distress.
v.13 Thou shouldest not have entered into the gate of my people in the day of their calamity; yea, thou shouldest not have looked on their affliction in the day of their calamity, nor have laid hands on their subtance in the day of their calamity;
v.14 Neither shouldest thou have stood in the crossway, to cut off those of his that did escape; neither shouldest thou have delivered up those of his that did remain in the day of distress.

Gen.36:1,note

v.1 Now these are the generations of Esau, who is Edom: note 2(36:1) Edom (called "Seir," Gen.32:3;36:8) is the name of the country lying south of the ancient kingdom of Judah and extending from the Dead Sea to the Gulf of Aqaba. It includes the ruins of Petra, and is bounded on the north Moab. Peopled by descendants of Esau(Gen.36:1-19), Edom has a remarkable prominence in the prophetic Word as (together with Moab)the scene of the final destruction of Gentile world-power in the Day of the LORD.

(l) | Raze | it; Rase
(m) | raze | it; rase

v.8 O daughter of Babylon, (n)who art to be destroyed; happy shall he be, that rewardeth thee as thou hast served us.

(n) who art to be destroyed;
(n) Isa.13:1-6;7:1;Jer.25:12;50:2;51:24,56

Isa.13:1-6

v.1 THE burden of Babylon, which Isaiah, the son of Amoz, did see.
v.2 Lift ye up a banner upon the high mountain, exalt the voice unto them, shake the hand, that they may go into the gates of the nobles.
v.3 I have commanded my sanctified ones, I have also called my mighty ones for mine anger, even them that rejoice in my highness.
v.4 The noise of a great people; a tumultuous noise of the kingdoms of nations gather. The LORD of hosts mustereth the host of the battle.
v.5 They come from a far country, from the end of heaven, even the LORD, and the weapons of his indignation, to destroy the whole land.
v.6 | Wail |; for the day of the LORD is at hand; it shall come as a destruction from the Almighty.

Isa.7:1

v.1 AND it came to pass in the days of Ahaz, the son of Jotham, the son of Uzzi'ah, king of Judah, that Rezin, the king of Syria, and Pekah, the son of Remali'ah, king of Israel, went up toward Jerusalem to war against it, but could not prevail against it.

Jer.25:12

v.12 And it shall come to pass, when seventy years are accomplished, that I will punish the king of Babylon, and that nation, saith the LORD, for their iniquity, and the land of the Chalde'ans, and will make it perpetual desolations.

Jer.50:2

v.2 Declare among the nations, and publish, and set up a standard; publish, and conceal not; say, Babylon is taken, Bel is confounded, Mer'odach is broken in pieces; her idols are confounded, her images are broken in pieces.

Jer.51:24,56

v.24 And I will render unto Babylon and to all the inhabitants of Chalde'a all their evil that they have done in Zion in your sight, saith the LORD.

v.56 Because the spoiler is come upon her, even upon Babylon, and her mighty men are taken, every one of their bows is broken: for the LORD God of recompenses shall surely requite.

v.9 Happy shall he be, that taketh and (a)dasheth thy little ones against the stones.

(a) dasheth
(a) 2 i.8:12;Isa.13:16;Hos.13:16;Nah.3:10

2 Ki.8:12

v.12 And Hazael said, Why weepeth my lord? And he answered, Because I know the evil that thou wilt do unto the children of Israel: their strongholds wilt thou

set on fire, and their young men wilt thou slay with
the sword, and wilt dash their children, and rip up
their women with child.*

Isa.13:16

v.16 Their children also shall be dashed to pieces before
their eyes; their houses shall be spoiled, and their
wives ravished.

Hos.13:16

v. 16 Samaria shall become desolate; for she hath rebelled
against her God: they shall fall by the sword: their
infants shall be dashed in pieces, and their women
with child shall be ripped up.

Nah.3:10

v.10 Yet was she carried away, she went into captivity:
her young children also were dashed in pieces at
the top of all the streets: and they cast lots for her
honorable men, and all he great men were bound in
chains.

Editor's note:

Inclosing the Psalm 137 is the best illustration of Cries to God to Avenge—The Imprecatory Psalms give full view of Prayers to God for oppressions during captivity; God's chosen people endured three captivities, The Egyptian, The Assyrian, and climaxed by the Babylonian captivity.

GOD'S ALL SEEING EYE

PSALM 139

v.1 O LORD, (a) thou hast searched me, and known me.

(a) thou hast searched me,
(a) Ps.17:3;Jer.12:3

Ps.17:3

v.3 Thou hast proved mine heart; thou hast visited me in the night; thou tried me, and shalt find nothing: I am purposed that my mouth shall not transgress.

Jer.12:3

v.3 But thou, O LORD, knowest me: thou hast seen me, and tried mine heart toward thee: pull them out like sheep for the slaughter, and prepare them for the day of slaughter.

v.2 (a) Thou knowest my downsitting and mine uprising; thou (b) understandest my thought afar off.

(a) thou
(a) 2 Ki.19:27
(b) understandest
(b) Isa.66:18;Mt.9:4

2 Ki.19:27

v.27 But I know thy abode, and thy going out, and thy coming in, and thy rage against me.

Isa.66:18

v.18 For I know their works and their thoughts: it shall come, that I will gather all nations and tongues; and they shall come, and see my glory.

Mt.9:4

v.4 And Jesus knowing their thoughts said, **Wherefore think ye evil in your hearts?**

v.3 (a) Thou 1 compassest my path and my lying down, and art acquainted with all my ways.

(a) thou
(a) Job 14:16;31:4
1 compassest;
[1 comprehendeth, lit winnow]

Job.14:16

v.16 For now thou numberest my steps:dost thou not watch over my sin?

Job.31:4

v.4 Doth not he see my ways, and count all my steps?

v.4 For there is not a word in my tongue, but lo, O LORD, (a)thou knowest it altogether.

(a) thou knowest it altogether.
(a) [Heb.4:13]

v.13 Neither is there any creature that is not manifest in his sight: but all things are naked and opened unto the eyes of him with whom we have to do.

v.5 Thou hast 1 beset me behind and before, and laid thine hand upon me.

1 beset;[enclosed or hedged]

v.6 (a) Such knowledge is too wonderful for me; it is high, I cannot attain unto it.

(a) Such knowledge is too wonderful for me;
(a) Job 42:3;Ps.40:5

Job 42:3

v.3 Who is he that hideth counsel without knowledge? Therefore have I uttered that I understood not; things too wonderful for me, which I knew not.

Ps.40:5

v.5 Many, O LORD my God, are thy wonderful works which thou hast done, and thy thoughts which are to us-ward: they cannot be reckoned up in order unto thee: if I would declare and speak of them, they are more than can be numbered.

v.7 (a) Whither shall I go from thy spirit? Or whither shall I flee from thy presence?

(a) Whither shall I go from thy spirit?
(a) Jer.23:24;Amos 9:2-4

Jer.23:24

v.24 Can any hide himself in secret places that I shall not see him? saith the LORD. Do not I fill heaven and earth? saith the LORD.

Amos 9:2-4

v.2 Though they dig hell, thence shall mine hand take them; though they climb up to heaven, thence will I bring them down.
v.3 And though they hide themselves in the top of Carmel, I will search and take them out thence; and though they be hidden from my sight in the bottom of the sea, thence will I command the serpent, and he shall bite them:
v.4 And though they go into captivity before their enemies, thence will I command the sword, and it shall slay them: and I will set mine eyes upon them for evil, and not for good.

v.8 (a) If I ascend up into heaven, thou art there: (b) if I make my bed in 1hell, behold, thou art there

(a) If I ascend into heaven,
(a) [Amos 9:2-4]
see the above v.7
(b) if I make my bed in 1hell,
(b) Job26:6;Prov.15:11]
[Sheol]Hab.2:5,Lk.16:23note
see note, Ps.6:5 [Penitential]

Job 26:6

v.6 Hell is naked before him, and destruction hath no covering.

Prov.15:11

v.11 Hell and destruction are before the Lord: how much more then the hearts of the children of men?

1 Sheol

v.9 If I take the wings of the morning, and dwell in the uttermost part of the sea;

v.10 Even there shall thy hand lead me, and thy right hand shall hold me.
v.11 If I say, Surely the darkness shall cover me; even the night shall be light about me.
v.12 Yea, the (cc) darkness hideth not from thee, but the night shineth as the day; the darkness and the light are both alike to thee.
v.13 For thou hast possessed my (a)[inward parts]; thou hast covered me in my mother's womb.

(a) [inward part's];
(a) KJV reins

v.14 I will praise thee; for I am fearfully and wonderfully made. Marvelous are thy works, and that my soul knoweth right well.
v.15 (b) My substance was not hidden from thee, when I was made in secret, and ©[intricately] wrought in the lowest parts of the earth.

(b) Job 10:8-9;
(b)Eccl.11:5
(c) | intricately |
(c) KJV curiously

Job 10:8-9

v.8 Thine hands have made me and fashioned me together round about; yet thou dost destroy me.
v.9 Remember, I beseech thee, that thou hast made me as the clay. And wilt thou bring me into dust again?

Eccl.11:5

v.5 As thou knowest not what is the way of the | wind |, nor how the bones grow in the womb of her who is with child, even so thou knowest not the works of God, who maketh all.

(c) | intricately |
(c) KJV curiously

v.16 Thine eyes did see my substance, yet being (d) | unformed | ; and in thy book all my members were written, which in continuance were fashioned, when as yet there was there was none of them.

(d) | unformed | ;
(d) KJV unperfect

v.17 (e) How precious also are thy thoughts unto me, O God! How great is the sum of them!

(e) how precious
(e) Rom.11:33

v.33 Oh, the depth of the riches both of the wisdom and knowledge of God! How unsearchable are his judgments, and his ways past finding out!

v.18 If I should count them, they are more in number than the sand; when I awake, I am still with thee.
v.19 (f) Surely, thou wilt slay the wicked, O God; depart from me therefore, ye bloody men.

(f) surely
(f) Isa.11:4

v.4 But with righteousness shall he judge the poor, and reprove with equity for the meek of the earth; and he shall smite the earth with the rod of his mouth, and with the breath of his lips shall he slay the wicked.

v.20 For they (g) speak against thee wickedly, and thine enemies take thy name in vain.

(g) speak
(g) Jude 15

v.15 To execute judgment upon all, and to |convict| all that are ungodly deeds which they have ungodly committed, and of all their hard speeches which ungodly sinners have spoken against him.

v.21 Do not I hate them, O LORD, that hate thee? And am not I grieved with those who rise up against thee?
v.22 I hate them with perfect hatred; I count them mine enemies.
v.23 (h) Search me, O God, and know my heart; (i)try me, know my thoughts;

(h) search me
(h) Job 31:6;Ps.26:2
(i) try me
(i)Test-tempt: vv.23-24
Prov.1:10.(Gen.3:1;Jas.1:14)

Job 31:6

v.6 Let me be weighed in an even balance, that God may know mine integrity.

Ps.26:2

v.2 Examine me, O LORD, and prove me; |test| my |heart| and my |mind|.

Prov.1:10

v.10 My son, if sinners entice thee, consent thou not.

Gen.3:1

v.1 Now the serpent was more subtle than any beast of the field which the LORD God had made. And he said unto the woman, Yea, hath God said, Ye shall not eat of every tree of the garden?

Jas.1:14

v.14 But every man is tempted, when he is drawn away of his own lust, and enticed.

v.24 And see if there be any wicked way in me, and (j) lead me in the way everlasting.

(j) lead
(j) Ps.5:8;143:10

Ps.5:8

v.8 Lead me, O Lord, in thy righteousness because of mine enemies; make thy way straight before my face.

Ps.143:10

v.10 Teach me to do thy will; for thou art my God. Thy Spirit is good; lead me into the land of uprightness.

IV

ETERNALITY OF GOD, MAN'S FRAILTY

THE ETERNAL GOD

PSALM 90

v.1 LORD, (u) thou hast been our dwelling place in all generations.

(u) thou hast been our dwelling place
(u)Dt.33:27; Ezek.11:16

Dt.33:27

v.27 The eternal God is thy refuge, and underneath are the everlasting arms; and he shall thrust out the enemy from before thee, and shall say, Destroy them.

Ezek.11:16

v.16 Therefore say, Thus saith the Lord God: Although I have cast them far off among the |nations|, and although I have scattered them among the countries, yet will I be to them a little sanctuary in the countries where they shall come.

v.2 (v) Before the mountains were brought forth, or ever thou hast formed the earth and the world, even from everlasting to everlasting, thou art God.

(v) before
(v)Prov.8:25-26

Prov.8:25-26

v.25 Before the mountains were settled, before the hills, was I brought forth;
v.26 While as yet he had not made the earth, nor the fields, nor the highest part of the dust of the world.

v.3 Thou turnest man to destruction, and sayest, Return, ye children of men.
v.4 For a (w) thousand years in thy sight are but as yesterday when it is past, and as a watch in the night.

(w) thousand
(w)2 Pet.3:8

2 Pet.3:8

v.8 But, beloved, be not ignorant of this one thing, that one day is with the Lord as a thousand years, and a thousand years as one day.

v.5 Thou carriest them away as with a flood; they ate like a (x) sleep; in the morning (y) they are like grass which growth up.

(x) sleep;
(x) i.e. a dream
(y) they;
(y) Ps.103:15;Isa.40:6

Ps.103:15

v.15 As for man, his days are like grass; as a flower of the field, so he flourisheth.

Isa.40:6

v.6 The voice said, Cry. And he said, What shall I cry? All flesh is grass, and all its |beauty| is like the flower of the field.

v.6 In the morning it flourisheth, and growth up; in the evening it is cut down, and withered.

v.7 For we are consumed by thine anger, and by thy wrath are we troubled.

v.8 (z) Thou hast set our iniquities before thee, our (aa) secret sins in the light of thy countenance.

(z) Thou hast set our iniquities before thee,
(z) Ps.50:21;Jer.16:17
(aa) secret;
(aa) Ps.19:12

Ps.50:21

v.21 These things hast thou done, and I kept silence. Thou thoughtest that I was altogether such an one as thyself, but I will reprove thee, and set them in order before thine eyes.

Jer.16:17

v.17 For mine eyes are upon all their ways; they are not hidden from my face, neither is their iniquity hidden from mine eyes.

Ps.19:12

v.12 Who can understand his errors? Cleanse thou me from secret faults.

v.9 For all our days are passed away in thy wrath; we spend our years as a tale that is told.

v.10 The days of our years are threescore years and ten; and if, by reason of strength, they be fourscore years, yet is their strength labor and sorrow; for it is soon cut off, and we fly away.

v.11 Who knoweth the power of thine anger? Even according to thy fear, so is thy wrath.

v.12 So (a) teach us to number our days, that we may apply our hearts unto wisdom.

(a) teach us
(a) Ps.39:4

v.4 Their young ones are |become strong|; they grow up |in the open field|; they go forth, and return not unto them.

v.13 Return, O LORD, how long? And let it (b) repent thee concerning thy servants.

(b) repent
(b) Zech.8:14, note

v.14 For thus saith the LORD of hosts: As I thought to punish you, when your fathers provoked me to wrath, saith the LORD of hosts, and I repented not,

Note, 4(8:14) Repentance (O.T.), Summary: In the O.T., "repentance" is the English word used to translate the Hebrew nacham, to be eased or comforted. It is used of both God and man. Notwithstanding the literal meaning of nacham, it is evident, from a study of all passages, that the sacred writers use it is the sense of metanoia in the N.T., meaning a change of mind. See Mt.3:2; Acts 17:30,note. As in the N.T., such change of mind is often accompanied by contrition and self-judgment. When applied to God, the word is used phenomenally, according to O.T. custom. God seems to change His mind. The phenomena are such as, in the case of a man, would indicate a change of mind.

v.14 Oh, satisfy us early with thy mercy, that we may rejoice and be glad all our days.
v.15 Make us glad according to the days wherein thou hast afflicted us, and the years wherein we have seen evil.

v.16 Let thy work appear unto thy servants, and thy glory unto their children.
v.17 And let the (c) beauty of the LORD our God be upon us, and (d) establish thou the work of our hands upon us; yea, the work of our hands establish thou it.

(c) beauty
(c) Ps.27:4
(d) establish
(d) Isa.26:12

Ps.27:4

v.4 One thing have I desired of the LORD, that will I seek after: that I may dwell in the house of the LORD all the days of my life, to behold the beauty of the LORD, and to inquire in his temple.

Isa.26:12

v.12 LORD, thou wilt ordain peace for us; for thou also hast wrought all our works in us.

SECRET PLACE OF SECURITY

PSALM 91

v.1 (e) HE who dwelleth in the secret place of the Most High shall abide under the (f) shadow of the Almighty.

(e) He who dwelleth in the secret place
(e) Ps.27:5;31:20;32:7
(f) shadow
(f) Assurance-security:
v.1;Isa.32:17. (Ps.23:1 Jude 1)

Ps.27:5

v.5 For the time of trouble he shall hide me in his pavilion; in the secret of his tabernacle shall he hide me; he shall set me up upon a rock.

Ps.31:20

v.20 Thou shalt hide them in the secret of thy presence from the pride of man; thou shalt keep them secretly in a pavilion from the strife of tongues.

Ps.32:7

v.7 Thou art my hiding place; thou shalt preserve me from trouble; thou shalt compass me about with songs of deliverance. Selah.

See the above v.1:

Isa.32:17

v.17 And the work of righteousness shall be peace; and the effect of righteousness, quietness and assurance forever.

Ps.23:1

v.1 THE LORD is my shepherd; I shall not want.

Jude 1

v.1 Jude, the servant of Jesus Christ, and brother of James, to them that are sanctified by God, the Father and preserved in Jesus Christ, and called:

v.2 I will say of the LORD, He is my refuge and my fortress, my God; in him will I (g) trust.

(g) trust
(g) Ps.2:12,note.Ps.16:1(Messianic Psalms)

v.3 Surely he shall (h) deliver thee from the snare of the fowler, and from the noisome pestilence.

(h) deliver
(h) Ps.124:7

Ps.124:7

v.7 Our soul is escaped like a bird out of the snare of the fowlers; the snare is broken, and we are escaped.

v.4 (i)He shall cover thee with his feathers, and under his wings shalt thou trust; his truth shall be thy shield and bucker.

(i) He shall cover thee
(i) Ps.17:8;57:1;61:4

Ps. 17:8

v.8 Keep me as the apple of the eye; hide me under the shadow of thy wings,

Ps.57:1

v.1 BE merciful unto me, O God, be merciful unto me; for my soul trusteth in thee. Yea, in the shadow of thy wings will I make my refuge, until these calamities be |passed by|.

Ps.61:4

v.4 I will abide in thy tabernacle forever; I will trust in the |shelter| of thy wings. Selah.

v.5 (j) Thou shalt not be afraid for the terror by night, nor for the arrow that flieth by day,

(j) Thou shalt not be afraid
(j) Job 5:19;Ps.112:7;121:7;
Prov.3:23-24;Isa.43:2

Job.5:19

v.19 He shall deliver thee in six troubles; yea, in seven there shall no evil touch thee.

Ps. 112:7

v.7 He shall not be afraid of evil tidings; his heart is fixed, trusting in the LORD.

Ps.121:7

v.7 The LORD shall preserve thee from all evil; he shall preserve thy soul.

Prov.3:23-24

v.23 Then shalt thou walk in thy way safely, and thy foot shall not stumble.
v.24 When thou liest down thou shalt not be afraid; yea thou shalt lie down, and thy sleep shall be sweet.

Isa.43:2

v.2 When thou passest through the waters, I will be with thee; and through the rivers, they walkest through the fire, thou shalt not be burned, neither shall the flame kindle upon thee.

v.6 Nor for the pestilence that walketh in darkness, nor for the destruction that wasteth at noonday.
v.7 A thousand shall fall at thy side, and ten thousand at thy right hand, but it shall come (k) |near| thee.

(k) |near| thee.
(k) KJV nigh

Only (l) with thine eyes shalt thou behold and see the reward of the wicked.

(l) with thine eyes
(l) Ps.37:34;cp.Mal.1:5

Ps.37:34

v.34 Wait on the LORD, and keep his way, and he shall exalt thee to inherit the land. When the wicked are cut off, thou shalt see it.

Mal.1:5

v.5 And your eyes shall see, and ye shall say, The LORD will be magnified from the border of Israel.

v.9 Because thou hast made the LORD, who is my refuge, even the Most High, thy (m) habitation,

(m) habitation,
(m) Ps.71:3;90:1

Ps.71:3

v.3 Be thou my strong habitation, whereunto I may continually resort. Thou hast given commandment to save me; for thou art my rock and my fortress.

Ps.90:1

v.1 LORD, thou hast been our dwelling place in all generations.

v.10 (n) There shall no evil befall thee, neither shall any plague come (k) | near | thy dwelling

(n) there shall no evil befall thee,
(n) Prov.12:21
(k) | near | ;
(k) KJV nigh

Prov.12:21

v.21 There shall no evil happen to the just, but the wicked shall be filled with mischief.

v.11 (o) For he shall give his (p) angels charge over thee, to keep thee in all thy ways.

(o) For he shall give his
(o) Ps.34:7;Heb.1:14;cp.Lk.4:10-11
(p) angels;
(p) Heb.1:4,note

Ps. 34:7

v.7 The angel of the LORD encampeth round about those who fear him, and delivered them.

Heb.1:14

v.14 Are they not all ministering spirits, sent forth to minister for them who shall be heirs of salvation?

Lk.4:10-11

v.10 For it is written, He shall give his angels charge over thee, to keep thee;
v.11 And in their hands they shall bear thee up, lest at any time thou dash thy foot against a stone.

(p) angels;Heb.1:4;
see Ps.68:17 [Messianic Ps.]

v.12 They shall bear thee up in their hands, (q) lest thou dash thy foot against a stone.

(q) lest thou dash thy foot
(q) Mt.4:6

v.6 And saith unto him, If thou be the Son of God, cast thyself down; for it is written, He shall give his angels charge concerning thee, and in their hands they shall bear thee up, lest at any time thou dash thy foot against a stone.

v.13 Thou shalt tread upon the lion and (r) adder; the young lion and the (s) | serpent | shalt thou trample under feet.

(r) adder;
(r) Or asp
(s) | serpent |
(s) KJV dragon

v.14 Because he hath set his love upon me, therefore will I deliver him; I will set him on high, because he hath (t) known my name.

(t) known my name.
(t) Ps.9:10

v.10 And they who know thy name will put their trust in thee; for thou, LORD, hast not forsaken those who seek thee.

v.15 He shall (u) call upon me, and I will answer him. I will be (v) with him in trouble; I will deliver him, and honor him.

(u) call upon me
(u) Ps.50:15
(v) with him in trouble;
(v) Isa.43:2

Ps.50:15

v.15 And call upon me in the day of trouble; I will deliver thee, and thou shalt glorify me.

Isa.43:2

v.2 When thou passest through the waters, I will be with thee; and through the rivers, they shall not overflow thee; when thou walkest through the fire, thou shalt not be burned, neither shall the flame kindle upon thee.

v.16 With long life will I satisfy him, and show him my salvation.

THE PROPRIETY OF PRAISE

PSALM 92

v.1 IT IS a (w) good thing to give thanks unto the LORD, and to sing praises unto thy name, O Most High;

(w) good thing to give thanks unto the LORD,
(w) Ps.147:1

v.1 PRAISE ye the LORD; for it is good to sing praises unto our God; for it is pleasant; and praise is |fitting|.

v.2 (x) To show forth thy loving-kindness in the morning, and thy faithfulness every night,

(x) to show forth thy loving-kindness-faithfulness
(x) Ps.89:1

v.1 I will sing of the mercies of the LORD forever; with my mouth will I make known thy faithfulness to all generations.

v.3 Upon an instrument of ten strings, and upon the psaltery; upon the harp with a solemn sound.
v.4 For thou, LORD, hast made me glad through thy work; I will triumph in the works of thy hands.
v.5 O LORD, how great are thy works ! And thy (y) thoughts are very deep.

(y) thoughts are very deep
(y) Ps.139:17-18;Isa.28:29
Rom.11:33-34

Ps.139:17-18

v.17 How precious also are thy thoughts unto me, O God! How great is the sum of them!
v.18 If I should count them, they are more in number than the sand; when I awake, I am still with thee.

Isa.28:29

v.29 This also cometh forth from the Lord of hosts, who is wonderful in counsel, and excellent in working.

Rom.11:33-34

v.33 Oh, the depth of the riches both of the wisdom and knowledge of God! How unsearchable are his judgments, and his ways past finding out!
v.34 For who hath known the mind of the Lord? Or who hath been his counselor?

v.6 A (z) |stupid| man knoweth not, neither doth a fool understand this.

(z) |stupid| man knoweth not,
(z) KJV brutish

v.7 (aa) When the wicked spring like the grass, and when all the workers of iniquity do flourish, it is that they shall be (bb) destroyed forever:

(aa) when the wicked
(aa) Job 12:6;Ps.37:1-2;Jer.12:1-2;Mal.3:15
(bb) destroyed forever:
(bb) Ps.37:38;73:17

Job 12:6

v.6 The |tents| of robbers prosper, and they that provoke God are secure; into whose hand God bringeth abundantly.

Ps.37:1-2

v.1 FRET not thyself because of evildoers, neither be thou envious against the workers of iniquity.
v.2 For they shall soon be cut down like the grass, and wither like the green herb.

Jer.12:1-2

v.1 RIGHTEOUS are thou, O LORD, when I plead with thee; yet let me talk with thee of thy judgments. | Why | doth the way of the wicked prosper? Why are all they happy that deal very treacherously?
v.2 Thou hast planted them, yea they bring forth fruit; thou art near in their mouth, and far from their | heart |.

Mal.3:15

v.15 And now we call the proud happy; yea, they that work wickedness are set up; yea, they that | test | God are even delivered.

Ps.37:38

v.38 But the transgressors shall be destroyed together; the end of the wicked shall be cut off.

Ps.73:13

v.13 Verily, I have cleansed my heart in vain, and washed my hands in innocence.

v.8 But thou, LORD, art most high for evermore.
v.9 For, lo, thine enemies, O LORD, for, lo, thine enemies shall perish; all the workers of iniquity shall be scattered.
v.10 But my (cc) horn shalt thou exalt like the horn of (dd) | a wild ox | ; I shall be (ee) anointed with fresh oil.

(cc) horn
(cc) See Dt.33:17,note

See Ps.89:17—Messianic Ps.
(dd) |a wild ox|;
(dd) KJV an unicorn
(ee) anointed
(ee) Ps.23:5

Ps.23:5

v.5 Thou prepares a table before me in the presence of mine enemies; thou anointest my head with oil; my cup runneth over.

v.11 (ff) Mine eye also shall see my desire on mine enemies, and mine ears shall hear my desire of the wicked that rise up against me.

(ff) mine eyes
(ff) Ps.54:7;59:10;112:8

Ps.54:7

v.7 For he hath delivered me out of all trouble, and mine eye hath seen his desire upon mine enemies.

Ps.59:10

v.10 The God of my mercy shall |meet| me; God shall let me see my desire upon mine enemies.

Ps.112:8

v.8 His heart is established; he shall not be afraid, until he see his desire upon his enemies.

v.12 The (gg) righteous shall flourish like the palm tree; he shall grow like a cedar in Lebanon.

(gg) righteous
(gg) vv.13:14;Ps.1:3;52:8

v.13 Those who are planted in the house of the LORD shall flourish in the courts of our God.
v.14 They shall bring forth (hh)fruit in old age; they shall be fat and (ii) flourishing,

Ps.1:3

v.1 BLESSED is the man who walketh not in the counsel of the ungodly. Nor standeth in the way of sinners, nor sitteth in the seat of the scornful.

Ps.52:8

v.8 But I am like a green olive tree in the house of God; I trust in the mercy of God forever and ever.

v.13 Those who are planted in the house of the LORD shall flourish in the courts of our God.
v.14 They shall still bring forth (hh) fruit in old age; they shall be fat and (ii) flourishing,

(hh) fruit in old age;
(hh) Ps.cp.Jn.15:2
(ii) flourishing
(ii) Lit. green

v.2 **Every branch in me that beareth not fruit he taketh away; and every branch that beareth fruit, he purgeth it, that it may bring forth more fruit.**

v.15 To show that the LORD is upright. He is my rock, and (jj) there is no unrighteousness in him.

(jj) there is no unrighteousness in him.
(jj) cp. Rom.9:14

v.14 What shall we say then? Is there unrighteousness with God? God forbid.

THE MAJESTY OF GOD

PSALM 93

v.1 THE LORD reigneth; he is clothed with majesty. The LORD is
clothed with strength, wherewith he hath girded himself;
the (a) world also is (b) | established | , that it cannot be
moved.

(a) world
(a) Ps.96:10
(b) | established | ;
(b) KJV stablished

Ps.96:10

v.10 Say among the | nations | that the LORD reigneth. The
world also shall be established that it shall not be
moved; he shall judge the peoples righteously.

v.2 Thy throne is established of old; thou art from everlasting.
v.3 The floods have lifted up, O LORD, the floods have lifted up
their voice; the floods lift up their waves.
v.4 The LORD on high is mightier than the noise of many waters,
yea, than the mighty waves of the sea.
v.5 Thy testimonies are very sure; holiness becometh thine
house, O LORD, forever.

VENGEANCE BELONGS TO GOD

PSALM 94

v.1 O LORD God, to whom (c) vengeance belongeth; O God, to whom vengeance belonged, (d) show thyself.

(c) vengeance belongeth,
(c) Dt.32:35;Rom.12:19
(d) show thyself;
(d) Lit. shine forth

Dt.32:35

v.35 To me belongeth vengeance, and recompence; their foot shall slide in due time. For the day of their calamity is at hand, and the things that shall come upon them made haste.

Rom.12:19

v.19 Dearly beloved, avenge not yourselves but, rather, give place unto wrath; for it is written, Vengeance is mine; I will repay, saith the Lord.

v.2 Lift up thyself, thou judge of the earth; render a reward to the proud.
v.3 LORD, how long shall the wicked, how long shall the wicked triumph?
v.4 How long shall they (e) utter and speak hard things, and all the workers of iniquity boast themselves?

(e) utter and speak hard things,
(e) Ps.31:18;Jude15

Ps.31:18

v.18 Let the lying lips be put to silence, which speak grievous things proudly and contemptuously against the righteous.

Jude 15

v.15 To execute judgment upon all, and to |convict| all that are ungodly among them of all their ungodly deeds which they have ungodly committed, and of all their hard speeches which ungodly sinners have spoken against him.

v.5 They break in pieces thy people, O Lord, and afflict thine heritage.
v.6 They slay the widow and the stranger, and murder the fatherless.
v.7 Yet they say, The Lord shall not see, neither shall the God of Jacob regard it.
v.8 Understand, ye (f) |stupid| among the people; and ye fools, when will ye be wise?

(f) |stupid|
(f) KJV brutish;Ps.92:6

v.6 A |stupid| man knoweth not, neither doth a fool understand this.

v.9 (g) He who planted the ear, shall he not hear? He who formed the eye, shall he not see?

(g) he who planted the ear
(g) Ex.4:11;Prov.20:12

Ex.4:11

v.11 And the LORD said unto him, Who hath made man's mouth? Or who maketh the dumb, or deaf, or the seeing, or the blind? Have not I, the LORD?

Prov.20:12

v.12 The hearing ear, and the seeing eye, the LORD hath made even both of them.

v.10 He who chastiseth the (h) |nations|, shall not he correct? He who teaches man knowledge, shall not he know?

(h) |nations|
(h) KJV heathen

v.11 The LORD (i) knoweth the thoughts of man, that they are vanity.

(i) knoweth the thoughts
(i) 1 Cor.3:20

v.20 And again, The Lord knoweth the thoughts of the wise, that they are vain.

v.12 Blessed is the man whom thou (j) chastenest, O LORD, and teachest him out of thy law,

(j) chastenest,
(j) Heb.12:5-7

v.5 And ye have forgotten the exhortation which speaketh unto you as unto |sons|, My son, despise not thou the chastening of the Lord, nor faint when thou art rebuked of him;

v.6 For whom the Lord loveth he chasteneth, and scourgeth every son whom he receiveth.
v.7 If ye endure chastening, God dealeth with you as with sons; for what son is he whom the father chasteneth not?

v.13 That thou mayest give him rest from the days of adversity, until the pit be digged for the wicked.
v.14 For the LORD will not cast off his people, neither will he forsake his inheritance
v.15 But judgment shall return unto righteousness, and all the upright in heart shall follow it.
v.16 Who will rise up for me against the evildoers? Or who will stand up for me against the workers of iniquity?
v.17 Unless the LORD had been my help, my soul had almost dwelt in silence.
v.18 When I said, My foot slippeth, thy mercy, O LORD, held me up.
v.19 In the multitude of my thoughts within me thy comforts delight my soul.
v.20 Shall the throne of iniquity have fellowship with thee, who frameth mischief by a (k) law?

(k) law
(k) cp.Isa.10:1

v.1 WOE onto them who decree unrighteous decrees, and who write grievousness which they have prescribed,

v.21 They gather themselves together against the soul of the righteous, and condemn the (l) innocent blood.

(l) innocent blood
(l) Ex.23:7;cp.Mt.27:4

Ex.23:7

v.7 Keep thee far from a false matter: and the innocent and righteous slay thou not: for I will not justify the wicked.

Mt.27:4

v.4 Saying, I have sinned in that I have betrayed innocent blood. And they said, What is that to us? See thou to that.

v.22 But the LORD is my defense, and my God is the rock of my refuge.
v.23 And he shall bring upon them their own iniquity, and shall cut them off in their own wickedness; yea, the LORD our God shall cut them off.

EXHORTATION TO WORSHIP

PSALM 95

v.1 OH, come, let us sing unto the LORD, let us make a joyful noise to the rock of our salvation.
v.2 Let us come before his presence with thanksgiving, and make a joyful noise unto him with (m) psalms.

(m) psalms
(m) Eph.5:19;Jas.5:13

Eph.5:19

v.19 Speaking to yourselves in psalms and hymns and spiritual songs, singing and making melody in your heart to the Lord,

Jas.5:13

v.13 Is any among you afflicted? Let him pray. Is any merry? Let him sing psalms.

v.3 For the LORD, is a great God, and a great King above all (n) gods.

(n) gods
(n) 1Cor.8:5-6;see Ps.16:4,note

1Cor.8:5-6

v.5 For though there be that are called gods, whether in heaven or in earth (as there are gods many, and lords many).

v.6 But to us there is but one God, the Father, of whom are all things, and we in him; and one Lord Jesus Christ, by whom are all things, and we by him.

Ps.16:4,note

v.4 Their sorrows shall be multiplied, who hasten after another god; their drink offerings of blood will I not offer, nor take up their names into my lips.

Note;1(16:4) Of course there is only one God(1Cor.8:5-6). The pagans had, however, those whom they called "gods", e.g. in David's day, Dagon and Baal. Then and now, whatever preempts the place in one's heart that belongs to the true God may be said to be god, e.g. self and the pleasures of this world (2 Tim.3:2,4).

v.4 In his hand are the deep places of the earth; the strength of the hills is his also.
v.5 The sea in his, and he made it, and his hands formed the dry land.
v.6 Oh, come, let us worship and bow down; let us kneel before the LORD our maker.
v.7 For he is our God, and we are the people of his pasture, and the sheep of his hand. (o) Today if ye will hear his voice,

(o) Today
(o) vv.7-11; Heb.3:7-11

v.7 For he is our God, and we are the people of his pasture, and the sheep of his hand. Today if ye will hear his voice,
v.8 Harden not your heart, as in the provocation, and as in the day of temptation in the wilderness,
v.9 When your father (p) | tried | me, (q) | tested | me, and saw my (r) work.
v.10 (s) Forty years long was I grieved with this generation, and said, It is a people that do err in their heart, and they have not known my ways;

v.11 Unto whom I (t) swore in my wrath that they should not enter into my rest.

Heb.3:7-11

v.7 Wherefore, as the Holy |Spirit| saith, Today if ye will hear his voice,
v.8 Harden not your hearts, as in the provocation, in the day of |trail| in the wilderness,
v.9 When your fathers |put me to the test|, proved me, and saw my works forty years.
v.10 Wherefore, I was grieved with that generation, and said, They do always err in their heart, and they have not known my ways.
v.11 So I swore in my wrath, They shall not enter into my rest.

v.8 Harden not your heart, as in the provocation, and as in the day of temptation in the wilderness,
v.9 When your fathers (p) |tried| me, (q) |tested| me, and saw my (r) work.

(p) |tried| me,
(p) KJV tempted. Test-tempt:
v.9; Ps.106:14.
(Gen.3:1;Jas.1:14)
(q) |tested| me,
(q) KJV proved
(r) work.
(r) cp.Num.14:22
Note, see above v.9

Ps.106:14

v.14 But lusted exceedingly in the wilderness, and |tested| God in the desert.

Gen.3:1

v.1 Now the serpent was more subtle than any beast of the field which the LORD God had made. And he said unto the woman, yea, hath God said unto Ye shall not eat of every tree of the garden?

Jas.1:14

v.14 But every man is tempted, when he is drawn away of his own lust, and enticed.

Num.14:22

v.22 Because all those men who have seen my glory, and my miracles, which I did in Egypt and in the wilderness, and have |put me to the test| now these ten times, and have not hearkened to my voice;

v.10 (s)Forty years long was I grieved with this generation, and said, It is a people that do err in their heart, and they have not known my ways;

(s) forty year
(s) Acts7:36;13:18;Heb.3:17

Acts7:36

v.36 He brought them out, after he had shown wonders and signs in the land of Egypt, and in the Red Sea, and in the wilderness forty years.

Acts13:18

v.18 And about the time of forty years |bore| he their manners in the wilderness.

Heb.3:17

v.17 But with whom was he grieved forty years? Was it not with them that had sinned, whose carcasses fell in the wilderness?

v.11 Unto whom I (t) swore in my wrath that they should not enter into my rest.

(t) swore
(t) Heb.4:3

v.3 For we who believed do enter into rest, as he said, As I have sworn in my wrath, if they shall enter into my rest; although the works were finished from the foundation of the world.

PRAISE OF GOD'S AND GLORY

PSALM 96

v.1 (u) OH, sing unto the LORD a new song; sing unto the LORD, all the earth.

(u) OH, sing unto the LORD
(u) vv.1-13;cp.1Chr.16:23-33

v.1 (u) OH, sing unto the LORD a new song; sing unto the LORD, all the earth.
v.2 Sing unto the LORD, bless his name; show forth his salvation from day to day.
v.3 Declare his glory among the (a) | nations |, his wonders among all people.
v.4 For the LORD, is great, and greatly to be praised; he is to be (b) feared above all (c) gods.
v.5 For all the (c) gods of the nations are idols; but the (d) LORD made the heavens.
v.6 Honor and majesty are before him; strength and beauty are in his sanctuary.
v.7 Give unto the LORD, o ye kindreds of the people; give unto the LORD glory and strength.
v.8 Give unto the LORD the glory due unto his name; bring an offering, and come into his courts.
v.9 Oh, worship the LORD in the beauty of holiness; fear before him, all the earth.
v.10 Say among the (a) | nations | that the (e) LORD reigneth. The world also shall be established that it shall not be moved; he shall judge the peoples righteously.
v.11 Let the heavens rejoice, and let the earth be glad; let the sea roar, and the fullness thereof.

v.12 Let the field be joyful, and all that is therein; then shall all the trees of the (f) | forest | rejoice
v.13 Before the LORD; for he (g) cometh, for he cometh to judge the earth; he shall judge the world with righteousness, and the people with his trust.

1Chr.16:23-33.

v.23 Sing unto the LORD, all the earth; show forth from day to day his salvation.
v.24 Declare his glory among the | nations |, marvelous works among all | peoples |.
v.25 For great is the LORD, and greatly to be praised; he also is to be feared above all gods.
v.26 For all the gods of the people are idols; but the LORD made the heavens.
v.27 Glory and honor are in his presence; strength and gladness are his place.
v.28 Give unto the LORD, ye kindreds of the people, give unto the LORD glory and strength
v.29 Give unto the LORD the glory due unto his name; bring an offering, and come before him; worship the LORD, in the beauty of holiness.
v.30 Fear before him, all the earth; the world also shall be stable, that it be not moved.
v.31 Let the heavens be glad, and let the earth rejoice; and let men say among the nations, The LORD reigneth.
v.32 Let the sea roar, and the fullness thereof; let the fields rejoice, and all that is therein.
v.33 Then shall the trees of the woods sing out at the presence of the LORD, because he cometh to judge the earth.

v.2 Sing unto the LORD, bless his name; show forth his salvation from day to day.
v.3 Declare his glory among the (a) | nations |, his wonders among all peoples.

(a) | nations |
(a)KJV heathen

v.4 For the LORD is great, and greatly to be praised; he is to (b) feared above all (c)gods.

(b) feared above all
(b)See Ps.19:9,note
See Ps. 22:25
(c) gods; See Ps. 95:3

v.5 For all the (c)gods of the nations are idols; but the (d)LORD make the heavens.

(c) gods; See Ps.95:3
(d) LORD
(d) Isa.42:5;Jer.10:12

Isa.42:5

v.5 Thus saith God, the LORD, he who created the heavens, and stretched them out; he who spread forth the earth, and that which cometh out of it; he who giveth breath unto the people upon it, and spirit to them that walk in it:

Jer.10:12

v.12 He hath made the earth by his power; he hath established the world by his wisdom, and hath stretched out the heavens by his |understanding|,

v.6 Honor and majesty are before him; strength and beauty are in his sanctuary.
v.7 Give unto the LORD, O ye kindreds of the peoples; give unto the LORD glory and strength.
v.8 Give unto the LORD the glory due unto his name; bring an offering, and come into his courts.
v.9 Oh, worship the LORD in the beauty of holiness; fear before him, all the earth.
v.10 Say among the (a)|nations| that the (e) LORD reigneth. The world also shall be established that it shall not be moved; he shall judge the peoples righteously.

(a) |nations|
(a) KJV heathen
(e) Lord reigneth
Ps.93:1;97:1;Rev.11:15;19:6

Ps.93:1

v.1 THE LORD reigneth, he is clothed with majesty. The LORD, is clothed with strength, wherewith he hath girded himself; the world also is |established|, that it cannot be moved.

Ps.97:1

v.1 THE LORD reigneth; let the earth rejoice; let the multitude of isles be glad thereof.

Rev.11:15

v.15 And the seventh angel sounded; and there were great voices in heaven, saying, The |kingdom| of the world is become the kingdom of our Lord, and his Christ, and he shall reign forever and ever.

Rev.19:6

v.6 And I heard, as it were, the voice of a great multitude, and like the voice of many waters, and like the voice of mighty |peals of thunder|, saying, |Hallelujah|! For the Lord God omnipotent reigneth.

v11 Let the heavens rejoice, and let the earth be glad; let the sea roar, and the fullness thereof.
v.12 Let the field be joyful, and all that is therein; then shall all the trees of the (f) |forest| rejoice

(f) |forest| rejoice
(f) KJV wood

v.13 Before the LORD; for he (g) cometh, for he cometh to judge the earth; he shall judge the world with righteousness, and the peoples with his trust.

(g) cometh;
(g) Christ (second advent):vv.10-13
Ps.110:1.(Dt.30:3Acts1:11,note)
See: above vv. 10-13

Ps.110:1

v.1 THE LORD said unto my Lord, Sit thou at my right hand, until I make thine enemies thy footstool.

Dt.30:3

v.3 That then the LORD thy God will turn thy captivity, and have compassion upon thee, and will return and gather thee from all the nations where the LORD thy God hath scattered thee.

Acts1:11,note

v.1 Who also said, Ye men of Galilee, why stand ye gazing up into heaven? This same Jesus, who is taken up from you into heaven, shall so come in like manner as ye have seen him go into heaven.

Note:1(1:11) The Two Advents, Summary:

(1) The O.T. fore view of the coming Messiah is in two aspects—that of rejection and suffering (e.g. in Isa.53); and that of earthly glory and power (e.g. in Isa.11; Jer.23;Ezek.37). Often these two aspects blend in one passage (e.g.Ps.22). The prophets themselves were perplexed by this seeming contradiction (1Pet.1:10-11). It was solved by partial fulfillment. In due time the Messiah, born of a virgin according to Isaiah's prophecy (7:14), appeared among men and began

His ministry by announcing the predicted kingdom as "at hand" (Mt.4:17,note 4). The rejection of King and kingdom followed.

(2) Thereupon the rejected king announced His approaching crucifixion, resurrection, departure, and return (Mt.12:38-40; 16:1-4,21,27;24;25; Lk.12:35-46; 17:20-36; 18:31-34;19:12-27).

(3) He uttered predictions concerning the course of events between His departure and return (Mt.13:1-50;16:18;24:4-26).

(4) this promised return of Christ is a prominent theme in The Acts, Epistles, and The Revelation.

Taken together the N.T. teaching concerning the return of Jesus Christ may be summarized as follows:

(1) The return of Christ is an event, not a process, and is personal and corporeal (Mt.23:39;24:30;25:31; Mk.14:62; Lk.17:24; Jn.14:3;Acts1:11;Phil.3:20-21; 1Th.4:14-17).

(2) His coming has a threefold relation: to the Church, to Israel, and to the nations:

(a) To the Church, the descent of the Lord into the air, to raise believers who have died and to change the living Christians, is a constant expectation and hope (1Cor.15:51-52; Phil.3:20;1Th.1:10;4:13-17;1Tim.6:14;Ti.2:13;Rev.22:20).

(b) To Israel, the return of the Lord to the earth is to accomplish the yet unfulfilled prophecies Davidic Covenant (2Sam. 7:16,note;cp.Acts15:14-17 with Zech. 14:1-9). See Kingdom (O.T.), 2Sam.7:8-17;Zech.12:8,note,(N.T.), Lk.1:31-33;1 Cor.15:24, note.

(c) To the Gentile nations, the return of Christ is to bring the destruction of the present political world system (Dan.2:34-35;Rev.19:11,note), and the judgment of Mt.25:31-46, followed by world-wide Gentile conversion and participation in the blessings of the kingdom (Isa.2:2-4;11:10;60:3; Zech.8:3,20-23;14:16-21).

THE POWER OF THE RIGHTEOUS LORD

PSALM 97

v.1 THE LORD (h) reigneth; let the earth rejoice; let the multitude of (i) isles be glad thereof.

(h) reigneth;
(h) Ps.96:10
(i) isles
(i) i. e. coasts

v.10 Say among the |nations| that the LORD reigneth. The world also shall be established that it shall not be moved; he shall judge the peoples righteously.
Clouds and darkness are round about him; righteousness and (j)|justice| are the habitation of his throne.

(j) |justice|
(j) KJV judgment

v.3 A fire goeth before him, and burneth up his enemies round about.
v.4 His lightnings (k)|lightened| the world; the earth saw, and trembled.

(k) |lightened|
(k) KJV enlightened

v.5 The hills melted like wax at the presence of the LORD of the whole earth.
v.6 The heavens declare his righteousness, and all the peoples see his glory.
v.7 Confounded be all those who serve (l) | carved | images, who boast themselves of idols; (m) worship him, all ye gods.

(l) | carved | images,
(l) KJV graven
(m) worship him,
(m) cp.Heb.1:6

Heb.1:6

v.6 And again, when he bringeth in the first-begotten into the world, he saith, And let all the angels of God worship him.

v.8 Zion heard, and was glad; and the daughters of Judah rejoiced because of thy judgments, O LORD.
v.9 For thou, LORD, art high above all the earth; (n) thou art exalted far above all (c) gods.

(n) thou
(n) Ex.18:11;Ps.95:3;96:4
(c) gods; Ps.16:7,note
(c) See :Ps.95:3

Ex.18:11

v.11 Now I know that the LORD is greater than all gods; for in the thing wherein they dealt proudly he was above them.

Ps. 96:4

v.4 For the LORD is great, and greatly to be praised; he is to be feared above all gods.

v.10 Ye who love the LORD, (o) hate evil. He (p) preserveth the souls of his saints; he delivereth them out of the hand of the wicked.

(o) hate evil
(o)Prov.8:13;Rom.12:9
(p) presereth; Ps.31:23;37:28;145:20;Prov.2:8

Prov.8:13

v.13 The fear of the LORD is to hate evil; pride, and arrogance, and the evil way, and the |perverse| mouth, do I hate.

Rom.12:9

v.9 Let love be without |hypocrisy|. Abhor that which is evil; |cling| to that which is good.

Ps.31:23

v.23 Oh, love the LORD, all ye his saints; for the LORD preserveth the faithful, and plentifully rewardeth the proud doer.

Ps.37:28

v.28 For the LORD loveth |justice|, and forsaketh not his saints; they are preserved forever, but the seed of the wicked shall be cut off.

Ps.145:20

v.20 The LORD preserveth all those who love him, but all the wicked will he destroy.

Prov.2:8

v.8 He keepeth the paths of |justice|, and preserveth the way of his saints.

v.11 Light is sown for the righteous, and gladness for the upright in heart.

v.12 Rejoice in the LORD, ye righteous, and give thanks at the remembrance of his holiness.

PRAISE TO THE LORD

PSALM 98

v.1 OH, (q) sing unto the LORD a new song: for he hath (r) done
marvelous things; his right hand, and his holy arm, have
gotten him the victory.

(q) sing
(q) Ps.33:3;96:1;Isa.42:10
(r) done marvelous things;
(r) Ex.15:11;Ps.77:14;86:10;105:5;136:4;139:14

Ps. 33:3

v.3 Sing unto him a new song; play skillfully with a loud noise.

Ps.96:1

v.1 OH, sing unto the LORD a new song; sing unto the LORD, all the earth.

Isa.42:10

v.10 Sing unto the LORD, a new song, and his praise from the end of the earth, ye that go down to the sea, and all that is in it; the |coasts|, and their inhabitants

Ex.15:11

v.11 Who is like unto thee, O LORD, among the gods? Who is like thee, glorious in holiness, fearful in praises, doing wonders?

Ps.77:14

v.14 Thou art the God who doest wonders; thou hast declared thy strength among the peoples.

Ps.86:10

v.10 For thou art great, and doest wondrous things; thou art God alone.

Ps.105:5

v.5 Remember his marvelous works that he hath done; his wonders, and the judgments of his mouth;

Ps.136:4

v.4 To him who alone doeth great wonders; for his mercy endureth forever;

Ps.139:14

v.14 I will praise thee; for I am fearfully and wonderfully made. Marvelous are thy works, and that my soul knoweth right well.

v.2 The LORD hath made (s) known his salvation; his righteousness hath he openly shown in the sight of the (a) | nations | .

(s) known;
(s) Isa.52:10;Lk.1:77;2:30-31
(a) | nations | ;
(a) KJV heathen

Isa.52:10

v.10 The LORD hath made bare his holy arm in the eyes of all the nations, and all the ends of the earth shall see the salvation of our God.

Lk.1:77

v.77 To give knowledge of salvation unto his people by the remission of their sins,

Lk.2:30-31

v.30 For mine eyes have seen thy salvation,
v.31 Which thou hast prepared before the face of all people, Israel.

(a) |nations|
(a) KJV heathen

v.3 He hath remembered his mercy and his truth toward the house of Israel; (t) all the ends of the earth have seen the salvation of our God.

(t) all the ends of the earth
(t) Isa.49:6;Lk.3:6;Acts13:47;28:28

Isa.49:6

v.6 And he said, It is a light thing that thou shouldest be my servant to raise up the tribes of Jacob, and to restore the preserved of Israel; I will also give thee for a light to the |nations|, that thou mayest be my salvation unto the end of the earth.

Lk.3:6

v.6 And all flesh shall see the salvation of God.

Acts13:47

v.47 For so hath the Lord commanded us, saying, I have set thee to be a light of the |nations|, that thou shouldest be for salvation unto the ends of the earth.

Acts28:28

v.28 Be it known, therefore, unto you, that the salvation of God is sent unto the Gentiles, and that they will hear it.

v.4 Make a joyful noise unto the LORD, all the earth; make a loud noise, and rejoice, and sing praise.
v.5 Sing unto the LORD with the harp; with the harp, and the voice of a psalm.
v.6 With trumpets and sound of cornet make a joyful noise before the LORD, the King.

v.7 Let the sea roar, and the fullness thereof; the world, and they that dwell therein.
v.8 Let the floods clap their hands; let the hills be joyful together
v.9 Before the LORD; for he (u) cometh to judge the earth; with righteousness shall he judge the world, and the peoples with equity.

(u) cometh
(u) Ps.96:10,13

Ps.96:10

v.10 Say among the |nations| that the LORD reigneth. The world also shall be established that it shall not be moved; he shall judge the peoples righteously.
v.13 Before the LORD; for he cometh, for he cometh to judge the earth; he shall judge the world with righteousness, and the peoples with his truth.

REVERENCE FOR GOD'S GREATNESS

PSALM 99

v.1 THE LORD reigneth; let the peoples tremble. (v) He sitteth between the cherubim, let the earth be moved.

(v) He sitteth between the cherubim,
(v) Ex.25:22;Ps.80:1

Ex.25:22

v.22 And there I will meet thee, and I will commune with thee from above the mercy seat, from between the two cherubim which are upon the ark of the testimony, of all things which I will give thee in commandment unto the children of Israel.

Ps.80:1

v.1 GIVE ear, O Shepherd of Israel, thou who leadest Joseph like a flock; thou who dwellest between the cherubim, shine forth.

v.2 The LORD is great in Zion, and he is high above all the peoples.
v.3 Let them praise thy great and (w) |awe-inspiring| name; for it is (x) holy.

(w) |awe-inspiring| name;
(w) KJV terrible.
Dt.28:58;cp.Rev.15:4

(x) holy
(x) Isa.6:3;cp.Rev.4:8

Dt.28:58

v.58 If thou wilt not observe to do all the words of the law that are written in this book, that thou mayest fear this glorious and fearful name, THE LORD THY GOD,

Rev.15:4

v.4 Who shall not fear thee, O Lord, and glorify thy name? For thou only art holy; for all nations shall come and worship before thee; for thy judgments are made manifest.

Isa.6:3

v.3 And one cried unto another, and said, Holy, holy, holy, is the LORD of hosts; the whole earth is full of his glory.

Rev.4:8

v.8 And the four |living creatures| had each of them six wings about him, and they were full of eyes within; and they rest not day and night, saying, Holy, holy, holy, Lord God Almighty, who was, and is to come.

v.4 The king's strength also loveth (j) |justice|; thou dost establish equity, thou executes (j) |justice| and righteousness in Jacob.

(j) |justice|
(j) KJV judgment
(j) |justice| thou dost establish equity,
(j) KJV judgment

v.5 Exalt ye the LORD our God, and worship at his footstool; for he is holy.

v.6 Moses and Aaron among his priests, and (a) Samuel among those who (b) call upon his name; they called upon the LORD, and he answered them.

(a) Samuel
(a) cp. Jer.15:1
(b) call upon his name;
(b) 1 Sam.7:9

Jer.15:1

v.1 THEN said the LORD unto me, Though Moses and Samuel stood before me, yet my mind could not be toward this people. Cast them out of my sight, and let them go forth.

1 Sam.7:9

v.9 And Samuel took a sucking lamb, and offered it for a burnt offering wholly unto the LORD. And Samuel cried unto the LORD for Israel; and the LORD heard him.

v.7 He spoke unto them in the cloudy pillar; they kept his testimonies, and the ordinance that he gave them.
v.8 Thou answeredst them, O LORD our God: thou wast a God who (c) forgavest them, though thou hast taken vengeance on their (d) | misdeeds | .

(c) forgavest them,
(c) Ps.79:11
(d) | misdeeds | ;
(d) Lit. the children of death

Ps. 79:11

v.11 Let the sighing of the prisoner come before thee; according to the greatness of thy power preserve thou those that are appointed to die;

v.9 Exalt the LORD, our God, and worship at his holy hill; for the LORD our God is holy.

GLADNESS AND THANKSGIVING

PSALM 100

v.1 MAKE a joyful noise unto the LORD, all ye lands.
v.2 Serve the LORD with gladness; come before his presence with singing.
v.3 Know ye that the LORD, he is God; it is he who hath (e) made us, and not we ourselves; (f) we are his people, and the sheep of his pasture.

(e) made us,
(e) Ps. 119:73;139:13-14;149:2
(f) we are his people:
(f) Ps.95:7;Ezek.34:30-31

Ps.119:73

v.73 Thy hands have made me and fashioned me; give me understanding, that I may learn thy commandments.

Ps.139:13-14

v.13 For thou hast possessed my |inward parts|, thou hast covered me in my mother's womb.
v.14 I will praise thee; for I am fearfully and wonderfully made. Marvelous are thy works, and that my soul knoweth right well.

Ps.149:2

v.2 Let Israel rejoice in him who made him; let the children of Zion be joyful in their King.

Ps.95:7

v.7 For he is our God, and we are the people of his pasture, and the sheep of his hand. Today if ye will hear his voice,

Ezek.34:30-31

v.30 Thus shall they know that I, the LORD their God, am with them, and that they, even the house of Israel, are my people, saith the Lord God.
v.31 And ye my flock, the flock of my pasture, are men, and I am your God, saith the Lord God.

v.4 (g) Enter into his gates with thanksgiving, and into his courts with praise; be thankful unto him, and bless his name.

(g) Enter;
(g) Ps.66:13;116:17-19

Ps.66:13

v.13 I will go into thy house with burnt offerings; I will pay thee my vows,

Ps.116:17-19

v.17 I will offer to thee the sacrifice of thanksgiving, and will call upon the name of the LORD.
v.18 I will pay my vows unto the LORD now in the presence of all his people,
v.19 In the courts of the LORD'S house, in the midst of thee, O Jerusalem. Praise ye the LORD.

v.5 For the LORD is good; his mercy is everlasting, and his truth endureth to all generations.

A VOW FOR A HOLY LIFE

PSLAM 101

v.1 I will sing of mercy and (h)|justice|; unto thee O LORD, will I sing.

(h) |justice|;
(h) KJV judgment.

Ps.94:15

v.15 But judgment shall return unto righteousness, and all the upright in heart shall follow it.

v.2 I will behave myself wisely in a (i) perfect way. Oh, when wilt thou come unto me? I will walk within my house with a perfect heart.

(i) perfect way;
(i) v.6 see 1 Ki.8:61,note

v.6 Mine eyes shall be upon the faithful of the land, that they may dwell with me; he that walketh in a perfect way, he shall serve me.

1 Ki.8:61,note

v. 61 Let your heart, therefore, be perfect with the LORD our God, to walk in his statutes, and keep his commandments, as at this day.

Note: 1(8:61) The word "perfect" implies wholeheartedness for God, single-mindedness, sincerity—not sinless perfection (e.g. Job 1:1)

v.3 I will set no wicked thing before mine eyes. I hate the work of those who turn aside; it shall not (j) | cling | to me.

(j) | cling | to me
(j) KJV cleave

v.4 A (k) | perverse | heart shall depart from me; I will not know a wicked person.

(k) | perverse |
(k) KJV forward

v.5 Whoso (l) | secretly | slandereth his neighbor, him will I cut off; him that hath an high look and a proud heart will not I (m) | tolerate |.

(l) | secretly |
(l) KJV privily
(m) | tolerate |
(m) KJV suffer

v.6 Mine eyes shall be upon the faithful of the land, that they may dwell with me; he that walketh in a perfect way, he shall serve me.
v.7 He that worketh deceit shall not dwell within my house; he that telleth lies shall not tarry in my sight.
v.8 I will early (n) destroy all the wicked of the land, that I may cut off all wicked doers from the (o) city of the LORD.

(n) destroy all the wicked
(n) Ps.75:10;cp.Jer.21:12
(o) city of the LORD;
(o) Ps.48:2,8

Ps.75:10

v.10 O God, how long shall the adversary reproach? Shall the enemy blaspheme thy name forever?

Jer.21:12

v.12 O house of David, thus saith the LORD, Execute |justice| in the morning, and deliver him that is spoiled out of the hand of the oppressor, lest my fury go out like fire, and burn that none can quench it, because of the evil of your doings.

Ps.48:2,8

v.2 Beautiful for situation, the joy of the whole earth, is Mount Zion, on the sides of the north, the city of the great King.

v.8 As we have heard so have we seen in the city of the LORDof hosts, in the city of our God; God will establish it forever. Selah.

CHRIST, THE AFFLICTION OF HIS HOLY SOUL

PSALM 102

v.1 1 Hear my prayer, O LORD, and let my cry come unto thee.

1 (102:1)

v.2 (p) Hide not thy face from me in the day when I am in trouble; incline thine ear unto me; in the day when I call, answer me speedily.

(p) hide not thy face
(p) Ps.27:9;69:17

Ps.27:9

v.9 Hide not thy face far from me; put not thy servant away in anger. Thou hast been my help; leave me not, neither forsake me, O God of my salvation.

Ps. 69:17

v.17 And hide not thy face from thy servant; for I am in trouble. Hear me speedily.

v.3 For my days are (q) consumed like smoke, and my bones are burned like an hearth.

(q) consumed like smoke,

(q) Jas. 4:14

v.14 Whereas ye know not what shall be on the |next day|. For what is your life? It is even a vapor that appeared for a little time, and then vanisheth away.

v.4 My heart is smitten, and withered like grass, so that I forget to eat my bread.
v.5 By reason of the voice of my groaning, my bones (j)|adhere| to my skin.

(j) |adhere|
(j) KJV cleave

v.6 I am like a pelican of the wilderness; I am like an owl of the desert.
v.7 I watch, and am like a sparrow alone upon the housetop.
v.8 Mine enemies reproach me all the day, and they that are mad against me are sworn against me.
v.9 For I have eaten ashes like bread, and mingled my drink with weeping,
v.10 Because of thine indignation and thy wrath; for thou hast lifted me up, and cast me down.
v.11 My days are like a shadow that declineth, and I am withered like grass.
v.12 But thou, O LORD, shalt endure forever, and thy remembrance unto all generations.
v.13 Thou shalt arise, and have mercy upon Zion; for the time to favor her, yea, the (r) set time, is come.

(r) set time,
(r) cp. Dan.8:19

v.19 Then I would know the truth of the fourth beast, which was diverse from all the others, exceedingly dreadful, whose teeth were of iron, and its nails of |bronze|, which devoured, broke in pieces, and stamped the residue with his feet;

v.14 For thy servants take pleasure in her stones, and favor the dust thereof.

v.15 So the (s) |nations| shall (t) fear the name of the LORD, and all the Kings of the earth thy glory.

(s) |nations|
(s) KJV heathen
(t) fear the name of the LORD,
(t) Ps.19:9, note

Ps.19:9,note

v.9 The fear of the LORD is clean, enduring forever; the |ordinances| of the LORD are true and righteous altogether.

Note: 2(19:9) "The fear of the LORD" is an O.T. expression meaning reverential trust including the hatred of evil.

v.16 When the LORD shall build up Zion, he shall appear in his glory.

v.17 He will (a) regard the prayer of the destitute, and not despise their prayer.

(a) regard the prayer of the destitute,
(a) cp. Neh.1:6,11;2:8

v.6 Let thine ear now be attentive, and thine eyes open, that thou mayest hear the prayer of thy servant, which I pray before thee now, day and night, for the children of Israel, thy servants, and confess the sins of the children of Israel, which we have sinned against thee; both I and my father's house have sinned.

v.11 O LORD, I beseech thee, let now thine ear be attentive to the prayer of thy servant, and the prayer of thy servants, who |delight| to fear thy name; and prosper, I pray thee, thy servant this day, and grant him mercy in the sight of this man. For I was the king's cupbearer.

Neh.2:8

v.8 And a letter unto A'saph, the keeper of the king's forest, that he may give me timber to make beams for the gates of the palace which |is near| to the house, and for the wall of the city, and for the house that I shall enter into. And the king granted me, according to the good hand of my GOD, upon me.

v.18 This shall be written for the generation to come; and the people who shall be created shall praise the LORD.
v.19 For he hath (b) looked down from the height of his sanctuary; from heaven did the LORD behold the earth,

(b) looked down
(b) cp. Ex.3:7

v.7 And the LORD said, I have surely seen the affliction of my people who are in Egypt, and have heard their cry by reason of their taskmasters; for I know their sorrows;

v.20 To (c) hear the groaning of the prisoner; to loose (d) those that are appointed to die;

(c) hear the groaning of the prisoner;
(c) Ps.79:11

v.11 Let the sighing of the prisoner come before thee; according to the greatness of thy power preserve thou those that are appointed to die;

(d) those that are appointed to die;
(d) lit. the children of death

v.21 To declare the name of the LORD in Zion, and his praise in Jerusalem,
v.22 (e) When the people are gathered together, and the kingdoms, to serve the LORD.

(e) When the people are gathered
(e) Isa.2:2-3;60:3

Isa.2:2-3

v.2 And it shall come to pass in the last days, that the mountain of the LORD'S house shall be established in the top of the mountains, and shall be exalted above the hills; and all nations shall flow unto it.
v.3 And many people shall go and say, Come ye, and let us go up to the mountain of the LORD, To the house of the God of Jacob; and he will teach us of his ways, and we will walk in his paths; for out of Zion shall go forth the law, and the word of the LORD from Jerusalem.

Isa.60:3

v.3 And the |nations| shall come to thy light, and kings to the brightness of thy rising.

v.23 He weakened my strength in the way; he shortened my days.
v.24 I said, O my God, take me not away in the midst of my days; thy years are throughout all generations.
v.25 Of old hast thou laid the (f) foundation of the earth, and the heavens are the work of thy hands.

(f) foundation of the earth,
(f) vv. 25-27; Heb.1:10-12

v.25 Of old hast thou laid the (f) foundation of the earth, and the heavens are the work of thy hands.

v.26 They shall (g) perish, but thou shalt endure; yea, all of them shall (h) |become| old like a garment; like a vesture shalt thou change them, and they shall be changed.

v.27 But thou art the (i) same, and thy years shall have no end.

Heb.1:10-12

v 10 And, Thou, Lord, in the beginning hast laid the foundation of the earth; and the heavens are the work of thine hands.

v.11 They shall perish, but thou remainest; and they all shall |become| old as doth a garment,

v.12 And as a vesture shalt thou fold them up, and they shall be changed; but thou art the same, and thy years shall not fail.

v.26 They shall (g) perish, but thou shalt endure; yea, all of them shall (h) |become| old like a garment; like a vesture shalt thou change them, and they shall be changed.

(g) perish, but thou shalt endure;
(g)Isa.34:4; 51:6;Mt. 24:35;
2 Pet.3:7,10-12;Rev.20:11
(h) |become|
(h) KJV wax

Isa.34:4

v.4 And all the host of heaven shall be dissolved, and the heavens shall be rolled together like a scroll; and all their host shall fall down, as the leaf falleth off from the vine, and like a falling fig from the fig tree.

Isa.51:6

v.6 Lift up your eyes to the heavens, and look upon the earth beneath; for the heavens shall vanish away like smoke, and the earth shall |grow| old like a garment, and they that dwell therein shall die in like manner; but my salvation shall be forever, and my righteousness shall not be abolished.

Mt.24:35

v.35 **Heaven and the earth shall pass away, but my words shall not pass away.**

2 Pet 3:7;10-12

v.7 But the heavens and the earth which are now, by the same word are kept in store, reserved unto fire against the day of judgment and perdition of ungodly men.

2 Pet. 3:10-12

v.10 But the day of the Lord will come as a thief in the night, in which the heavens shall pass away with a great noise, and the elements shall melt with fervent heat; the earth also, and the works that are in it shall be burned up.

v.11 Seeing, then, that all these things shall be dissolved, what manner of persons ought ye to be in all holy |living| and godliness,

v.12 Looking for and hasting unto the coming of the day of God, in which the heavens, being on fire, shall be dissolved, and the elements shall melt with fervent heat?

Rev.20:11

v.11 And I saw a great white throne, and him that sat on it, from whose face the earth and the heaven fled away, and there was found no place for them.

v.27 But thou art the (i) same, and thy years shall have no end.

(i) same
(i) Mal.3:6;Heb.13:8;Jas.1:17

Mal.3:6

v.6 For I am the LORD, I change not; therefore ye sons of Jacob are not consumed.

Heb.13:8

v.8 Jesus Christ, the same yesterday, and today, and forever.

Jas.1:17

v.17 Every good gift and every perfect gift is from above, and cometh down from the Father of lights, with whom is no variableness, neither shadow of turning.

v.28 The children of thy servants shall continue, and their seed shall be established before thee.

Finally, the remaining section heightens the contrast between frail man and unchanging God by bringing both theme together (vv.23-28).

1 (102:1) The reference of vv.25-27 to Christ (Heb.1:10-12). is assurance that, in the preceeding verses of this Psalm, there is shown, prophetically, the affliction of His holy soul in the days of His humiliation and rejection

A PSALM OF UNMIXED PRAISE

PSALM 103

v.1 BLESS the LORD, O my soul, and all that is within me, bless his holy name.
v.2 Bless the LORD, O my soul, and (j) forget not all his benefits,

(j) forget not all his benefits,
(j)cp.Dt.6:11-12

Dt.6:11-12

v.11 And the priest shall offer the one for a sin offering, and the other for a burnt offering, and make an atonement for him, because he sinned by the dead, and shall hallow his head that same day.
v.12 And he shall consecrate unto the LORD the days of his separation, and shall bring a lamb of the first year for a trespass offering; but the days that were before shall be lost, because his separation was defiled.

v.3 Who (k) forgiveth all thine iniquities, who (l)healeth all thy diseases,

(k) forgiveth all thine iniquities,
(k) Ps.130:8;Isa.33:24;cp.Mt.9:2,6;
Mk.2:5,10-11;Lk.7:47
(l) healeth all thy diseases,
(l)Ex.15:26;Isa.53:5;Ps.147:3;Jer.17:14

Ps.130:8

 v.8 And he shall redeem Israel from all his iniquities.

Isa.33:24

v.24 And the inhabitant shall not say, I am sick; the people that dwell therein shall be forgiven their iniquity.

Mt.9:2,6

v.2 And, behold, they brought to him a man sick of the palsy, lying on a bed; and Jesus, seeing their faith, said unto the sick of the palsy,
v.6 **But that ye may know that the Son of man hath power on earth to forgive sins** (then saith he to the sick of the palsy), **Arise, take up thy bed, and go unto thine house.**

Mk.2:5,10-11

v.5 When Jesus saw their faith, he said unto the sick of the palsy, **Son, thy sins are forgiven thee.**
v.10 **But that ye may know that the Son of man hath |authority| on earth to forgive sins** (he saith to the sick of the palsy),
v.11 **I say unto thee, Arise, and take up thy bed, and go thy way into thine house.**

Lk.7:47

v.47 **Wherefore, I say unto thee, Her sins, which are many, are forgiven; for she loved much. But to whom little is forgiven, the same loveth little.**

Ex.15:26

v.26 And said, If thou wilt diligently hearken to the voice of the LORD thy God, and wilt do that which is right is his sight, and wilt give ear to his commandments, and keep all his statutes, I will put none of these diseases upon thee, which I have brought upon the Egyptians; for I am the LORD that healeth thee.

Isa.53:5

v.5 But he was wounded for our transgressions, he was bruised for our iniquities; the chastisement | for | our peace was upon him, and with his strips we are healed.

Ps.147:3

v.3 He healeth the broken in heart, and bindeth up their wounds.

Jer.17:14

v.14 Heal me, O LORD, and I shall be healed; save me, and I shall be saved; for thou art my praise.

v.4 Who (m) redeemed thy life from destruction, who crowneth thee with loving-kindness and tender mercies,

(m) redeemed thy life from destruction,
(m) Redemption (Kinsman type):v4
(m) Ps.106:10.(Gen.48:16;Isa.59:20,note)
(m) See Ps.72:14—Messianic Ps.
See: above v.4

Ps.106:10

v.10 And he saved them from the hand of him that hated them, and redeemed them from the hand of the enemy.

Gen.48:16

v.16 | An angel | who redeemed me from all evil, bless the lads; and let my name be named on them, and the name of my fathers, Abraham and Isaac; and let them grow into a multitude in the midst of the earth. Kinsman Redeemer: See Ps.72:14 Messianic Ps.

v.5 Who satisfieth thy mouth with good things, so that thy youth is (n) renewed like the eagle's.

Isa.40:31

v.31 But they that wait upon the LORD shall renew their strength; they shall mount up with wings like eagles; they shall run, and not be weary; and they shall walk, and not faint.

The LORD executeth righteousness and judgment for all who are oppressed.

v.7 He made known his (o) ways unto Moses, his acts unto children of Israel.

(o) ways unto Moses,
(o)Ex.33:12-17

v.12 And Moses said unto the LORD, See, thou sayest unto me, Bring up this people: and thou hast not let me know whom thou wilt send with me. Yet thou hast said, I know thee by name, and thou hast also found grace in my sight.
v.13 Now therefore, I pray thee, if I have found grace in thy sight, show me now thy way, that I may know thee, that I may find grace in thy sight; and consider that this nation is thy people.
v.14 And he said, My presence shall go with thee, and I will give thee rest.
v.15 And he said unto him, If thy presence shall go not with me, carry us not up from here.
v.16 For wherein shall it be known here that I and thy people have found grace in thy sight? Is it not in that thou goest with us? So shall we be separated, I and thy people, from all the people that are upon the face of the earth.
v.17 And the LORD said unto Moses, I will do this thing also that thou hast spoken; for thou hast found grace in my sight, and I know thee by name.

v.8 (p) The LORD is merciful and gracious, slow to anger, and plenteous in mercy.

(p) The LORD is merciful and gracious,
(p) Ex.34:6-7;Num.14:18;Dt.5:10;
(p) Neh.9:17;Ps.86:15;Jer.32:18

Ex.34:6-7

v.6 And the LORD passed by before him, and proclaimed, The LORD, The LORD God, merciful and gracious, long-suffering, and abundant in goodness and truth,
v.7 Keeping mercy for thousands, forgiving iniquity and transgression and sin, and who will by no means clear the guilty, visiting the iniquity of the fathers upon the children, and upon the children's children, unto the third and to the fourth generation.

Num.14:18

v.18 The LORD is long-suffering, and of great mercy, forgiving iniquity and transgression, and by no means clearing the guilty, visiting the iniquity of the fathers upon the children unto the third and fourth generation.

Dt.5:10

v.10 And showing mercy unto thousands of them who love me and keep my commandments.

Neh.9:17

v.17 And refused to obey, neither were mindful of thy wonders that thou didst among them; but hardened their necks, and in their rebellion appointed a captain to return to their bondage. But thou art a God ready to pardon, gracious and merciful, slow to anger, and of great kindness, and forsookest them not.

Ps.86:15

v.15 But thou, O Lord, art a God full of compassion, and gracious, long-suffering, and plenteous in mercy and truth.

Jer.32:18

v.18 Thou showest loving-kindness unto thousands, and recompensest the iniquity of the fathers into the bosom of their children after them; the Great, the Mighty God, the LORD of host is his name,

v.9 (q) He will not always chide; neither will he keep his anger forever.

(q) He will not always chide;
(q) Ps.30:5;Isa.57:16;Jer.3:5;Mic.7:18

Ps.30:5

v.5 For his anger endureth but a moment; in his favor is life. Weeping may endure for a night, but joy cometh in the morning.

Isa.57:16

v.16 For I will not contend forever, neither will I be always | anger | ; for the spirit should fail before me, and the souls which I have made.

Jer.3:5

v.5 Will he reserve his anger forever? Will he keep it to the end? Behold, thou hast spoken and done evil things as thou couldest.

Mic.7:18

v.18 Who is a God like unto thee, who pardoned iniquity, and passeth by the transgression of the remnant of his heritage? He retained not his anger forever, because he delighted in mercy.

v.10 He hath not dealt with us after our sins, nor rewarded us according to our iniquities.
v.11 For as the heavens are high above the earth, so great is his mercy toward them that (r) fear him.

(r) fear
(r) v.13; see Ps.19:9,note

v.13 As a father pitieth his children, (u) so the LORD pitieth them that fear him.

See: fear; Ps.19:9,note—Ps.23:4 Messianic Ps.

v.12 As far as the east is from the west, so far hath he (s) removed our transgressions (t) from us.

(s) removed
(s) see Ex.29:33,note
(t) from us
(t) Forgiveness: v.12;Isa.38:17.
(t) (Lev.4:20;Mt.26:28, note)

Ex.29:33

v.33 And they shall eat those things wherewith the atonement was made, to consecrate and to sanctify them; but a stranger shall not eat thereof, because they are holy.

Note :1(29:33) Hebrew kaphar, to atone sin. According to Scripture the sacrifice of the law only covered the offerer's sin and secured the divine forgiveness. The O.T. sacrifices never removed man's sin. "It is not possible that the blood of bulls and of goats should take away sins" (Heb.10:4). The Israelite's offering implied confession of sin and recognized its due penalty as death; and God "passed over" (Rom.3:25, lit.) his sin in anticipation of Christ's sacrifice which did, finally, "put away" the sins "done previously [lit] in the forbearance of God" (Rom.3:25; Heb.9:15,26). See Rom.3:25,note The word "atonement" does not occur in the N.T.; the word in Rom.5:11 is "reconciliation." See Gen.4:4; with marginal ref., Sacrifice, and Lev.16:6,note.

See the above v.12

Isa.38:17

v.17 Behold, for peace I had great bitterness, but thou hast in love to my soul delivered it from the pit of corruption; for thou hast cast all my sins behind thy back.

Lev.4:20

v.20 And he shall do with the bullock as he did with the bullock for a sin offering, so shall he do with this: and the priest shall make an atonement for them, and it shall be forgiven them.

Mt.26:28,note

v.28 **For this is my blood of the new testament, which is shed for many for the remission of sins.**

Note: 1(26:28) Forgiveness, Summary: The Greek word here translated "remission" (also in Acts 10:43;Heb.9:22), is elsewhere rendered "forgiveness." It means, to send off or away. And this, throughout Scripture, is the one fundamental meaning of forgiveness-to separate the sin from the sinner. Distinction must be made between divine and human forgiveness:

(1) Human forgiveness means the remission of a penalty deserved, whereas the divine forgiveness, in type and fulfillment in both O.T. and N.T., always follows the execution of the penalty. "The priest shall make an atonement for his sin that he hath committed, and it shall be forgiven him" (Lev.4:35). "This is the blood of the new testament, which is shed for many for the remission (sending away, forgiveness) of sin" (Mt.26:28). "Without shedding of blood is no remission" (Heb.9:22). See Sacrifice (Gen.4:4 and Heb.10:18, note). The sin of the justified believer interrupts his fellowship; It is forgiven upon confession, but always on the ground of Christ's propitiating sacrifice (1 Jn.1:6-9; 2:2). And

(2) human forgiveness rests upon and results from the divine forgiveness. In many passages this is assumed rather than stated, but the principle is declared in Mt.18:32-33; Ehp.4:32.

v.13 As a father pitieth his children, (u) so the LORD pitieth them that fear him.

(u) so the LORD pitieth them
(u) cp.

Lk.11:11-13

v.11 **If a son shall ask bread of any of you that is a father, will he give him a stone? Or if he ask a fish, will he for a fish give him a serpent?**
v.12 **Or if he shall ask an egg, will he offer him a scorpion.?**
v.13 **If ye then, being evil, know how to give good gifts unto your children, how much more shall your heavenly Father give the Holy Spirit to them that ask him?**

v.14 For he knoweth our frame; he remembered that we are dust.

v.15 As for man, his days are like (v) grass; as a flower of the field, so he flourisheth.

(v) grass;
(v) Isa.40:6-8;Jas.1:10-11;1Pet.1:24

v.6 The voice said, Cry. And he said, What shall I cry? All flesh is grass, and all its |beauty| is like the flower of the field.
v.7 The grass withered, the flower fadeth, because the |breath| of the LORD bloweth upon it; surely the people are grass.
v.8 The grass withered, the flower fadeth, but the word of our God shall stand forever.

Jas.1:10-11

v.10 But the rich, in that he is made low, because as the flower of the grass he shall pass away.
v.11 For the sun is no sooner risen with a burning heat, but it withered the grass, and its flower falleth, and the grace of the fashion of it perisheth; so also shall the rich man fade away in his ways.

1 Pet.1:24

v.24 For all flesh is like grass, and all the glory of man like the flower of grass. The grass withered, and its flower falleth away,

v.16 For the wind passeth over it, and it is gone; and the place thereof shall know it no more.
v.17 But the mercy of the LORD is from everlasting to everlasting upon those who fear him, and his righteousness unto children's children,
v.18 To such as keep his covenant, and to those that remember his commandments to do them.

v.19 The Lord hath prepared his throne in the heavens, and his kingdom ruleth over (w) all.

(w) all.
(w) Ps.83:18;Dan.4:17

Ps.83:18

v.18 That men may know that thou, whose name alone is | the Lord |, art the Most High over all the earth.

Dan.4:17

v.17 This matter is by the decree of the watchers, and the demand by the word of the holy ones, to the intent that the living may know that the Most High ruleth in the kingdom of men, and giveth it to whomsoever he will, and setteth up over it the basest of men.

v.20 Bless the Lord, all ye his (x) angels, that excel in strength, that do his commandments, hearkening unto the voice of his word.

(x) angels,
(x) Heb.1:4,note. See:Ps.8:5—Messianic Ps.

v.21 Bless ye the Lord, all ye his hosts, ye ministers of his, that do his pleasure.
v.22 Bless the Lord, all his works in all places of his dominion; bless the Lord, O my soul.

PRAISE TO THE GOD OF CREATION

PSALM 104

v.1 (y) BLESS the LORD, O my soul, O LORD my God, thou art very great; thou art clothed with honor and majesty,

(y) BLESS the LORD,
(y) Ps.103:1

v.1 BLESS the LORD, O my soul, and all that is within me, bless his holy name.

v.2 Who coverest thyself with light as with a garment; who stretchest out the heavens like a curtain;
v.3 Who layeth the beams of his chambers in the waters; who maketh the clouds his chariot; who walketh upon the wings of the wind;
v.4 Who maketh his (x) angels spirits, his ministers a flaming fire;

(x) angels spirits,
(x) See Heb.1:4,note;Ps.8:5—Messianic Ps.

v.5 Who laid the foundations of the earth, that it should not be removed forever.
v.6 Thou (z) coveredst it with the deep as with a garment; the waters stood above the mountains.

(z) coveredst
(z) Gen.1:6

v.6 But there went up a mist from the earth, and watered the whole face of the ground.

v.7 At thy rebuke they fled; at the voice of thy thunder they hastened away.
v.8 They go up by the mountains; they go down by the valleys unto the place which thou hast founded for them.
v.9 Thou hast (a) set a bound that they may not pass over, (b) that they turn not again to cover the earth.

(a) set a bound
(a) Job 26:10; Ps.33:7;Jer.5:22
(b) that they turn not again;
(b) Gen.9:11-15

Job 26:10

v.10 He hath compassed the waters with |a boundary|, until the day and night come to an end.

Ps.33:7

v.7 He gathered the waters of the sea together as an heap; he layeth up the depth in storehouses.

Jer.5:22

v.22 Fear ye not me? saith the Lord. Will ye not tremble at my presence, who have placed the sand for the bound of the sea by a perpetual decree, that it cannot pass it; and though its waves toss themselves, yet can they not prevail; though they roar, yet can they not pass over it?

Gen.9:11-15

v.11 And I will establish my covenant with you; neither shall all flesh be cut off any more by the waters of a flood; neither shall there any more be a flood; to destroy the earth.

v.12 And God said, This is the token of the covenant which I make between me and you and every living creature that is with you, for perpetual generations:

v.13 I do set my bow in the cloud, and it shall be for a token of a covenant between me and the earth.

v.14 And it shall come to pass, when I bring a cloud over the earth, that the bow shall be seen in the cloud;

v.15 And I will remember my covenant, which is between me and you and every living creature of all flesh; and the waters shall no more become a flood to destroy all flesh.

v.10 He sendeth the springs into the valleys, which run among the hills.

v.11 They give drink to every beast of the field; the wild asses quench their thirst.

v.12 By them shall the fowls of the heavens have their (c) habitation, that sing among the branches.

(c) habitation,
(c) cp. Mt.8:20

v.20 And Jesus saith unto him, The foxes have holes, and the birds of the air have nests, but the Son of man hath not where to lay his head.

v.13 He (d) watereth the hills from his chambers; the earth is satisfied with the fruit of thy works.

(d) watereth
(d) Ps.147:8

v.8 Who covereth the heaven with clouds, who prepareth rain for the earth, who maketh grass to grow upon the mountains.

v.14 He causeth the grass to grow for the cattle, and herb for the service of man, that he may bring forth food out of the earth.
v.15 And (e) wine that maketh glad the heart of man, and oil to make his face to shine, and bread which strengtheneth man's heart.

(e) wine maketh glad
(e) Jud.9:13;Ps.23:5; Prov.31:6

Jud.9:13

v.13 And the vine said unto them, Should I leave my wine, which cheereth God and man, and go to be promoted over the trees?

Ps.23:5

v.5 Thou prepares a table before me in the presence of mine enemies; thou anointest my head with oil; my cup runneth over.

Prov.31:6

v.6 Give strong drink unto him that is ready to perish, and wine unto those that are of heavy hearts.

v.16 The trees of the LORD are full of sap; the cedars of Lebanon, which he hath planted,
v.17 Where the birds make their nests; as for the stork, the fir trees are her house.
v.18 The high hills are a refuge for the wild goats; and the rocks for the (f) | badgers | .

(f) | badgers |
(f) KJV conies

v.19 He (g) appointed the moon for seasons; the (h)sun knowneth its going down.

(g) appointed the moon
(g) Gen:1:14
(h) sun;
(h) Job 38:12;Ps.19:6

Gen.1:14

v.14 And God said, Let there be lights in the firmament of the heaven to divide the day from the night; and let them be for signs, and for seasons, and for days, and years;

Job.38:12

v.12 Hast thou commanded the morning since thy days, and caused the dayspring to know its place.

Ps.19:6

v.6 His going forth is from the end of the heaven, and his circuit unto the ends of it; and there is nothing hidden from the heat thereof.

v.20 Thou makest (i) darkness, and it is night, wherein all the beasts of the forest do creep forth.

(i) darkness
(i) Isa.45:7

v.7 I form the light, and create darkness; I make peace, and create evil; I, the Lord, do all these things.

v.21 The young (j) lions roar after their prey, and seek their (k) | food | from God.

(j) lions
(j) cp. Job 38:39;Joel 1:20
(k) | food |
(k) KJV meat

Job 38:39

v.39 Wilt thou hunt the prey for the lion; or fill the appetite of the young lions.

Joel 1:20

v.20 The beasts of the field cry also unto thee; for the rivers of waters are dried up, and the fire hath devoured the pastures of the wilderness.

v.22 The sun riseth; they gather themselves together, and lay them down in their dens.

v.23 Man goeth forth unto (l) his work and to his labor until the evening.

(l) his works
(l) Gen.3:19

v.19 In the sweat of thy face shalt thou eat bread, till thou return unto the ground; for out of it wast thou taken: for dust thou art, and unto dust shalt thou return.

v.24 O LORD, how (m) manifold are thy works! In wisdom hast thou made them all; the earth is full of thy (n) riches.

(m) manifold are thy works!
(m) Ps.40:5
(n) riches;
(n) Ps. 65:9

v.5 Many, O LORD, my God, are thy wonderful works which thou hast done, and thy thoughts which are | toward us | ; they cannot be reckoned up in order unto thee. If I would declare and speak of them, they are more than can be numbered.

Ps.65:9

v.9 Thou visitest the earth, and waterest it; thou greatly enriches it with the river of God, which is full of water; thou prepares them |grain|, when thou hast so provided for it.

v.25 So is this great and wide sea, wherein are things creeping innumerable, both small and great beasts.
v.26 There go the ships; there is that (o) leviathan, whom thou hast made to play therein.

(o) leviathan,
(o) Perhaps the crocodile; Job 41:1

Job.41:1

v.1 CAST thou draw out leviathan with an hook, or his tongue with a cord which thou lettest down?

v.27 (p) These all wait upon thee, that thou mayest give them their (k)|food| in due season.

(p) these all wait upon thee,
(p) Ps.136:25;145:15;147:9;cp.Mt.6:26-30
(k)|food|
(k) KJV meat

Ps.136:25

v.25 Who giveth food to all flesh; for his mercy endureth forever.

Ps.145:15

v.15 The eyes of all wait upon thee; and thou givest them their |food| in due season.

Ps.147:9

v.9 He giveth to the beast food, and to the young ravens which cry.

Mt.6:26-30

v.26 **Behold the fowls of the air; for they sow not, neither do they reap, nor gather into barns, yet your heavenly Father feedeth them. Are ye not much better than they?**
v.27 **Which of you by |being anxious| can add one cubit unto his stature?**
v.28 **And why |are ye anxious| for raiment? Consider the lilies of the field, how they grow; they toil not, neither do they spin,**
v.29 **And yet I say unto you that even Solomon, in all his glory, was not arrayed like one of these.**
v.30 **Wherefore, if God so clothe the grass of the field, which today is, and tomorrow is cast into the oven, shall he not much more clothe you, O ye of little faith?**

v.28 That which thou givest them they gather; thou openest thine hand, they are filled with good.
v.29 Thou hidest thy face, they are troubled; thou takest away their breath, they die, and (q) return to their dust.

(q) return to their dust.
(q) Eccl.12:7

v.7 Then shall the dust return to the earth as it was, and the spirit shall return unto God, who gave it.

v.30 (r) Thou sendest forth thy (s) Spirit, they are created; and thou renewest the face of the earth.

(r) Thou sendest forth thy
(r)Isa.32:15;cp.Ezek.37:9-10

(s) Spirit,
(s) Holy Spirit (O.T.):v.30; Ps.139:7
(Gen.1:2;Zech.12:10)

Isa.32:15

v.15 Until the Spirit be poured upon us from on high, and the wilderness be a fruitful field, and the fruitful field be counted as a forest.

Ezek.37:9-10

v.9 Then said he unto me, Prophesy unto the wind, prophesy, son of man, and say to the wind, Thus saith the Lord God: Come from the four winds, O breath, and breathe upon these slain, that they may live.
v.10 So I prophesied as he commanded me, and the breath came into them, and they lived, and stood up upon their feet, an exceedingly great army.

See: above v.30

Ps.139:7

v.7 Whither shall I go from thy Spirit? Or whither shall I flee from thy presence?

Gen.1:2

v.2 And the earth was without form, and void; and darkness was upon the face of the deep. And the Spirit of God moved upon the face of the waters.

Zech.12:10

v.10 And I will pour upon the house of David, and upon the inhabitants of Jerusalem, the Spirit of Grace and of supplications; and they shall look upon me whom they have pierced, and they shall mourn for him, as one mourned for his only son, and shall be in bitterness for his first-born.

v.31 The glory of the Lord shall endure forever; the Lord shall (t) rejoice in his works.

(t) rejoice
(t)Gen.1:31;Prov.8:31

Gen.1:31

v.31 And God saw every thing that he had made, and, behold, it was very good. And the evening and the morning were the sixth day.

Prov.8:31

v.31 Rejoicing in the habitable part of his earth; and my delight was with the sons of men.

v.32 He looketh on the earth, and it (u) trembleth; he toucheth the hills, and they smoke.

(u) trembleth;
(u)Hab.3:10

v.10 The mountains saw thee, and they trembled; the overflowing of the water passed by; the deep uttered its voice, and lifted up its hands on high.

v.33 I will sing unto the Lord as long as I live; I will sing praise to my God while I have my being.
v.34 My (v) meditation of him shall be sweet; I will be glad in the Lord.

(v) meditation;
(v) Ps.19:14

v.14 Let the words of my mouth, and the meditation of my heart, be acceptable in thy sight, O LORD, my strength, and my redeemer.

v.35 Let the sinners be consumed out of the earth, and let the wicked be no more. Bless thou the LORD, O my soul. Praise ye the LORD.

GOD'S FAITHFULNESS TO ISRAEL

PSALM 105

v.1 OH, (w) give thanks unto the LORD; call upon his name; (x) make known his deeds among the peoples.

(w) give thanks unto the LORD;
(w) vv.1-45;cp.1Chr.16:7-36;Isa.12:4
(x) make known his deeds;
(x)cp.Ps.78:3-72;106:1-48

v.1 OH, (w) give thanks unto the LORD, call upon his name; (x) make known his deeds among the peoples.
v.2 Sing unto him, sing psalms unto him; talk ye all his wondrous works.
v.3 Glory ye in his holy name; let the heart of them rejoice who seek the LORD.
v.4 Seek the LORD, and his strength; (y) seek his face evermore.
v.5 (z) Remember his marvelous works that he hath done; his wonders, and the judgments of his mouth;
v.6 O ye seed of Abraham, his servant, ye children of Jacob, his chosen.
v.7 He is the LORD our God; his (aa) judgments are in all the earth.
v.8 He hath (bb) remembered his covenant forever, the word which he commanded to a thousand generations,

v.9 Which (cc) covenant he made with Abraham, and his oath unto Isaac,
v.10 And confirmed the same unto Jacob for a law, and to Israel for an everlasting covenant,
v.11 Saying, (dd) Unto thee will I give the land of Ca'naan, the (ee) lot of your inheritance;
v.12 When they were but a (ff) few men in number; yea, very few, and (gg) | sojourners | in it.
v.13 When they went from one nation to another, from one kingdom to another people,
v.14 He (a) | permitted | no man to do them wrong; yea, he reproved kings for their sakes,
v.15 Saying, Touch not mine anointed, and do my (h) prophets no harm.
v.16 Moreover, he called for a famine upon the land; he broke the whole staff of bread.
v.17 He sent a man before them, even Joseph, who was (c) sold for a servant,
v.18 Whose feet they hurt with fetters; he was laid in iron,
v.19 Until the time that his word (d) came; the word of the LORD (e) | tested | him.
v.20 The king sent and loosed him. Even the ruler of the people, and let him go free.
v.21 He made him lord of his house, and ruler of all his substance,
v.22 To bind his princes at his pleasure, and teach his (f) | elders | wisdom.
v.23 Israel also came into Egypt, and Jacob sojourned in the land of Ham.
v.24 And he (g) increased his people greatly, and made them stronger than their enemies.
v.25 (h) He turned their heart to hate his people, to deal subtly with his servants.
v.26 (i) He sent Moses, his servant, and Aaron, whom he had chosen.
v.27 They (j) showed his signs among them, and wonders in the land of Ham.

v.28 He sent darkness, and made it dark, and they rebelled not against his word.
v.29 He turned their waters into (k) blood, and slew their fish.
v.30 Their land brought forth frogs in abundance, in the chambers of their kings.
v.31 He spoke, and there came (l) | various | sorts of flies, and lice in all their (m) | borers | .
v.32 He gave them hail for rain, and flaming fire in their land.
v.33 He smote their vines also, and their fig trees, and broke the trees of their (m) | borders | .
v.34 He spoke, and the locusts came, and caterpillars, and that without number,
v.35 And did eat up all the herbs in their land, and devoured the fruit of their ground.
v.36 He smote also all the firstborn in their land, the chief of all their strength.
v.37 (n) He brought them forth also with silver and gold; and there was not one feeble person among their tribes.
v.38 Egypt was glad when they departed; for the fear of them fell upon them.
v.39 (o) He spread a cloud for a covering, and fire to give light in the night.
v.40 The people asked, and he brought quails, and satisfied them with the (p) bread of heaven.
v.41 He opened the rock, and the waters gushed out; they ran in the dry places like a river;
v.42 For he remembered his holy promise, and Abraham, his servant.
v.43 And he brought forth his people with joy, and his (q) chosen with gladness,
v.44 And gave them the lands of the (r) | nations | ; and they inherited the labor of the peoples,
v.45 That they might observe his statutes, and keep his laws. Praise ye the LORD.

1Chr.16:7-36

v.7 Then on that day David delivered first this psalm, to thank the LORD, into the hand of A'saph and his brethren:
v.8 Give thanks unto the LORD, call upon his name, make known his deeds among the people.
v.9 Sing unto him, sing psalms unto him, talk ye of his wondrous works.
v.10 Glory ye in his holy name; let the heart of them rejoice who seek the LORD.
v.11 Seek the LORD and his strength, seek his face continually.
v.12 Remember his marvelous works that he hath done, his wonders, and the judgments of his mouth;
v.13 O ye seed of Israel, his servant, ye children of Jacob, his chosen ones.
v.14 He is the LORD our God; his judgments are in all the earth.
v.15 Be ye mindful always of his covenant; the word which he commanded to a thousand generations,
v.16 Even of the covenant which he made with Abraham, and of his oath unto Isaac,
v.17 And hath confirmed the same to Jacob for a law, and to Israel for an everlasting covenant,
v.18 Saying, Unto thee will I give the land of Canaan the lot of your inheritance,
v.19 When ye were but few, even a few |sojourners| in it.
v.20 And when they went from nation to nation, and from one kingdom to another people,
v.21 He suffered no man to do them wrong; yea, he reproved kings for their sakes,
v.22 Saying, Touch not mine anointed, and do my prophets no harm.
v.23 Sing unto the LORD, all the earth; show forth from day to day his salvation.
v.24 Declare his glory among the |nations|, his marvelous works among all |peoples|.

v.25 For great is the Lord, and greatly to be praised; he also is to be feared above all gods.
v.26 For all the gods of the people are idols; but the Lord made the heavens.
v.27 Glory and honor are in his presence; strength and gladness are in his place.
v.28 Give unto the Lord, ye kindreds of the people, give unto the Lord glory and strength.
v.29 Give unto the Lord the glory due unto his name; bring an offering, and come before him, worship the Lord in beauty of holiness.
v.30 Fear before him, all the earth; the world also shall be stable, that it be not moved.
v.31 Let the heavens be glad, and let the earth rejoice; and let men say among the nations, The Lord reigneth.
v.32 Let the sea roar, and the fullness thereof; let the fields rejoice, and all that is therein.
v.33 Then shall the trees of the woods sing out at the presence of the Lord, because he cometh to judge the earth.
v.34 Oh, give thanks unto the Lord; for he is good; for his mercy endureth forever.
v.35 And say ye, Save us, O God of our salvation, and gather us together, and deliver us from the | nations |, that we may give thanks to thy holy name, and glory in thy praise.
v.36 Blessed be the Lord God of Israel forever and ever. And all the people said Amen, and praised the Lord.

Isa.12:4

v.4 And in that day ye say, Praise the Lord, call upon his name, declare his doings among the people, make mention that his name is exalted.

Ps.78:3-72

v.3 Which we have heard known, and our fathers have told us.

v.4 We will not hide them from their children, showing to the generation to come the praises of the LORD, and his strength, and his wonderful works that he hath done.
v.5 For the established a testimony in Jacob, and appointed a law in Israel, which he commanded our fathers, that they should make them known to their children;
v.6 That the generation to come might know them, even the children who should be born, who should arise and declare them to their children;
v.7 That they might set their hope in God, and not forget the works of God, but keep his commandments;
v.8 And might not be as their fathers, a stubborn and rebellious generation, a generation that set not their heart aright, and whose spirit was not steadfast with God.
v.9 The children of Ephraim, being armed, and carrying bows, turned back in the day of battle.
v.10 They kept not the covenant of God, and refused to walk in his law,
v.11 And forgot his works, and his wonders that he had shown them.
v.12 Marvelous things did he in the sight of their fathers, in the land of Egypt, in the field of Zoan.
v.13 He divided the sea, and caused them to pass through; and he made the waters to stand as an heap.
v.14 In the daytime also he led them with a cloud, and all the night with a light of fire.
v.15 He |split| the rocks in the wilderness, and gave them drink as out of the great depths.
v.16 He brought streams also out of the rock, and caused waters to run down like rivers.
v.17 And they sinned yet more against him by provoking the Most High in the wilderness.
v.18 And they |tested| God in their heart by asking |food| according to their |desire|.
v.19 Yea, they spoke against God; they said, Can God furnish a table in the wilderness?
v.20 Behold, he smote the rock, that the waters gushed

out, and the streams overflowed. Can he give bread also? Can he provide flesh for his people?

v.21 Therefore, the LORD heard this, and was |angry|; so a fire was kindled against Jacob, and anger also came up against Israel,

v.22 Because they believed not in God, and trusted not in his salvation,

v.23 Though he had commanded the clouds from above, and opened the doors of heaven,

v.24 And had rained down manna upon them to eat, and had given them of the |grain| of heaven.

v.25 Man did eat angels' food; he sent them |food| to the full.

v.26 He caused an east wind to blow in the heavens, and by his power he brought in the south wind.

v.27 He rained flesh also upon them like dust, and feathered fowls like the sand of the sea;

v.28 And he let it fall in the midst of their camp, round about their habitations.

v.29 So they did eat, and were well filled; for he gave them their own desire.

v.30 They were not estranged from their |desire|. But while their |food| was yet in their mouths,

v.31 The wrath of God came upon them, and slew the fattest of them, and smote down the chosen men of Israel.

v.33 Therefore, their days did he consume in vanity, and their years in trouble.

v.34 When he slew them, then they sought him, and they returned and inquired early after God.

v.35 And they remembered that God was their rock, and the high God their redeemer.

v.36 Nevertheless, they did flatter him with their mouth, and they lied unto him with their tongues.

v.37 For their heart was not right with him, neither were they steadfast in his covenant.

v.38 But he, being full of compassion, forgave their iniquity, and destroyed them not; yea, many a time turned he his anger away, and did not stir up all his wrath.

v.39 For he remembered that they were but flesh, a wind that passeth away, and cometh not again.
v.40 How often did they provoke him in the wilderness, and grieve him in the desert!
v.41 Yea, they turned back and |tested| God, and limited the Holy One of Israel.
v.42 They remembered not his hand, nor the day when he delivered them from the enemy;
v.43 How he had wrought his signs in Egypt, and his wonders in the field of Zoan,
v.44 And had turned their rivers into blood, and their |streams|, that they could not drink.
v.45 He sent |various| sorts of flies among them, which devoured them, and frogs, which destroyed them.
v.46 He gave also their increase unto the caterpillar, and their labor unto the locust.
v.47 He destroyed their vines with hail, and their sycamore trees with frost.
v.48 He gave up their cattle also to the hail, and their flocks to hot thunderbolts.
v.49 He cast upon them the fierceness of his anger, wrath, and indignation, and trouble, by sending evil angels among them.
v.50 He made a way to his anger; he spared not their soul from death, but gave their life over to the pestilence;
v.51 And smote all the first-born in Egypt, the chief of their strength in the tabernacles of Ham;
v.52 But made his own people to go forth like sheep, and guided them in the wilderness like a flock.
v.53 And he led them on safely, so that they feared not; but the sea overwhelmed their enemies.
v.54 And he brought them to this mountain, which his right hand had purchased.
v.55 He cast out the |nations| also before them, and divided them an inheritance by line, and made the tribes of Israel to dwell in their tents.

v.56 Yet they |tested| and provoked the most high God, and kept not his testimonies,
v.57 But turned back, and dealt unfaithfully like their fathers; they were turned aside like a deceitful bow.
v.58 For they provoked him to anger with their high places, and moved him to jealousy with their |carved| images.
v.59 When God heard this, he was |angry|, and greatly abhorred Israel;
v.60 So that he forsook the tabernacle of Shiloh, the tent which he placed among men,
v.61 And delivered his strength into captivity, and his glory into the enemy's hand.
v.62 He gave his people over also unto the sword, and was |angry| with his inheritance.
v.63 The fire consumed their young men; and their maidens were not given marriage.
v.64 Their priests fell by the sword, and their widows made no lamentation.
v.65 Then the Lord awakened as one out of sleep, and like a mighty man who shouted by reason of wine.
v.66 And he smote his enemies in the hinder parts; he put them to a perpetual reproach.
v.67 Moreover, he refused the tabernacle of Joseph, and chose not the tribe of E'phraim,
v.68 But chose the tribe of Judah, the Mount Zion which he loved.
v.69 And he built his sanctuary like high palaces, like the earth which he hath established forever.
v.70 He chose David his servant, and took him the sheepfolds;
v.71 From following the ewes great with young, he brought him to feed Jacob, his people, and Israel, and his inheritance.
v.72 So he fed them according to the integrity of his heart, and guided them by the skillfulness of his hands.

Ps.106:1-48

v.1 PRAISE ye the LORD, Oh, give thanks unto the LORD, for he Is good; for his mercy endureth forever.
v.2 Who can utter the mighty acts of the LORD? Who can show forth all his praise?
v.3 Blessed are they that (s) | observe justice |, and he that doeth righteousness at all times.
v.4 Remember me, O LORD, with the favor that thou bearest unto thy (t) people; oh, visit me with thy salvation.
v.5 That I may see the good of thy (q) chosen, that I may rejoice in the gladness of thy nation, that I may glory with thine inheritance.
v.6 (u) We have sinned with our fathers, we have committed iniquity, we have done wickedly.
v.7 Our fathers understood not thy wonders in Egypt; they remembered not multitude of thy mercies, but (v) provoked him at the sea, even at the Red Sea.
v.8 Nevertheless, he saved them (w) for his name's sake, (x) that he might make his mighty power to be known.
v.9 (y) He rebuked the Red Sea also, and it was dried up; so he (z) led them through the depths, as through the wilderness.
v.10 And he (aa) saved them from the hand of him that hated them, and (a) redeemed them from the hand of the enemy.
v.11 And the waters covered their enemies; there was not one of them left.
v.12 Then believed they his words; they sang his praise.
v.13 They soon forgot his works; they waited not for his counsel,
v.14 But lusted exceedingly in the wilderness, and (b) | tested | God in the desert.
v.15 And he gave them their request, but sent leanness into their soul.

v.16 They (c) envied Moses also in the camp, and Aaron, the saint of the LORD.
v.17 The (d) earth opened and swallowed up Dathan, and covered the company of Abi'ram.
v.18 And a fire was kindled in their company; the flame burned up the wicked.
v.19 They (e) made a calf in Horeb, and worshiped the (f) | melted | image.
v.20 Thus they (g) changed their glory into the similitude of an ox that eateth grass.
v.21 They forgot God, their Savior, who had done great things in Egypt,
v.22 Wondrous works in the land of Ham, and (h) | awesome | things by the Red Sea.
v.23 Therefore, he said that he would destroy them, had not Moses, his chosen, stood before him in the breach, to turn away his wrath, lest he should destroy them.
v.24 Yea, they despised the pleasant land; they (i) believed not his word,
v.25 But (j) murmured in their tents, and hearkened not unto the voice of the LORD.
v.26 (k) Therefore, he lifted up his hand against them, to overthrow them In the wilderness,
v.27 To overthrow their seed also among the nations, and to (l) scatter them in the lands.
v.28 They joined themselves also unto Ba'al-pe'or, and ate the sacrifices of the dead.
v.29 Thus they provoked him to angry with their (m) | doings |, and the plague broke in upon them.
v.30 (n) Then stood up Phin'ehas, and executed judgment; and so the plague was (o) | checked |.
v.31 And that was (p) counted unto him for righteousness unto all generation for evermore.
v.32 (q) They angered him also at the waters of strife, (r) so that it went ill with Moses for their sakes,
v.33 Because they provoked his spirit, so that he (s) spoke unadvisedly with his lips.
v.34 They did not (t) destroy the nations, concerning whom the LORD commanded them,

v.35 But were mingled among the (u) | nations | , and learned their works.
v.36 And they served their idols, which were a snare unto them.
v.37 Yea, they sacrificed their sons and their daughters unto (v) | demons | ,
v.38 And shed innocent blood, even the blood of their sons and of their daughters, whom they sacrificed unto the idols of Canaan; and the land was polluted with blood.
v.39 Thus were they defiled with their own works, and (w) | played the harlot in | their (m) | doings | .
v.40 Therefore was the wrath of the LORD kindled against his people, insomuch that he abhorred his own inheritance.
v.41 And he gave them into the hand of the (u) | nations | , and they that hated them ruled over them.
v.42 Their enemies also oppressed them, and they were brought into subjection under their hand.
v.43 (x) Many times did he deliver them; but they provoked him with their counsel, and were brought low for their iniquity.
v.44 Nevertheless, he regarded their affliction, when he heard their cry;
v.45 And he remembered for them his covenant, and (y) reopened according to the multitude of his mercies.
v.46 He made them also to be (z) pitted of all those that carried them captives.
v.47 (aa) Save us, O LORD our God, and gather us from among the (u) | nations | , to give thanks unto thy holy name, and to triumph in thy praise.
v.48 (bb) Blessed be the LORD God of Israel from everlasting to everlasting; and let all the people say, Amen. Praise ye the LORD.

v.2 Sing unto him, sing psalms unto him; talk ye of all his wondrous works.
v.3 Glory ye in his holy name; let the heart of them rejoice who seek the LORD.

v.4 Seek the LORD, and his strength; (y) seek his face evermore.

(y) seek
(y)Ps.27:8

v.8 When thou saidst, Seek ye my face, my heart said unto thee, Thy face, LORD, will I seek.

v.5 (z) Remember his marvelous works that he hath done; his mouth;

(z) Remember
(z)Ps.77:11

v.11 I will remember the works of the LORD; surely I will remember thy wonders of old.

v6 O ye seed of Abraham, his servant, ye children of Jacob, his chosen.
v.7 He Is the LORD our God; his (aa) judgments are in all the earth.

(aa) judgments
(aa) Isa.26:9

v.9 With my soul have I desired thee in the night; yea, with my spirit within me will I seek thee early; for when thy judgments are in the earth, the inhabitants of the world will learn righteousness.

v.8 He hath (bb) remembered his covenant forever, the word which he commanded to a thousand generations,

(bb) remembered
(bb) Lk.1:72

v.72 To perform the mercy promised to our fathers, and to remember his holy covenant;

v.9 Which (cc) covenant he made with Abraham, and his oath unto Isaac,

(cc) covenant he made with Abraham,
(cc)Gen.17:2;22:16-18;26:3;28:13,35:11;Lk.1:73;Heb.6:17

Gen.17:2

v.2 And I will make my covenant between me and thee, and will multiply thee exceedingly.

Gen.22:16-18

v.16 And said, By myself have I sworn, saith the LORD; for because thou hast done this thing, and hast not withheld thy son, thine only son;
v.17 That in blessing I will bless thee, and In multiplying I will multiply thy seed as the stars of the heaven, and as the sand which is upon the seashore; and thy seed shall possess the gate of his enemies;
v.18 And in thy seed shall all the nations of the earth be blessed, because thou hast obeyed my voice.

Gen.26:3

v.3 Sojourn in this land, and I will be with thee, and will bless thee; for unto thee, and thy seed, I will give all these countries, and I will perform the oath which I swore unto Abraham thy father;

Gen.28:13

v.13 And, behold, the LORD stood above it, and said, I am the LORD God of Abraham, thy father, and the God of Isaac: the land whereon thou liest, to thee will I give it, and to thy seed;

Gen.35:11

v.11 And God said unto him, I am God Almighty: be fruitful and multiply; a nation and a company of nations shall be of thee, and kings shall come out of thy loins;

Lk.1:73

v.73 The oath which he swore to our father, Abraham,

Heb.6:17

v.17 Wherein God, willing more abundantly to show unto the heirs of promise the immutability of his counsel, confirmed it by an oath,

v.10 And confirmed the same unto Jacob for a law, and to Israel for an everlasting covenant,
v.11 Saying, (dd) Unto thee will I give the land of Ca'naan, the (ee) lot of your Inheritance;

(dd) Unto thee
(dd)Gen.13:15;15:18
(ee) lot of your inheritance;
(ee) Lit. the cord

Gen.13:15

v.15 For all the land which thou seest, to thee will I give it, and to thy seed forever.

Gen.15:18

v.18 In the same day the LORD made a covenant with Abram, saying, Unto thy seed have I given this land, from the river, of Egypt unto the great river, the river Euphra'tes:

v.12 When they were but a (ff) few men in number; yea, very few, and (gg) | sojourners | In it.

(ff) few men
(ff)Gen.34:30;Dt.7:7;26:5
(gg) | sojourners |
(gg) KJV strangers; Heb.11:9

Gen.34:30

v.30 And Jacob said to Simeon and Levi, Ye have troubled me to make me | odious | among the Canaanites and the Periz'zites: and I being few in number, they shall gather themselves together against me, and slay me; and I shall be destroyed, I and my house.

Dt.7:7

v.7 The LORD did not set his love upon you, nor choose you, because ye were more in number than any people; for ye were the fewest of all people.

Dt.26:5

v.5 And thou shalt speak and say before the LORD thy God, A Syrian ready to perish was my father, and he went down Into Egypt and sojourned there with a few, and became there nation, great, mighty, and populous.

Heb.11:9

v.9 By faith he sojourned in the land of promise, as in a | foreign | country, dwelling In | tents | with Isaac and Jacob, the heirs with him of the same promise;

v.13 When they went from one nation to another, from one kingdom to another people, v.14 He (a) | permitted | no man to do them wrong; yea, he reproved kings for their sakes,

(a) | permitted |
(a) KJV suffered. Gen.35:5

v.5 And they journeyed: and the terror of God was upon the cities that were round about them, and they did not pursue after the sons of Jacob.

v.15 Saying, Touch not mine anointed, and do my (b) prophets no harm.

(b) prophets no harm.
(b) cp.Gen.20:7

v.7 Now therefore restore the man his wife; for he is a prophet, and he shall pray for thee, and thou shalt live: and If thou restore her not, know thou that thou shalt surely die, thou, and all that are thine.

v.16 Moreover, he called for a famine upon the land; he broke the whole staff of bread.

v.17 He sent a man before them, even Joseph, who was (c) sold for a servant,

(c) sold
(c) Acts 7:9

v.9 And the patriarchs, moved with envy, sold Joseph into Egypt; but God was with him,

v.18 Whose feet they hurt with fetters; he was laid In iron,

v.19 Until the time that his word (d) came; the word of the LORD (e) | tested | him.

(d) came;
(d)Gen.40:20-21,23

(e) | tested | him.
(e) KJV tried

Gen.40:20-21,23

v.20 And it came to pass the third day, which was Pharaoh's birthday, that he made a feast unto all his servant: and he lifted up the head of the chief butler and of the chief baker among his servants.
v.21 And he restored the chief butler unto his butlership again; and he gave the cup Into Pharaoh's hand.
v.23 Yet did not the chief butler remember Joseph, but forgot him.

v.20 The king sent and loosed him, even the ruler of the people, and let him go free.
v.21 He made him lord of his house, and ruler of all his substance,
v.22 To bind his princes at his pleasure, and teach his (f) | elders | wisdom.

(f) | elders | wisdom.
(f) KJV senators

v.23 Israel also came into Egypt, and Jacob sojourned in the land of Ham.
v.24 And he (g) increased his people greatly, and made them stronger than their enemies.

(g) increased
(g) Ex.1:7,12

v.7 And the children of Israel were fruitful, and Increased abundantly, and multiplied, and | became | exceedingly mighty, and the land was filled with them.
v.12 But the more they afflicted them, the more they multiplied and grew. And they were grieved because of the children of Israel.

v.25 (h) He turned their heart to hate his people, to deal subtly with his servants.

(h) He turned their heart
(h) Ex.1:8-10

v.8 Now there arose a new king over Egypt, who knew not Joseph.
v.9 And he said unto his people, Behold, the people of the children of Israel are more and mightier than we.
v.10 Come on, let us deal wisely with them, lest they multiply, and It come to pass, that, when |war occurs|, they join also unto our enemies, and fight against us, and so get them up out of the land.

v.26 (i) He sent Moses, his servant, and Aaron, whom he had chosen.

(i) He sent Moses, his servant,
(i) Ex.3:10;4:12-15;Num.16:5;17:5

Ex.3:10

v.10 Come now therefore, and I will send thee unto Pharaoh, that thou mayest bring forth my people, the children of Israel, out of Egypt.

Ex.4:12-15

v.12 Now therefore go, and I will be with thy mouth and teach thee what thou shalt say.
v.13 And he said, O my Lord, send, I pray thee, by the hand of him whom thou wilt send.
v.14 And the anger of the Lord was kindled against Moses, and he said, Is not Aaron, the Levite, thy brother? I know that he can speak well. And also, behold, he cometh forth to meet thee; and when he seeth thee, he will be glad In his heart.

v.15 And thou shalt speak unto him, and put words in his mouth; and I will be with thy mouth, and with his mouth, and will teach you what ye shall do.

Num. 16:5

v.5 And he spoke unto Korah and unto all his company, saying, Even tomorrow the LORD will show who are his, and who is holy, and will cause him to come near unto him; even him whom he hath chosen will he cause to come near unto him.

Num.17:5

v.5 And it shall come to pass that the man's rod, whom I shall choose, shall blossom; and I will make to cease from me the murmurings of the children of Israel, whereby they murmur against you.

v.27 They (j) showed his signs among them, and wonders in the land of Ham.

(j) showed his signs among them,
(j) Ex.7-12;Ps.78:43

Ex.7-12

v.7 And Moses was fourscore years old, and Aaron fourscore and three years old, when they spake unto Pharaoh.
v.8 And the LORD, spake unto Moses and unto Aaron, saying,
v.9 When Pharaoh shall speak unto you: saying, Show a miracle for you: then thou shalt say unto Aaron, Take thy rod, and cast it before Pharaoh, and it shall become a serpent.
v.10 And Moses and Aaron went in unto Pharaoh, and they did so as the LORD had commanded: and Aaron

cast down his rod before Pharaoh, and before his servants, and it became a serpent.
v.11 Then Pharaoh also called the wise men and the sorcerers: now the magicians of Egypt, they also did in like manner with their enchantments.
v.12 For they cast down every man his rod, and thy became serpents: but Aaron's rod swallowed up their rods.

Ps.78:43

v.43 How he had wrought his signs in Egypt, and his wonders in the field of Zoah:

v.28 He sent darkness, and made it dark; and they rebelled not against his word.
v.29 He turned their waters into (k) blood, and slew their fish.

(k) blood,
(k) Ex.7:20;Ps.78:44

Ex.7:20

v.20 And Moses and Aaron did so, as the LORD commanded: and he lifted up the rod, and smote the waters that were in the river, in the sight of Pharaoh and in the sight of his servants; and all the waters that were in the river were turned to blood.

Ps.78:44

v.44 And had turned their rivers into blood, and their |streams|, that they could not drink. Their land brought forth frogs in abundance, in the chambers of their kings.

v.31 He spoke, and there came (l)|various| sorts of flies, and lice in all their (m)|borders|.

(l) |various|
(l) KJV divers
(m) |borders|
(m) KJV coasts

v.32 He gave them hail for rain, and flaming fire in their land.
v.33 He smote their vines also, and their fig trees, and broke the
trees of their (m) |borders|.

(m) |borders|.
(m) KJV coasts

v.34 He spoke, and the locusts came, and the caterpillars, and
that without number,
v.35 And did eat up all the herbs in their land, and devoured
the fruit of their ground.
v.36 He smote also all the first-born in their land, the chief of all
their strength.
v.37 (n) He brought them forth also with silver and gold; and
there was not one feeble person among their tribes.

(n) He brought them forth
(n)Ex.12:35

v.35 And the children of Israel did according to the word
of Moses; and they |asked| of the Egyptians jewels
of silver, and jewels of gold, and raiment.

v.38 Egypt was glad when they departed; for the fear of them
fell upon them.
v.39 (o) He spread a cloud for a covering, and fire to give light in
the night.

(o) He spread a cloud
(o) Ex.13:21;Neh.9:12

Ex.13:21

v.21 And the LORD went before them by day in a pillar of a cloud, to lead them the way; and by night in a pillar of fire, to give them light; to go by day and night.

Neh.9:12

v.12 Moreover, thou leddest them in the day by a cloudy pillar; and in the night by a pillar of fire, to give them light in the way in which they should go.

v.40 The people asked, and he brought quails, and satisfied them with the (p) bread of heaven.

(p) bread of heaven
(p) Ps.78:24

v.24 And had rained down manna upon them to eat, and had given them of the |grain| of heaven.

v.41 He opened the rock, and the waters gushed out; they ran in the dry places like a river;
v.42 For he remembered his holy promise, and Abraham, his servant.
v.43 And he brought forth his people with joy, and his (q) chosen with gladness,

(q) chosen
(q) Election (corporate):v.43;
106:5;Ps.135:4.(Dt.7:6;1Pet.5:13)
See : above v.43

Ps.106:5

v.5 That I may see the good of thy chosen, that I may rejoice in the gladness, of thy nation, that I may glory with thine inheritance.

Ps.135:4

v.4 For the LORD hath chosen Jacob unto himself, and Israel for his peculiar treasure.

Dt.7:6

v.6 For thou art an holy people unto the LORD thy God; the LORD thy God hath chosen thee to be a special people unto himself, above all people who are upon the face of the earth.

1Pet.5:13

v.13 The church that is at Babylon, elected together with you, |greeteth| you; and so doth Mark, my son.

v.44 And gave them the lands of the (r) |nations|; and they Inherited the labor of the peoples,

(r) |nations|;
(r) KJV heathen

v.45 That they might observe his statutes, and keep his laws. Praise ye the LORD.

CONFESSION OF ISRAEL'S UNFAITHFULNESS

PSALM 106

v.1 PRAISE ye the LORD. Oh, give thanks unto the LORD, for he is good; for his mercy endureth forever.
v.2 Who can utter the mighty acts of the LORD? Who can show forth all his praise?
v.3 Blessed are they that (s) |observe justice|, and he that doeth righteousness at all times.

(s) |observe justice|,
(s) KJV keep judgment.

Lev.19:15,35

v.15 Ye shall do no unrighteousness in judgment; thou shalt not respect the person of the poor, nor honor the person of the mighty, but in righteousness shalt thou judge thy neighbor.
v.35 Ye shall do no unrighteousness in judgment, in |measure of length|, in weight, or in |quantity|,

v.4 Remember me, O LORD, with the favor that thou bearest unto thy (t) people; oh, visit me with thy salvation.

(t) people;
(t) Israel (history):vv.1-45;
Isa.1:25.(Gen.12:2;Rom.11:26)

vv.1-45

v.1 PRAISE ye the LORD, O, give thanks unto the LORD, for he is good; for his mercy endureth forever.

v.2 Who can utter the mighty acts of the LORD? Who can show forth all his praise?

v.3 Blessed are they that (s) | observe justice | , and he that doeth righteousness at all times.

v.4 Remember me, O LORD, with the favor that thou bearest unto thy (t) people; oh, visit me with thy salvation,

v.5 That I may see the good of thy (q) chosen, that I may rejoice in the gladness of thy nation, that I may glory with thine inheritance.

v.6 (u) We have sinned with our fathers, we have committed iniquity, we have done wickedly.

v.7 Our fathers understood not thy wonders in Egypt; they remembered not the multitude of thy mercies, but (v) provoked him at the sea, even at the Red Sea.

v.8 Nevertheless, he saved them (w) for his name's sake, (x) that he might make his mighty power to be known.

v.9 (y) He rebuke the Red Sea also, and it was dried up; so he (z) led them through the depths, as through the wilderness.

v.10 And he (aa) saved them from the hand of him that hated them, and (a) redeemed them from the hand of the enemy.

v.11 And the waters covered their enemies; there was not one of them left.

v.12 Then believed they his words; they sang his praise.

v.13 They soon forgot his works; they waited not for his counsel,

v.14 But lusted exceedingly in the wilderness, and (b) | tested | God in the desert.

v.15 And he gave them their request, but sent leanness into their soul.

v.16 They (c) envied Moses also in the camp, and Aaron, the saint of the LORD.
v.17 The (d) earth opened and swallowed up Dathan, and covered the company of Abi'ram.
v.18 And a fire was kindled in their company; the flame burned up the wicked.
v.19 They (e) made a calf in Horeb, and worshiped the (f) | melted | image.
v.20 Thus they (g) change their glory into the similitude of an ox that eateth grass.
v.21 They forgot God, their Savior, who had done great things in Egypt,
v.22 Wondrous works in the land of Ham, and (h) | awesome | things by the Red Sea
v.23 Therefore, he said that he would destroy them, had not Moses, his chosen, stood before him in the breach, to turn away his wrath, lest he should destroy them.
v.24 Yea, they despised the pleasant land; they (i) believed not his word,
v.25 But (j) murmured in their tents, and hearkened not the voice of the LORD.
v.26 (k) Therefore, he lifted up his hand against them, to overthrow them in the wilderness,
v.27 To overthrow their seed also among the nations, and to (l) scatter them in the lands.
v.28 They joined themselves also unto Ba'al-pe'or, and ate the sacrifices of the dead.
v.29 Thus they provoked him to anger with their (m) | doings |, and the plague broke in upon them.
v.30 (n) Then stood up Phin'ehas, and executed judgment; and so the plague was (o) | checked |.
v.31 And that was (p) counted unto him for righteousness unto all generations for evermore.
v.32 (q) They angered him also at the waters of strife, (r) so that it went ill with Moses for their sakes,
v.33 Because they provoked his spirit, so that he (s) spoke unadvisedly with his lips.
v.34 They did not (t) destroy the nation, concerning whom the LORD commanded them,

v.35 But were mingled among the (u) | nations | , and learned their works.
v.36 And they served unto their idols, which were a snare unto them.
v.37 Yea, they sacrificed their sons and their daughters unto (v) | demons | ,
v.38 And shed innocent blood, even the blood of their sons and of their daughters, whom they sacrificed unto the idols of Canaan; and the land was polluted with blood.
v.39 Thus were they defiled with their own works, and (w) | played the harlot in | their (m) | doings | .
v.40 Therefore was the wrath of the LORD kindled against his people, insomuch that he abhorred his own inheritance.
v.41 And he gave them into the hand of the (u) | nations | , and they that hated them ruled over them.
v.42 Their enemies also oppressed them, and they were brought into subjection under their hand.
v.43 (x) Many times did he deliver them; but they provoked him with their counsel, and were brought low for their iniquity.
v.44 Nevertheless, he regarded their affliction, when he heard their cry;
v.45 And he remembered for them his covenant, and (y) repented according to the multitude of his mercies.

Isa.1:25

v.25 And I will turn my hand upon thee, and | thoroughly | purge away thy dross, and take away all thy tin.

Gen.12:2

v.2 And I will make of thee a great nation, and I will bless thee, and make thy name great; and thou shalt be a blessing.

Rom.11:26

v.26 And so all Israel shall be saved; as it is written, Thereshall come out of Zion the Deliverer, and shall turn away ungodliness from Jacob;

v.5 That I may see the good of thy (q) chosen, that I may rejoice in the gladness of thy nation, that I may glory with thine inheritance.

(q) chosen,
(q) Election (corporate):v.43;106:5;
Ps.135:4.(Dt.7:6;1Pet.5:13)
See: (q) chosen; Psalm 105:43

v.6 (u) We have sinned with our fathers, we have committed iniquity, we have done wickedly.

(u) We have sinned
(u) Dan.9:5;cp.Lev.26:40;1Ki.8:47

Dan.9:5

v.5 We have sinned, and have committed iniquity, and have done wickedly, and have rebelled, even by departing from thy precepts and from thine |ordinances|,

Lev.26:40

v.40 If they shall confess their iniquity, and the iniquity of their fathers, with their trespass which they trespassed against me, and that also they have walked contrary unto me,

1 Ki.8:47

v.47 Yet if they shall |take it to their hearts| in the land where they were carried captives, and repent, and make supplication unto thee in the land of them who carried them captives, saying, We have sinned, and have done perversely, we have committed wickedness;

v.7 Our fathers understood not thy wonders in Egypt; they remembered not the multitude of thy mercies, but (v) provoked him at the sea, even at the Red Sea.

(v) provoked him
(v)Ex.14:11-12

v.11 And they said unto Moses, Because there were no graves in Egypt, hast thou taken us away to die in the wilderness? Wherefore hast thou dealt thus with us, to carry us forth out of Egypt?
v.12 Is not this the word that we did tell thee in Egypt, saying, Let us alone, that we may serve the Egyptians? For it had been better for us to serve the Egyptians, than that we should die in the wilderness.

v.8 Nevertheless, he saved them (w) for his name's sake, (x) that he might make his mighty power to be known.

(w) for his name sake:
(w)cp.Ezek.20:14
(x) that he might;
(x) Ex.9:16

Ezek.20:14

v.14 But I wrought for my name's sake, that it should not be polluted before the |nations|, in whole sight I brought them out.

Ex.9:16

v.16 And in very deed for this cause have I raised thee up, to show in thee my power; and that my name may be declared throughout all the earth.

v.9 (y) He rebuked the Red Sea also, and it was dried up; so he
(z) led them through the depths, as through the wilderness.

(y) He rebuked
(y) Ex.14:21;cp.Ps.18:15;Nah.1:4
(z) led them;
(z) Isa.63:11-14

Ex.14:21

v.21 And Moses stretched out his hand over the sea; and the LORD cause the sea to go back by a strong east wind all that night, and made the sea dry land, and the waters were divided.

Ps.18:15

v.15 Then the channels of waters were seen, and the foundations of the world were |laid bare| at thy rebuke, O LORD, at the blast of the breath of thy nostrils.

Nah.1:4

v.4 He rebuketh the sea, and maketh it dry, and drieth up all the rivers; Bashan languisheth, and Carmel; and the flower of Lebanon languisheth.

Isa.63:11-14

v.11 Then he remembered the days of old, Moses, and his people, saying, Where is he who brought them

up out of the sea with the shepherd of his flock? Where is he who put his Holy Spirit within him?
v.12 Who led them by the right hand of Moses with his glorious arm, dividing the water before them, to make himself an everlasting name?
v.13 Who led them through the deep, like a horse in the wilderness, that they should not stumble?
v.14 As a beast goeth down into the valley, the Spirit of the LORD caused him to rest; so didst thou lead thy people, to make thyself a glorious name.

v.10 And he (aa) saved them from the hand of him that hated them, and (a) redeemed them from the hand of the enemy.

(aa) saved them
(aa) Ex.14:30
(a) redeemed them
(a) Redemption (Kinsman type):
v.10;107:2;Ps.119:154
(Gen.48:16;Isa.59:20,note)

Ex.14:30

v.30 Thus the LORD saved Israel that day out of the hand of the Egyptians; and Israel saw the Egyptians dead upon the seashore.

See above v.10

Ps.107:2

v.2 Let the redeemed of the LORD say so, whom he hath redeemed from the hand of the enemy,

Ps.119:154

v.154 Plead my cause, and deliver me; |revive| me according to thy word.

Gen.48:16

v.16 |An angel| who redeemed me from all evil, bless the lads; and let my name be named on them, and the name of my fathers, Abraham and Isaac; and let them grow into a multitude in the midst of the earth.

Isa.59:20,note

v.20 And the Redeemer shall come to Zion, and unto those who turn from transgression in Jacob, saith the LORD.

Note: 1(59:20) Redemption, Kinsman type, Summary: The goel, or Kinsman-redeemer, is a beautiful type of Christ:

(1) The kinsman redemption was of persons and an inheritance (Lev.25:25,48; Gal.4:5;Eph.1:7,11,14).
(2) The redeemer must be a kinsman (Lev.25:48-49; Ruth 3:12-13, see v.9, note; Gal.4:4;Heb.2:14-15).
(3) The redeemer must be able to redeem (Ruth 4:4-6; Jer.50:34;Jn.10:11,18).
(4) Redemption is effected by the goel paying the just demand in full (Lev.25:27;Gal.3:13;1Pet.1:18-19). See notes at Ex.6:6 and Rom.3:24.

2(59:20) The time when the "Redeemer shall come to Zion" is fixed, relatively, by Rom.11:23-29, as following the completion of the Church. This is also the order of the great dispensational passage, Acts 15:14-17, In both, the return of the Lord to Zion follows the outcalling of the Church.

v.11 And the waters covered their enemies; there was not one of them left.
v.12 Then believed they his words; they sang his praise.
v.13 They soon forgot his works; they waited not for his counsel,
v.14 But lusted exceedingly in the wilderness, and (b)|tested| God in the desert.

(b) |tested| God in the desert.
(b) KJV tempted. Test-tempt:
v.14; Ps.139:23.(Gen.3:1;Jas.1:14)
See: above v.14

Ps.139:23

v.23 Search me, O God, and know my heart; try me, and know my thoughts;

Gen.3:1

v.1 Now the serpent was more subtle than any beast of the field which the LORD God had made. And he said unto the woman, Yea, hath God said, Ye shall not eat of every tree of the garden?

Jas.1:14

v.14 But every man is tempted, when he is drawn away of his own lust, and enticed.

v.15 And he gave them their request, but sent leanness into their soul.
v.16 They (c) envied Moses also in the camp, and Aaron, the saint of the LORD.

(c) envied;
(c) Num.16:2-3

v.2 And they rose up before Moses, with certain of the children of Israel, two hundred and fifty princes of the assembly, famous in the congregation, men renown;
v.3 And they gathered themselves together against Moses and against Aaron, and said unto them, Ye take too much upon you, seeing all the congregation is holy, everyone of them, and the LORD is among them: wherefore, then, lift ye up yourselves above the congregation of the LORD?

v.17 The (d) earth opened and swallowed up Dathan, and covered the company of Abi'ram.

(d) earth opened
(d) Num.16:31-33;Dt.11:6

Num.16:31-33

v.31 And it came to pass, as he had |finished| speaking all these words, that the ground |split open| that was under them;
v.32 And the earth opened its mouth, and swallowed them up, and their houses, and all the men that appertained unto Korah, and all their goods.
v.33 They, and all that appertained to them, went down alive into |sheol|, and the earth closed upon them; and they perished from among the congregation.

Dt.11:6

v.6 And what he did unto Dathan and Abi'ram, the sons of Eli'ab, the son of Reuben—how the earth opened its mouth and swallowed them up, and their households, and their tents, and all the substance that was in their possession, in the midst of all Israel.

v.18 And a fire was kindled in their company; the flame burned up the wicked.
v.19 They (e) made a calf in Horeb, and worshiped the (f)|melted| image.

(e) made a calf
(e) Ex.32:1-4
(f) |melted| image
(f) KJV molten

v.1 And when the people saw that Moses delayed to come down out of the mount, the people gathered themselves together unto Aaron, and said unto him,

Up, make us gods, which shall go before us; for as for this Moses, the man who brought us up out of the land of Egypt, we |know| not what is become of him.

v.2 And Aaron said unto them, Break off the golden earrings, which are in the ears of your wives, of your sons, and of your daughters, and bring them unto me.

v.3 And all the people broke off the golden earrings which were in their ears, and brought them unto Aaron.

v.4 And he received them at their hand, and fashioned it with an |engraving| tool, after he had made it a |melted| calf: and they said, These are thy gods, O Israel, which brought thee up out of the land of Egypt.

v.20 Thus they (g) changed their glory into the similitude of an ox that eateth grass.

(g) changed
(g)Jer.2:11;Rom.1:23

Jer.2:11

v.11 Hath a nation changed their gods, which are yet no gods? But my people have changed their glory for that which doth not profit.

Rom.1:23

v.23 And changed the glory of the incorruptible God into an image made like corruptible man, and birds, and four-footed beasts, and creeping things.

v.21 They forgot God, their Savior, who had done great things in Egypt,

v.22 Wondrous works in the land of Ham, and (h) |awesome| things by the Red Sea.

(h) |awesome|
(h) KJV terrible

v.23 Therefore, he said that he would destroy them, had not Moses, his chosen, stood before him in the breach, to turn away his wrath, lest he should destroy them.
v.24 Yea, they despised the pleasant land; they (i) believed not his word,

(i) believed not his word;
(i) Heb.3:18

v.18 And to whom swore he that they should not enter into his rest, but to them that believed not?

v.25 But (j) murmured in their tents, and hearkened not unto the voice of the LORD.

(j) murmured,
(j) Num.14:2,27

v.2 And all the children of Israel murmured against Moses and against Aaron: and the whole congregation said unto them, Would God that we had died in the land of Egypt! Or would God we had died in this wilderness!
v.27 How long shall I bear with this evil congregation, who murmur against me? I have heard the murmurings of the children of Israel, which they murmur against me.

v.26 (k) Therefore, he lifted up his hand against them, to overthrow them in the wilderness,

(k) Therefore,
(k) Num.14:28-30;Ps.95:11;
Ezek.20:15-16;Heb.3:11,18

Num.14:28-30

v.28 Say unto them, As truly as I live, saith the LORD, as ye have spoken in mine ears, so will I do to you.
v.29 Your carcasses shall fall in this wilderness; and all who were numbered of you, according to your whole number, from twenty years old and upward, who have murmured against me,
v.30 Doubtless ye shall not come into the land, concerning which I swore to make you dwell therein, except Caleb, the son of Jephun'neh, and Joshua, the son of Nun.

Ps.95:11

v.11 Unto whom I swore in my wrath that they should not enter into my rest.

Ezek.20:15-16

v.15 Yet also I lifted up mine hand unto them in the wilderness, that I would not bring them into the land which I had given them, flowing with milk and honey, which is the glory of all lands,
v.16 Because they despised mine |ordinances|, and walked not in my statutes, but polluted my sabbaths; for their heart went after their idols.

Heb.3:11,18

v.11 So I swore in my wrath, They shall not enter into my rest.
v.18 And to whom swore he that they should not enter his rest, but to them that believed not?

v.27 To overthrow their seed also among the nations, and to (1) scatter them in the lands.

(1) scatter;

(l) Lev.26:33;Ps.44:11;
Ezek.20:23

Lev.26:33

v.33 And I will scatter you among the |nations|, and will draw out a sword after you; and your land shall be desolate, and your cities waste.

Ps.44:11

v.11 Thou hast given us like sheep appointed for |food|, and hast scattered us among the |nations|.

Ezek.20:23

v.23 I lifted up mine hand unto them also in the wilderness, that I would scatter them among the |nations|, and disperse them through the countries,

v.28 They joined themselves also unto Ba'al-pe'or, and ate the sacrifices of the dead.
v.29 Thus they provoked him to anger with their (m) |doings|, and the plague broke in upon them.

(m) |doings|;
(m) KJV inventions

v.30 (n) Then stood up Phin'ehas, and excuted judgment; and so the plague was (o)|checked|.

(n) Then stood
(n) Num.25:7-8
(o) |checked|
(o) KJV stayed

Num.25:7-8

v.7 And when Phin'ehas, the son of Elea'zar, the son of Aaron the priest, saw it he rose up from among the congregation, and took a javelin in his hand;

v.8 And he went after the man of Israel into the tent, and thrust both of them through, the man of Israel, and the woman through her |abdomen|. So the plague was stayed from the children of Israel.

v.31 And that was (p) counted unto him for righteousness unto all generations for evermore.

(p) counted unto him
(p) Num.25:11-13

v.11 Phin'ehas, the son of Elea'zar, the son of Aaron the priest, hath turned my wrath away from the children of Israel, while he was zealous for my sake among them, that I consumed not the children of Israel in my jealousy.

v.12 Wherefore say, Behold, I give unto him my covenant of peace;

v.13 And he shall have it, and his seed after him, even the covenant of an everlasting priesthood, because he was zealous for his God, and made an atonement for the children of Israel.

v.32 (q) They angered him also at the waters of strife, (r) so that it went ill with Moses for their sakes,

(q) They angered him
(q) Num.20:3-13;Ps.81:7
(r) so that it went ill
(r) Dt.1:37;3:26

Num.20:3-13

v.3 And the people |strove| with Moses, and spoke, saying, Would God that we had died when our brethren died before the LORD!

v.4 And why have ye brought up the congregation of the LORD into this wilderness, that we and our cattle should die there?

v.5 And wherefore have ye made us to come up out of Egypt, to bring us in unto this evil place? It is no place of seed, or of figs, or of vines, or of pomegranates; neither is there any water to drink.

v.6 And Moses and Aaron went from the presence of the assembly unto the door of the tabernacle of the congregation, and they fell upon their faces; and the glory of the LORD appeared unto them.

v.7 And the LORD spoke unto Moses, saying,

v.8 Take the rod, and gather thou the assembly together, thou, and Aaron, thy brother, and speak ye unto the rock before their eyes; and it shall give forth its water, and thou shalt bring forth to them water out of the rock: so thou shalt give the congregation and their beast drink.

v.9 And Moses took the rod from before the LORD, as he commanded him.

v.10 And Moses and Aaron gathered the congregation together before the rock, and he said unto them, Hear now, ye rebels; must we fetch you water out of this rock?

v.11 And Moses lifted up his hand, and with his rod he smote the rock twice; and the water came out abundantly, and the congregation drank, and their beast also.

v.12 And the LORD spoke unto Moses and Aaron, Because ye believed me not, to sanctify me in the eyes of the children of Israel, therefore ye shall not bring this congregation into the land which I have given them.

v.13 This is the water of Mer'ibah; because the children of Israel strove with the LORD, and he was sanctified in them.

Ps.81:7

v.7 Thou calledst in trouble, and I delivered thee; I answered thee in the secret place of thunder; I |tested| thee at the waters of Meribah. Selah.

Dt.1:37;3:26

v.37 Also the LORD was angry with me for your sakes, saying, Thou also shalt not go in there.

Dt.3:26

v.26 But the LORD was |angry| with me for your sakes, and would not hear me; and the LORD said unto me, Let it suffice thee; speak no more unto me of this matter.

v.33 Because they provoked his spirit, so that he (s) spoke unadvisedly with his lips.

(s) spoke unadvisedly
(s) cp.Mt.26:69-75

v.69 Now Peter sat |outside| in the |court|, and a |maid| came unto him, saying, Thou also wast with Jesus of Galilee.
v.70 But he denied it before them all saying, I know not what thou sayest.
v.71 And when he was gone out into the porch, another maid saw him, and said unto them that were there, This fellow was also with Jesus of Nazareth.
v.72 And again he denied with an oath, I do not know the man.

v.73 And after a while came unto him they that stood by, and said to Peter, Surely thou also art one of them; for thy speech |betrayed| thee.
v.74 Then began he to curse and to swear, saying, I know not the man. And immediately the cock |crowed|.
v.75 And Peter remembered the word of Jesus, who said unto him, Before the cock crows, thou shalt deny me thrice. And went out, and wept bitterly.

v.34 They did not (t) destroy the nations, concerning whom the LORD commanded them,

(t) destroy the nations,
(t)Dt.7:2,16;Jud.2:2

Dt.7:2,16

v.2 And when the LORD thy God shall deliver them before thee, thou shalt smite them, and utterly destroy them; thou shalt make no covenant with them, nor show mercy unto them.
v.16 And thou shalt consume all the people whom the LORD Thy God shall deliver to thee; thine eye shall have no pity upon them, neither shalt thou serve their gods; for that will be a snare unto thee.

Jud.2:2

v.2 And ye shall make no league with the inhabitants of this land; ye shall throw down their altars. But ye have not obeyed my voice. Why have ye done this?

v.35 But were mingled among the (u) |nations|, and learned their works.

(u) |nations|,
(u) KJV heathen

v.36 And they served their idols, which were a snare unto them.
v.37 Yea, they sacrificed their sons and their daughters into
(v) | demons | ,

(v) | demons | ,
(v) KJV devils

v.38 And shed innocent blood, even the blood of their sons and
of their daughters, whom they sacrificed unto the idols of
Ca'naan; and the land was polluted with blood.
v.39 Thus were they defiled with their own works, and
(w) | played the harlot in | their (m) | doings | .

(w) | played the harlot in |
(w) KJV went a whoring with
(m) | doings |
(m) KJV inventions

v.40 Therefore was the wrath of the LORD kindled against his
people, insomuch that he abhorred his own inheritance.
v.41 And he gave them into the hand of the (u) | nations | , and
they that hated them ruled over them.

(u) | nations |
(u) KJV heathen

v.42 Their enemies also oppressed them, and they were brought
into subject under their hand.

v.43 (x) Many times did he deliver them; but they provoked him
with their counsel, and were brought low for their iniquity.

(x) Many times
(x) Jud.2:16;Neh.9:27

Jud.2:16

v.16 Nevertheless the LORD raised up Judges, who delivered them out of the hand of those who spoiled them.

Neh.9:27

v.27 Therefore, thou deliveredst them into the hand of their enemies, who vexed them; and in time of their trouble, when they cried unto thee, thou heardest them from heaven; and according to thy manifold mercies thou gavest them saviors, who saved them out of the hand of their enemies.

v.44 Nevertheless, he regarded their affliction, when he heard their cry;
v.45 And he remembered for them his covenant, and (y) repented according to the multitude of his mercies.

(y) repented
(y) See Zech.8:14,note

v.14 For thus saith the LORD of hosts: As I thought to punish you, when your fathers provoked me to wrath saith the LORD of hosts, and I repented not

Note: 4(8 :14) Repentance (O.T.), Summary: In the O.T. "repentance" is the English word used to translate the Hebrew nacham, to be eased or comforted. It is used of both God and man. Notwithstanding the literal meaning of nacham, It is evident, from a study of all the passages, that the sacred writers use it is the sense of metanoia in the N.T., meaning a change of mind. See Mt.3:2;Acts17:30, note. As in the N.T., such change of mind is often accompanied by contrition and self-judgment, When applied to God, the word is used phenomenally, according to O.T. custom. God seems to change His mind. The phenomena are such as, the case of a man, would indicate a change of mind.

v.46 He made them also to be (z) pitted of all those that carried them captives.

(z) pitted,
(z) Ezra 9:9;Jer.42:10-12

Ezra 9:9

v.9 For we were |slaves|; yet our God hath not forsaken us in our bondage, but hath extended mercy unto us in the sight of the kings of Persia, to give us a reviving, to set up the house of our God, and to repair the desolations of it, and to give us a wall in Judah and in Jerusalem.

Jer.42:10-12

v.10 If ye will still abide in this land, then will I build you, and not pull you down, and I will plant you, and not pluck you up; for I repent of the evil that I have done unto you.
v.11 Be not afraid of the king of Babylon, of whom ye are afraid; be not afraid of him, saith the LORD; for I am with you from his hand.
v.12 And I will show mercies unto you, that he may have mercy upon you, and cause you to return to your own land.

v.47 (aa) Save us, O LORD God, and gather us from among the (u)|nations|, to give thanks unto thy holy name, and to triumph in thy praise.

(aa) Save us,
(aa) 1Chr.16:35-36

v.35 And say ye, Save us, O God of our salvation, and gather us together, and deliver us from the |nations|, that we may give thanks to thy holy name, and glory in thy praise.

v.36 Blessed be the LORD God of Israel forever and ever. And all the people said, Amen, and praised the LORD.

v.48 (bb) Blessed be the LORD God of Israel from everlasting to everlasting; and let all the people say, Amen. Praise ye the LORD.

(bb) Blessed be the LORD God
(bb)Ps.41:13;72:19;89:52

Ps.41:13

v.13 Blessed be the LORD God of Israel from everlasting, and to everlasting. Amen, and Amen.

Ps.72:19

v.19 And blessed be his glorious name forever; and let the whole earth be filled with his glory, Amen, and Amen.

Ps.89:52

v.52 Blessed be the LORD for evermore. Amen, and Amen.

Author's Note: Ps.78:3-72;105:1-45;106:1-48 give a complete survey of God's dealings with His chosen people, Israel in history. JMD

V

HALLEL OR HALLELUJAH PSALMS,

SONG'S OF PRAISE

PRAISE FOR GOD'S WONDERFUL WORKS

PSALM 111

v.1 PRAISE ye the LORD. I will praise the LORD with my whole heart, in the assembly of the upright, and in the congregation.
v.2 The works of the LORD are great, sought out of all them who have pleasure therein.
v.3 His work is honorable and glorious, and his righteousness endureth forever.
v.4 He hath made his wonderful works to be remembered; the LORD is gracious and full of compassion.
v.5 He hath given (m) | food | unto those who (n) fear him; he will ever be mindful of his covenant.

(m) | food |,
(m) KJV meat
(n) fear him;
(n) See Ps.19:9, note
See Ps.23:4 Messianic Psalm

v.6 He hath shown his people the power of his works, that he may give them the heritage of the (l) | nations |.

(l) | nations |,
(l) KJV heathen

v.7 The works of his hands are verity and (o) | justice |; all his commandments are sure.

(o) | justice | ;
(o) KJV judgment

v.8 They stand fast for ever and ever, and are done in truth and uprightness.
v.9 He sent (p) redemption unto his people; he hath commanded his covenant forever; holy and reverend is his name.

(p) redemption
(p) See Ex.6:6,note

Ex.6:6

v.6 Wherefore say unto the children of Israel, I am the LORD, and I will bring you out from under the burdens of the Egyptians, and I will rid you out of their bondage, and I will redeem you with | an outstretched | arm, and with great judgments;

Note: 2(6:6) Redemption: (Exodus) Summary. Exodus is the book of redemption and teaches:

(1) redemption is wholly from God (Ex.3:7-8; Jn.3:16);
(2) redemption is by blood (Ex.12:13,23,27; 1Pet.1:18-19);and
(3) redemption is by power (Ex.6:6;13:14;Rom.8:2.See Isa.59:20 and Rom.3:24,note).

The blood of Christ redeems the believer from the guilt and penalty of sin (1Pet.1:18-19) and the power of the Holy Spirit delivers from the dominion of sin on the basis of Calvary (Rom.8:2; Gal.5:16).

v.10 The (n) fear of the LORD is the (q) beginning of wisdom. A good understanding have all they that do his commandments; his praise endureth. Forever.

(n) fear;

(n) See Ps.19:9,note
See Ps.23:4 Messianic Psalm
(q) beginning of wisdom.
(q) Prov.1:7

v.7 The fear of the LORD is the beginning of knowledge,
but fools despise wisdom and instruction.

BLESSINGS OF THE GOD-FEARING MAN

PSALM 112

v.1 PRAISE ye the LORD, (a) Blessed is the man who feareth the LORD, who delighteth greatly in his commandments.

(a) Blessed is the man
(a) Ps.128:1

v.1 BLESSED is every one that feareth the LORD, that walketh in his ways.

v.2 His (b) seed shall be mighty upon earth; the generation of the upright shall be blessed.

(b) seed shall be mighty
(b)Ps.25:13;37:26;102:28

Ps.25:13

v.13 His soul shall dwell at ease, and his seed shall inherit the earth.

Ps.37:26

v.26 He is ever merciful, and lendeth; and his seed is blessed.

Ps.102:28

v.28 The children of thy servants shall continue, and their seed shall be established before thee

v.3 Wealth and riches shall be in his house; and his righteousness endureth forever.
v.4 (c) Unto the upright there ariseth light in the darkness; he is gracious, and full of compassion, and righteous.

(c) Unto the upright
(c) Job 11:17;Ps.97:11

Job 11:17

v.17 And thine age shall be clearer than the noonday. Thou shalt shine forth, thou shalt be as the morning.

Ps.97:11

v.11 Light is sown for the righteous, and gladness for the upright in heart.

v.5 A good man showed favor, and (d) lendeth; he will guide his affairs (e) with discretion.

(d) lendeth;
(d) Ps.37:26;Lk.6:35
(e) with discretion
(e) Eph.5:15;Col.4:5

Ps.37:26

v.26 He is ever merciful, and lendeth; and his seed is blessed.

Lk.6:35

v.35 **But love ye your enemies, and do good, and lend, hoping for nothing again; and your reward shall be great, and ye shall be the |sons| of the Highest; for he is kind unto the unthankful and to the evil.**

Eph.5:15

v.15 See, then, that ye walk circumspectly, not as fools but as wise,

Col.4:5

v.5 Walk in wisdom toward them that are |outside|, redeeming the time.

v.6 Surely he shall not be moved forever; the (f) righteous shall be in everlasting remembrance.

(f) righteous
(f) Prov.10:7

v.7 The memory of the just is blessed, but the name of the wicked shall rot.

v.7 (g) He shall not be afraid of evil tidings; his heart is fixed, (h) trusting in the Lord.

(g) He shall not be afraid
(g) Prov.1:33
(h) trusting
(h) See Ps. 2:12,note
See Ps.40:4 Messianic Psalm

Prov.1:33

v.33 But whoso hearkeneth unto me quite from fear of evil.

v.8 His (i)heart is established; he shall not be afraid, until he see his desire upon his enemies.

(i) heart is established;
(i)Heb.13:9
See Ps.2:12,note
See Ps.40:4 Messianic Psalm

v.9 Be not carried about with |various| and strange doctrines, For it is a good thing that the heart be established with grace, not with |foods|, which have been occupied with them.

v.9 He hath (j) |distributed|, he hath given to the poor; his righteousness endureth forever; his (k) horn shall be exalted with honor.

(j) |distributed|
(j) KJV dispersed. 2Cor.9:9
(k) horn
(k) See Dt.33:17,note

2Cor.9:9

v.9 (As it is written, He hath dispersed abroad; he hath given to the poor; his righteousness remained forever.

See Dt.33:17,note
See Ps. 89:17 Messianic Psalm

v.10 The wicked shall see it, and be grieved; he shall gnash with his teeth, and melt away. The desire of the wicked shall perish.

GOD'S CONTINUAL PRAISE

PSALM 113

v.1 1 PRAISE ye the LORD, Praise, O ye servants of the LORD, praise the name of the LORD

v.2 (l) Blessed be the name of the LORD from this time forth and for evermore.

(l) Blessed be the name of the LORD
(l) Dan.2:20

v.20 Daniel answered and said, Blessed be the name of God forever and ever; for wisdom and might are his,

v.3 (m) From the rising of the sun unto the going down of the same, the LORD'S name is to be praised.

(m) From the rising
(m) Isa.59:19;Mal.1:11

Isa.59:19

v.19 So shall they fear the name of the LORD from the west, and his glory from the rising of the sun. When the enemy shall come in like a flood, the Spirit of the LORD shall lift up a standard against him.

Mal.1:11

v.11 For from the rising of the sun even unto the going down of the same, my name shall be great among the |nations|, and in every place incense shall be offered unto my name, and a pure offering; for my name shall be great among the |nations|, saith the LORD of hosts.

v.4 The LORD is high above all nations, and his (n) glory above the heavens.

(n) glory
(n) Ps.8:1

v.1 O LORD, our Lord, how excellent is thy name in all the earth, who hast set thy glory above the heavens!

v.5 Who is like unto the LORD, our God, who dwelleth on (o) high,

(o) high
(o) Ps.11:4;138:6;Isa.57:15

Ps.11:4

v.4 The LORD is in his holy temple, the LORD'S throne is in heaven; his eyes behold, his eyelids |test| the children of men.

Ps.138:6

v.6 Though the LORD be high, yet hath he respect unto the lowly; but the proud he knoweth afar off.

Isa.57:15

v.15 For thus saith the high and lofty One who inhabiteth eternity, whose name is Holy: I dwell in the high and holy place, with him also who is of a contrite and humble spirit, to revive the spirit of the humble, and to revive the heart of the contrite ones.

v.6 Who humbleth himself to behold the things that are in heaven, and in the earth!

v.7 He (p) raised up the poor out of the dust, and lifted the (q) needy out of the dunghill.

(p) raised up
(p) 1Sam.2:8;Ps.107:41
(q) needy;
(q) Ps.72:12

1 Sam.2:8

v.8 But Abner, the son of Ner, captain of Saul's host, took Ishbosh'eth, the son of Saul, and brought him over to Mahana'im;

Ps.107:41

v.41 Yet setteth he the poor on high from affliction, and maketh their families like a flock.

Ps.72:12

v.12 For he shall deliver the needy when he crieth; the poor also, and him that hath no helper.

v.8 That he may (r) set him with princes, even with the princes of his people.

(r) set him with princes,
(r) Job 36:7

v.7 He withdraw not his eyes from the righteous; but with kings are they on the throne; yea, he doth establish them forever, and they are exalted.

v.9 He maketh the barren woman to keep house, and to be joyful mother of children. Praise ye the LORD.

1(113:1) The Hallelujah Psalms are the following: Ps.104-106; 111-113;115-117;135;146-150. Of these, Ps.135-136 and 146-150 were used in daily synagogue worship. Psalms 113-118 were called the Egyptian Hallel and were used in connection with the feasts of Passover, Pentecost, Tabernacles, and Dedication. At the Passover celebration the earlier portion of these Psalms was sung before the feast; Ps.115-118(the Great Hallel) were sung after the last cup (cp.Mt.26:30)

IN PRAISE OF THE EXODUS

PSALM 114

v.1 WHEN Israel went out of Egypt, the house of Jacob from a people of (s) strange language,

(s) strange language,
(s) Ps.81:5

v.5 This he ordained in Joseph for a testimony, when he went out through the land of Egypt, where I heard a language that I understood not.

v.2 (t) Judah was his sanctuary, and Israel his dominion.

(t) Judah was
(t) Ex.6:7;19:6;25:8; 29:45-46;Dt.27:9

Ex.6:7

v.7 And I will take you to me for a people, and I will be to you a God: and ye shall know that I am the LORD your God, who bringeth you out from under the burdens of the Egyptians

Ex.19:6

v.6 And ye shall be unto me a kingdom of priests, and an holy nation. These are the words which thou shalt speak unto the children of Israel.

Ex.25:8

v.8 And let them make me a sanctuary, that I may dwell among them

Ex.29:45-46

v.45 And I will dwell among the children of Israel, and will be their God.
v.46 And they shall know that I am the LORD their God, who brought them forth out of the land of Egypt, that I may dwell among them: I am the LORD their God.

Dt.27:9

v.9 And Moses and the priests, the Levites, spoke unto all Israel, saying Take heed, and hearken, O Israel: this day thou art become the people of the LORD thy God.

v.3 The sea (u) saw it, and fled; the (v) Jordan was driven back.

(u) saw it
(u) Ex.14:21;Ps.77:16
(v) Jordan
(v) v.5 Josh.3:13-16

(u) Ex.14:21

v.21 And Moses stretched out his hand over the sea ; and the LORD caused the sea to go back by a strong east wind all that night, and made the sea dry land, and the waters were divided.

Ps.77:16

v.16 The waters saw thee, O God, the waters saw thee; they were afraid; the depths also were troubled.
v.5 (w) What ailed thee, O thou sea, that thou fleddest? Thou Jordan, that thou wast driven back?

Josh.3:13-16

v.13 And it shall come pass, as soon as the soles of the feet of the priests who bear the ark of the LORD, the Lord of all the earth, shall rest in the waters of the Jordan, that the waters of the Jordan shall be cut off above, and they shall stand |in one| heap.
v.14 And it came to pass, when the people removed from their tents to pass over the Jordan, and the priests bearing the ark of the covenant before the people,
v.15 And, as they who bore the ark were come unto the Jordan and the feet of the priests who bore the ark were dipped in the brim of the water (for the Jordan overfloweth all its banks all the time of harvest),
v.16 That the waters which came down from above stood and rose up |in one| heap very far from the city Adam, that is beside Zar'ethan; and those that came down toward the sea of the |Ar'abah|, even the Salt Sea, failed, and were cut off; and the people passed over right against Jericho.

v.4 The mountain skipped like rams, and the little hills like lambs.
v.5 (w) What ailed thee, O thou sea, that thou feddest? Thou Jordan, that thou wast driven back?

(w) What ailed thee,
(w) Hab.3:8

v.8 Was the LORD displeased against the rivers ? Was thine anger against the rivers? Was thy wrath against the sea, that thou didst ride upon thine horses and thy chariots of salvation?

v.6 Ye mountains, that ye skipped like rams, and ye little hills, like lambs?
v.7 Tremble, thou earth, at the presence of the Lord, at the presence of the God of Jacob,

v.8 (x) Who turned the rock into a (y) |pool of | water, the flint into a fountain of waters.

(x) Who turned the rock
(x) Ex.17:6;Num.20:11;Ps.107:35
(y) |pool of|
(y) KJV standing

Ex.17:6

v.6 Behold, I will stand before thee there upon the rock in Horeb; and thou shalt smite the rock, and there shall come water out of it, that the people may drink. And Moses did so in the sight of the elders of Israel.

Num.20:11

v.11 And Moses lifted up his hand, and with his rod he smote the rock twice; and the water came out abundantly, and the congregation drank, and their beasts also.

Ps.107:35

v.35 He turneth the wilderness into a |pool of | water, and dry ground into water springs;

TO GOD ALONE BE THE GLORY

PSALM 115

v.1 (z) NOT unto us, O LORD, not unto us, but unto thy name give glory, for thy mercy, and for thy truth's sake.

(z) NOT unto us,
(z) Isa.48:11;Ezek.36:32

Isa.48:11

v.11 For mine own sake, even for mine own sake, will I do it; for how should my name be polluted? And I will not give my glory unto another.

Ezek.36:32

v.32 Not for your sakes do I this, saith the Lord God, be it known unto you; be ashamed and confounded for your own ways, O house of Israel.

v.2 Wherefore should the (aa) | nations | say, Where is now their God?

(aa) | nations | say,
(aa) KJV heathen

v.3 But our (bb) God is in the heavens; he hath done whatsoever he hath pleased.

(bb) God is in the heaven;
(bb) Ps.103:19;135:6;Dan.4:35

Ps.103:19

v.19 The LORD hath prepared his throne in the heavens, and his kingdom ruleth over all.

Ps.135:6

v.6 Whatsoever the LORD pleased, that did he in heaven, and in earth, in the seas, and all deep places.

Dan.4:35

v.35 And all the inhabitants of the earth are reputed as nothing; and he doeth according to his will in the army of heaven, and among the inhabitants of the earth, and none can stay his hand, or say unto him, What doest thou?

v.4 (cc) Their idols are silver and gold, the work of men's hands.

(cc) Their idols
(cc) vv.4-8;cp.Ps.135:15-18

v.4 (cc) Their idols are silver and gold, the work of men's hands.
v.5 They have mouths, but they speak not; eyes have they, but they see not.
v.6 They have ears, but they hear not; noses have they, but they smell not.
v.7 They have hands, but they handle not; feet have they, but they walk not; neither speak they through their throat.
v.8 They who make them are like unto them; so is every one who trusteth in them.

Ps.135:15-18

v.15 But overthrew Phar'aoh and his host in the Red Sea; for his mercy endureth forever;

v.16 To him who led the people through the wilderness; for his mercy endureth forever;
v.17 To him who smote great kings; for his mercy endureth forever;
v.18 And slew famous kings; for his mercy endureth forever:

v.5 They have mouths but they speak not; eyes have they, but they see not.
v.6 They have ears, but they hear not; noses have they, but they smell not.
v.7 They have hands, but they handle not; feet have they, but they walk not; neither speak they through their throat.
v.8 They who make them are like unto them; so is every one who trusteth in them.
v.9 O Israel, (a) trust thou in the LORD; he is their help and their shield.

(a) trust;
(a) See Ps.2:12,note
See Ps.55:23 Penitential Psalm

v.10 O house of Aaron, trust in the LORD; he is their help and their shield.
v.11 Ye that (b) fear the LORD; (a) trust in the LORD; he is their help and their shield.

(b) fear the LORD;
(b) See Ps.19:9,note
See Ps.23:4 Messianic Psalm
(a) trust in the LORD;
(a) See Ps.2:12,note
See Ps.55:23 Penitential Psalm

v.12 The LORD hath been mindful of us; he will bless us, he will bless the house of Israel, he will bless the house of Aaron.
v.13 He will (c) bless those who (b) fear the LORD, both small and great.

(c) bless those who,
(c) Ps.128:1,4
(b) fear the LORD,
(b) See Ps.19:9,note
See Ps.23:4 Messianic Psalm

Ps.128:1,4

v.1 BLESSED is every one that feareth the LORD, that walketh in his ways.
v.4 Behold, that thus shall the man be blessed who feareth the LORD.

v.14 The LORD shall increase you more and more, you and your children.
v.15 Ye are blessed by the LORD who made heaven and earth.
v.16 The heaven, even the heavens, are the LORD'S; but the earth hath he given to the children of men.
v.17 The (d) dead praise not the LORD, neither any that go down into silence.

(d) dead praise
(d) See Eccl.9:10,note

Eccl.9:10,note

v.10 Whatsoever thy hand findeth to do, do it with thy might; for there is no work, nor device, nor knowledge, nor wisdom in |sheol|, whither thou goest.

Note: 1(9:10) This statement is no more a divine revelation concerning the state of the dead than any other conclusion of "the Preacher" (1:1). No one would quote 9:2 as a divine revelation. These reasonings of man apart from divine revelation are set down by inspiration just as the words of Satan (Gen.3:4;Job.2:4-5;etc.) are so recorded. But that life and consciousness continue between death and resurrection is directly affirmed in Scripture (Isa.14:9-11; Mt.22:32; Mk.9:43-48; Lk.16:19-31; 2Cor.5:6-8; Phil.1:21-23; Rev.6:9-11).

v.18 But we will bless the LORD from this time forth and for evermore. Praise the LORD.

THE GRATITUDE OF THE REDEEMED

PSALM 116

v.1 I LOVE the LORD, because he hath heard my voice and my supplications.
v.2 Because he hath incline his ear unto me, therefore will I call upon him as long as I live.
v.3 The (e) sorrows of death compassed me, and the pains of (f) | sheol | (g) got hold upon me; I found trouble and sorrow.

(e) sorrows
(e) Ps.18:4-6
(f) | sheol |
(f) KJV hell. See Hab.2:5,note;
Lk.16:23,note
See Ps.6:5 Penitential Psalm
(g) got hold
(g) Lit. found me.

Ps.18:4-6

v.4 The sorrows of death compassed me, and the floods of ungodly men made me afraid.
v.5 The sorrows of | sheol | compassed me about; the snares of death | were round about | me.
v.6 In my distress I called upon the LORD, and cried unto my God; he heard my voice out of his temple; and my cry came before him, even into his ears.

v.4 Then called I upon the name of the LORD: I beseech thee, deliver my soul.
v.5 Gracious is the LORD, and (h) righteous; yea, our God is merciful.

(h) righteous;
(h) Ezra9:15;Neh.9:8;
Ps.119:137;145:17

Ezra9:15

v.15 O LORD God of Israel, thou art righteous; for we remain yet escaped, as is this day. Behold, we are before thee in our trespasses; for we cannot stand before thee because of this.

Neh.9:8

v.8 And foundest his heart faithful before thee, and madest a covenant with him to give the land of the Ca'naanites, the Hittites, the Amorites, and the Periz'zites, and the Jeb'usites, and the Gir'gashites, to give it, I say, to his seed, and hast performed thy words; for thou art righteous,

Ps.119:137

v.137 Righteous art thou, O LORD, and upright are thy judgments.

Ps.145:17

v.17 The LORD is righteous in all his ways, and holy in all his works.

v.6 The LORD preserveth the simple; I was brought low, and he helped me.
v.7 (i) Return unto thy rest, O my soul; for the LORD hath (j) dealt bountifully with thee.

(i) Return unto thy rest,
(i) Cp.Jer.6:16;Mt.11:29
(j) dealt bountifully
(j) Ps.13:6;119:17

Jer.6:16

v.16 Thus saith the LORD, Stand in the ways, and see, and ask for the old paths, where is the good way, and walk in it, and ye shall find rest for your souls. But they said, We will not walk in it.

Mt.11:29

v.29 **Take my yoke upon you, and learn of me; for I am meek and lowly in heart, and ye shall find rest unto your souls.**

Ps.13:6

v.6 I will sing unto the LORD, because he hath dealt bountifully with me.

Ps.119:17

v.17 Deal bountifully with thy servant, that I may live, and keep thy word.

v.8 (k) For thou hast delivered my soul from death, mine eyes from tears, and my feet from falling.

(k) For thou hast
(k) Ps.56:13

v.13 For thou hast delivered my soul from death. Wilt not thou deliver my feet from falling, that I may walk before God in the light of the living?

v.9 I will walk before the LORD in the land of the living.

v.10 (l) I believed, therefore have I spoken. I was greatly afflicted;

(l) I believed,
(l) 2Cor.4:13

v.13 We, having the same spirit of faith, according as it is written, I believed, and therefore have I spoken; we also believe, and therefore speak,

v.11 I said in my haste, All men are liars.
v.12 What shall I render unto the Lord for all his benefits toward me?
v.13 I will take the cup of salvation, and call upon the name of the Lord.
v.14 I will pay my vows unto the Lord now in the presence of all his people.
v.15 (m) Precious in the sight of the Lord is the death of his saints.

(m) Precious
(m) Rev.14:13cp.Ps.72:14

Rev.14:13

v.13 And I heard a voice from heaven saying unto me, Write, Blessed are the dead who die in the Lord from henceforth. Yea, saith the Spirit, that they may rest from their labors, and their works do follow them.

Ps.72:14

v.14 He shall redeem their soul from deceit and violence, and precious shall be given of the gold of Sheba; prayer also shall be made for him continually, and daily shall he be praised.

v.16 O Lord, truly I am thy servant; I am thy servant, and the son of thine handmaid; thou hast loosed my bonds.

v.17 I will offer to thee the (n) sacrifice of thanksgiving, and will call upon the name of the LORD.

(n) sacrifice of thanksgiving,
(n) Lev.7:12;Ps.50:14;107:22

Lev.7:12

v.12 If he offer it for a thanksgiving, then he shall offer with the sacrifice of thanksgiving unleavened cakes |mixed| with oil, and unleavened wafers anointed with oil, and cakes |mixed| with oil, of fine flour, fried.

Ps.50:14

v.14 Offer unto God thanksgiving, and pay thy vows unto the Most High,

Ps.107:22

v.22 And let them sacrifice the sacrifices of thanksgiving, and declare his works with rejoicing.

v.18 I will pay my vows unto the LORD now in the presence of all his peope,
v.19 In the courts of the LORD'S house. In the midst of thee, O Jerusalem. Praise ye the LORD.

THE UNIVERSAL PRAISE OF GOD

PSALM 117

v.1 OH, (o) praise the LORD, all ye nations; praise him, all ye people.

(o) praise the LORD,
(o) Rom.15:11

v.11 And again Praise the Lord, all ye | nations | ; and laud him, all ye peoples.

v.2 For his merciful kindness is great toward us; and the truth of the LORD endureth forever. Praise ye the LORD.

CHRIST AS THE STONE OR ROCK

PSALM 118

v.1 OH, give thanks unto the LORD, for he is good; (p) because
his mercy endureth forever.

(p) because his mercy endureth forever.
(p) Ps.136:1-26

v.1 OH, give thanks unto the LORD, for he is good; for his mercy endureth forever.
v.2 Oh, give thanks unto the God of gods; for his mercy endureth forever.
v.3 Oh, give thanks unto the Lord of lords; for his mercy endureth forever;

v.4 To him who alone doeth great wonders; for his mercy endureth forever;
v.5 To him who by wisdom made the heavens; for his mercy endureth forever;
v.6 To him who stretched out the earth above the waters; for his mercy endureth forever;
v.7 To him who made great lights; for his mercy endureth forever;
v.8 The sun to rule by day; for his mercy endureth forever;
v.9 The moon and stars to rule by night; for his mercy endureth forever;
v.10 To him who smote Egypt in their first-born; for his mercy endureth forever;
v.11 And brought out Israel from among them; for his mercy endureth forever;
v.12 With a strong hand, and with | an outstretched | arm; for his mercy endureth forever;
v.13 To him who divided the Red Sea into parts; for his mercy endureth forever;
v.14 And made Israel to pass through the midst of it; for his mercy endureth forever;
v.15 But overthrew Phar'aoh and his host in the Red Sea; for his mercy endureth forever;
v.16 To him who led his people through the wilderness; for his mercy endureth forever;
v.17 To him who smote great kings; for his mercy endureth forever;
v.18 And slew famous king's for his mercy endureth forever;
v.19 Sihon, king of the Amorites; for his mercy endureth forever;
v.20 And Og, the king of Bashan; for his mercy endureth forever;
v.21 And gave their land for an heritage; for his mercy endureth forever;
v.22 Even an heritage unto Israel, his servant; for his mercy endureth forever;
v.23 Who remembered us in our low estate; for his mercy endureth forever;

v.24 And hath redeemed us from our enemies; for his mercy endureth forever;
v.25 Who giveth food to all flesh; for his mercy endureth forever;
v.26 Oh, give thanks unto the God of heaven; for his mercy endureth forever;

v.2 Let Israel now say that his mercy endureth forever.
v.3 Let the house of Aaron now say that his mercy endureth forever;
v.4 Let them now who (b)fear the LORD say that his mercy endureth forever.

(b) fear
(b) Ps.19:9,note

v.9 The fear of the LORD is clean, enduring forever; the |ordinances| of the LORD are true and righteous altogether. 2(19:9) "The fear of the LORD" is an O.T. expression meaning reverential trust, including the hatred of evil.

v.5 I called upon the LORD in distress; the LORD answered me, and set me in a large place.
v.6 The (q) LORD is on my side; I will not fear. What can a man do unto me?

(q) LORD is on my side;
(q) Ps.56:9;Rom.8:31;Heb.13:6

Ps.56:9

v.9 When I cry unto thee, then shall mine enemies turn back: this I know; for God is for me.

Rom.8:31

v.31 What shall we then say to these things ? If God be for us, who can be against us?

Heb.13:6

v.6 So that we may boldly say, The Lord is my helper, and I will not fear what man shall do unto me.

v.7 The Lord taketh my part with those who help me; therefore shall I see my desire upon those who hate me.
v.8 It is better to trust in the Lord than to put confidence in (r) man.

(r) man
(r) Cp. 2Chr.32:7-8;Isa. 31:1-3

2Chr.32:7-8

v.7 Be strong and courageous, be not afraid nor for all the king of Assyria, nor for all the multitude who are with him; for there are more with us than with him.
v.8 With him is an arm of flesh; but with us is the Lord, our God, to help us, and to fight our battles. And the people rested themselves upon the words of Hezeki'ah, king of Judah.

Isa.31:1-3

v.1 Woe to those who go down to Egypt for help, and |rely| on horses, and trust in chariots, because they are many; and in horsemen, because they are very strong; but they look not unto the Holy One of Israel, neither seek the Lord!
v.2 Yet he also is wise, and will bring evil, and will not call back his words, but will arise against the house of the evildoers, and against the help of those who work iniquity.
v.3 Now the Egyptians are men, and not God; and their horses flesh, and not God; and their horses flesh, and not spirit. When the Lord shall stretch out his hand, both he that helpeth shall fall down, and he that is |helped| shall fall down, and they all shall fail together.

v.9 It is better to (a) trust in the LORD than to put trust confidence in princes.

(a) trust
(a)Ps.2:12,note

v.12 Kiss the Son, lest he be angry, and ye perish from the way, when his wrath is kindled but a little. Blessed are they who put their trust in him.

Note 1(2:12) Trust is the characteristic O.T. word the N.T. "faith," and "believe." It occur 152 times in the O.T., and is the rendering of Hebrew words signifying to take refuge (e.g. Ruth 2:12); to lean on (e.g. Ps.56:3); to roll on (e.g. Ps. 22:8); to wait for (e.g. Job.35:14).

v.10 All nations compassed me about, but in the name of the LORD will I destroy them.
v.11 (s) They compassed me about; yea, they compassed me about, but in the name of the LORD I will destroy them.

(s) They compassed me about;
(s) Ps.88:17

Ps. 88:17

v.17 They came round about me daily like water; they compassed me about together.

v.12 They compassed me about like (t) bee; they are quenched (u) like the fire of thorns, for in the name of the LORD I will destroy them.

(t) bee;
(t) cp. Dt.1:44
(u) like the fire of thorns.
(u) cp.Nah.1:10

Dt.1:44

v.44 And the Amorites, who dwelt in that mountain, came out against you, and chased you as bees do, and destroyed you in Seir, even unto Hormah.

Nah.1:10

v.10 For while they are |entangled| together like thorns, and while they are drunk like drunkards, they shall be devoured like stubble fully dry.

v.13 Thou hast thrust (v)|hard| at me that I might fall, but the LORD helped me.

(v) |hard|
(v) KJV sore

v.14 The (a) LORD is my strength and song, and is become my salvation.

(a) LORD
(a) Ex.15:2; Isa.12:2

Ex.15:2

v.2 The Lord is my strength and song, and he is become my salvation; he is my God, and I will prepare him an habitation; my father's God, and I will exalt him.

Isa.12:2

v.2 Behold, God is my salvation; I will trust, and not be afraid; for the LORD, even |the LORD|, is my strength and my song; he also is become my salvation.

v.15 The voice of rejoicing and salvation is in the tabernacles of the righteous; the right hand of the LORD doeth valiantly.

v.16 The right hand of the LORD is exalted; the right hand of the LORD doeth valiantly.
v.17 I shall (b) not die, but live, and declare the works of the LORD.

(b) not die,
(b) Ps.116:8-9;cp.Ps.6:5;Hab.1:12

Ps.116:8-9

v.8 For thou hast delivered my soul from death, mine eyes from tears, and my feet from falling.
v.9 I will walk before the LORD in the land of the living.

Ps.6:5

v.5 For in death there is no remembrance of thee; in |sheol| who shall give thee thanks?

Hab.1:12

v.12 Art thou not from everlasting, O LORD, my God, mine Holy One? We shall not die. O LORD, thou hast ordained them for judgment; and, O Mighty God, thou hast established them for correction.

v.18 The LORD (c) hath chastened me (d)|very much|, but he hath not given me over unto death.

(c) hath chastened me
(c) 2Cor.6:9
(d)|very much|
(d) KJV sore

2Cor.6:9

v.9 As unknown, and yet always well known; as dying, and, behold, we live; as chastened, and not killed;

(d) |very much|
(d) KJV sore

v.19 (e) Open to me the gates of righteousness; I will go into them, and I will praise the LORD,

(e) Open
(e) Isa.26:2;cp. Ps.24:7

Isa.26:2

v.2 Open ye gates, that the righteous nation that keepeth the truth may enter in.

Ps.24:7

v.7 Lift up your heads, O ye gates; and be ye lifted up, ye everlasting doors; and the King of glory shall come in.

v.20 This gate of the LORD, (f) into which the righteous shall enter.

(f) into which the righteous shall enter.
(f) Isa.35:8;Rev.21:27;22:14-15

Isa.35:8

v.8 And an highway shall be there, and a way, and it shall be called The way of holiness; the unclean shall not pass over it, but it shall be for those; the wayfaring men, though fools, shall not err therein.

Rev.21:27

v.27 And there shall in no |way| enter into it anything that defileth, neither he that worketh abomination, or maketh a lie, but they who are written in the Lamb's book of life.

Rev.22:14-15

v.14 Blessed are they that |wash their robes|, that they may have right to the tree of life, and may enter in through the gates into the city.

v.15 For |outside| are dogs, and sorcerers, and |fornicators|, and whosoever loveth and maketh a lie.

v.21 I will praise thee; for thou hast heard me, and art become my salvation.

v.22 The 1(g) stone which the builders refused is become the head of the corner.

1(g) stone which the builders;
(g) 1(118:22) Christ (Stone):v.22;
Isa.8:14.(Gen.49:24;1Pet.2:8).

Ps. 118 looks beyond the rejection of the Stone (Christ) to His final exaltation in the kingdom, See above,v.22

Isa.8:14

v.14 And he shall be for a sanctuary; but for a stone of stumbling and for a rock of offense to both the houses of Israel, for a |trap| and for a snare to the inhabitants of Jerusalem.

Gen.49:24

v.24 But his bow abode strength, and the arms of his hands were made strong by the hands of the mighty God of Jacob (from there is the shepherd, the stone of Israel),

1 Pet.2:8

v.8 And a stone of stumbling, and a rock of defense, even to them who stumble at the word, being disobedient; whereunto also they were appointed.

v.23 (h) This is the LORD'S doing; it is marvelous in our eyes.

(h) This is the LORD'S doing;
(h) lit. This is from the LORD

v.24 This is the day which the LORD hath made; we will rejoice and be glad in it.
v.25 Save now, I beseech thee, O LORD! O LORD, I beseech thee, send now prosperity!
v.26 (i) Blessed is he that cometh in the name of the LORD; we have blessed you out of the house of the LORD.

(i) Blessed is he that cometh;
(i) Mt.21:9;23:39;Mk.11:9;
Lk.13:35;19:38;Jn.12:13

Mt. 21:9

v.9 And the multitudes that went before, and that followed, cried, saying, Hosanna to the Son of David! Blessed is he that cometh in the name of the Lord! Hosanna in the highest!

Mt.23:39

v.39 For I say unto you, Ye shall not see me henceforth, till ye shall say, Blessed is he that cometh in the name of the Lord.

Mk.11:9

v.9 And they that before, and they that followed, cried, saying, Hosanna! Blessed is he that cometh in the name of the Lord.

Lk.13:35

v.35 **Behold, your house is left unto you desolate; and verily I say unto you, Ye shall not see me, until the**

time come when ye shall say, Blessed is he that cometh in the name of the Lord.

Lk.19:38

v. 38 Saying, Blessed be the king who cometh in the name of the Lord; peace in heaven, and glory in the highest.

Jn.12:13

v.13 Took branches of palm trees, and went forth to meet him, and cried, Hosanna! Blessed is the King of Israel, cometh in the name of the Lord.

v.27 God is the LORD, who hath shown us light; bind the sacrifice with cords, even unto the horns of the altar.
v.28 Thou art my God, and I will praise thee; thou art my God, I will exalt thee.
v.29 2 Oh, give thanks unto the LORD, for he is good; for his mercy endureth forever.

2(118:29) The Messianic Psalms: Summary. That the Psalms contain a testimony to Christ, our Lord Himself affirmed (Lk.24:44,etc.), and the N.T. quotations from the Psalter point unerringly to those Psalms which have the Messianic character. A similar spiritual and prophetic character identifies others. See Ps.2:1,note.

(1) Christ is seen in the Psalms in two general attitudes: as suffering (e.g. Ps.22), and as entering into His kingdom glory (e.g.Ps.2 and 24. Cp.Lk.24:25-27).
(2) Christ is seen in His Person as (a) Son of God (Ps.2:7), and very God (Ps.45:6-7;102:25;110:1); (b) Son of man (Ps.8:4-6); and (c) Son of David (Ps.89:3-4,27,29).
(3) Christ is seen in His offices as (a) Prophet (Ps.22:22,25;40:9-10);(b) Priest (Ps.110:4);and (c) King (e.g.Ps.2 and 24).
(4) Christ is seen in His varied work, As Priest He offers Himself in sacrifice (Ps.22;40:6-8,with Heb.10:5-12), and, in resurrection, as the Priest—Shepherd, ever

living to make intercession (Ps.23, with Heb.7:21-25; 13:20). As Prophet He proclaims the name of the LORD as Father (Ps.22:22, with Jn.20:17). As King He fulfills the Davidic Covenant (Ps.89) and restore alike the dominion of man over creation (Ps.8:4-8;Rom.8:17-21) and the Father over all (1Cor.15:25-28).

(5) The Messianic Psalms give also the inner thoughts, the exercises of soul, of Christ in His earthly experiences (e.g. Ps.16:8-11;22:1-21;40:1-17).

118—Messianic Psalm—Scofield
Hallelujah (Hallel)—Scofield
Thanksgiving—King James Study Bible (Nelson)

VI
IN PRAISE OF GOD'S WORD

PSALM 119

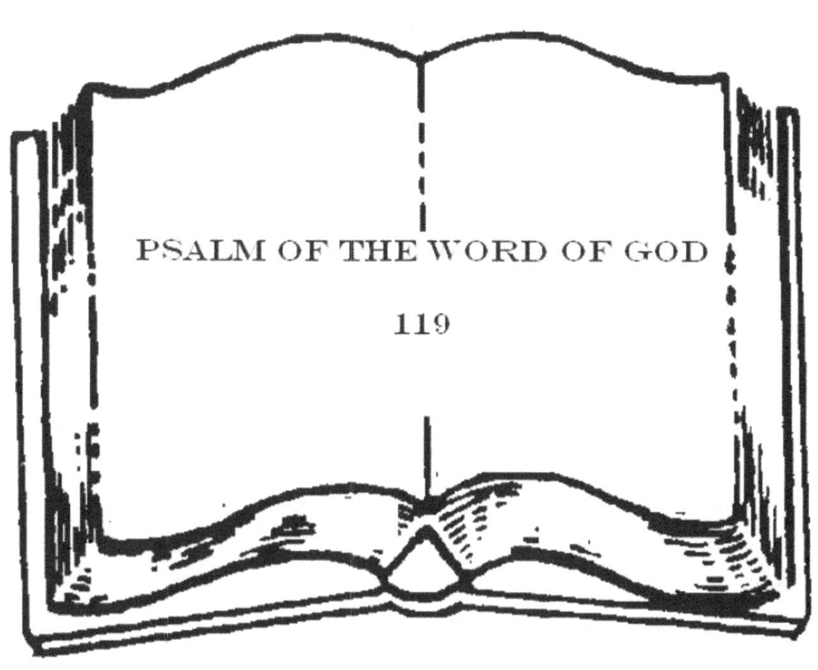

IN PRAISE OF GOD'S WORD

PSALM 119

3 A'LEPH
(1)

v.1 BLESSED are the undefiled in the way, who walk in the (4j) law of the LORD.

(4j) law
(j) Law (of Moses):vv.1-176;
Isa.1:10.(Ex.19:1;Gal.3:24)

v.1 BLESSED are the undefiled in the way, who walk in the (4j) law of the LORD.
v.2 Blessed are they that keep his testimonies, and that seek him with the (a) whole heart.
v.3 (b) They also do no iniquity; they walk in his ways.
v.4 Thou hast commanded us to keep thy precepts diligently.
v.5 Oh, that my ways were directed to keep thy statutes!
v.6 Then shall I not be ashamed, when I have respect unto thy commandments.
v.7 I will praise thee with uprightness of heart, when I shall have learned thy righteous judgments.
v.8 I will keep thy statutes; oh, forsake me not utterly.

BETH

v.9 Wherewithal shall a young man cleanse his way? By taking heed thereto according to thy word.

v.10 (c) With my whole heart have I sought thee; oh, let me not wander from thy commandments.
v.11 Thy word have I hidden in mine heart, that I might not sin against thee.
v.12 Blessed art thou, O LORD; teach me thy statutes.
v.13 With my lips have I declared all the (d) | ordinances | of thy mouth.
v.14 I have rejoiced in the way of thy testimonies, as much as in all riches.
v.15 I will meditate in thy precepts, and have respect unto thy ways.
v.16 I will delight myself in thy statutes; I will not forget thy word.

GI'MEL

v.17 (e) Deal bountifully with thy servant, that I may live, and keep thy word.
v.18 Open thou mine eyes, that I may behold wondrous things out of thy law.
v.19 I am a (f) | sojourner | in the earth; hide not thy commandments from me.
v.20 My soul breaketh for the longing that it hath unto thine (d) | ordinances | at all times.
v.21 Thou hast rebuked the proud who are cursed, who do err from thy commandments.
v.22 (g) Remove from me reproach and contempt; for I have kept thy testimonies.
v.23 Princes also did sit and speak against me, but thy servant did meditate in thy statutes.
v.24 Thy testimonies also are my delight and my counselors.

DA'LETH

v.25 My soul (h) | clingeth to | the dust; (i) | revive | me according to thy word.
v.26 I have declared my ways, and thou heardest me; teach me thy statutes.

v.27 Make me to understand the way of thy precepts; (j) so shall I talk of thy wondrous works.
v.28 My soul (k) melteth for heaviness; (l) strengthen thou me according unto thy word.
v.29 Remove from me the way of lying, and grant me thy law graciously.
v.30 I have chosen the way of truth; thine (d) | ordinances | have I laid before me.
v.31 I have (m) | clung | unto thy testimonies; O LORD, put me not to shame.
v.32 I will run the way of thy commandments, when thou shalt (n) enlarge my heart.

HE

v.33 Teach me, O LORD, the way of thy statutes, and I shall keep it unto the end.
v.34 (o) Give me understanding, and I shall keep thy law; yea, I shall observe it with my whole heart.
v.35 Make me to go in the path of thy commandments; for therein do I delight
v.36 Incline my heart unto thy testimonies, and not to (p) covetousness.
v.37 Turn away mine eyes from beholding vanity, and (i) | revive | thou me in thy way.
v.38 (q) | Establish | thy word unto thy servant, who is devoted to thy (r) fear.
v.39 Turn away my reproach which I fear; for thine (d) | ordinances | are good.
v.40 Behold, I have longed after thy precepts; (s) | give me life | in thy righteousness.

VAV

v.41 Let thy mercies come also unto me, O LORD, even thy salvation, according to thy word.
v.42 So shall I have wherewith to answer him that reproacheth me; for I trust in thy word.

v.43 And take not the word of truth utterly out of my mouth; for I have hoped in thine (d) | ordinances |.
v.44 So shall I keep thy law continually forever and ever.
v.45 And I will walk at (a) liberty; for I seek thy precepts.
v.46 (b) I will speak of thy testimonies also before kings, and will not be ashamed.
v.47 And I will delight myself in thy commandments, which I have loved.
v.48 My hands also will I lift up unto thy commandments, which I have loved; and I will meditate in thy statutes.

ZA'YIN

v.49 Remember the word unto thy servant, upon which thou hast caused me to hope.
v.50 This is my comfort in my affliction; for thy word hath (c) | given me life |.
v.51 The proud have had me greatly in derision; yet have I not declined from thy law.
v.52 I remembered thine (d) | ordinances | of old, O LORD, and have comforted myself.
v.53 (e) Horror hath taken hold upon me because of the wicked who forsake thy law.
v.54 Thy statutes have been my songs in the house of my pilgrimage.
v.55 I have remembered thy name, O LORD, in the night, and have kept thy law.
v.56 This I had, because I kept thy precepts.

KHETH

v.57 (f) Thou art my portion, O LORD; I have said that I would keep thy words.
v.58 I entreated thy (g) favor with my whole heart; be merciful unto me according to thy word.
v.59 I (h) thought on my ways, and turned my feet unto thy testimonies.
v.60 I made haste, and delayed not to keep thy commandments.

v.61 The bands of the wicked have robbed me, but I have not forgotten thy law.
v.62 At midnight I will rise to give thanks unto thee, because of thy righteous (d) | ordinances | .
v.63 I am a companion of all those who (i) fear thee, and of those who keep thy precepts.
v.64 The earth, O LORD, is full of thy mercy; teach me thy statutes.

TETH

v.65 Thou hast dealt well with thy servant, O LORD, according unto thy word.
v.66 Teach me good judgment and (j) knowledge; for I have believed thy commandments.
v.67 Before I was (k) afflicted I went astray, but I kept thy word.
v.68 Thou art good, and doest good; teach me thy statutes.
v.69 The proud have forged a lie against me, but I will keep thy precepts with my whole heart.
v.70 Their heart is as fat as grease, but I delight in thy law.
v.71 It is good for me that I have been afflicted, that I might learn thy statutes.
v.72 The law of thy mouth is better unto me than thousands of gold and silver.

YODH

v.73 Thy hands have made me and (l) fashioned me; give me understanding, that I may learn thy commandments.
v.74 They that (i) fear thee will be (m) glad when they see me, because I have hoped in thy word.
v.75 I know, O LORD, that thy judgments are right, and (n) that thou in faithfulness hast afflicted me.
v.76 Let, I pray thee, thy merciful kindness be for my comfort, according to thy word unto thy servant.
v.77 Let thy tender mercies come unto me, that I may live; for thy law is my (o) delight.

v.78 Let the proud be ashamed; for they dealt perversely with me without a cause; but I will meditate in thy precepts.
v.79 Let those who fear thee turn unto me, and those who have known thy testimonies.
v.80 Let my heart be sound in thy statutes, that I be not ashamed.

KAPH

v.81 (p) My soul fainteth for thy salvation, but I hope in thy word.
v.82 Mine eyes fail for thy word, saying, When wilt thou comfort me?
v.83 For I am become like a (q) | wine skin | in the smoke; yet do I not forget thy statutes.
v.84 How many are the days of thy servant? (r) When wilt thou execute judgment on those who persecute me?
v.85 The proud have digged pits for me, which are not after thy law.
v.86 All thy commandments are faithful. They persecute me wrongfully; help thou me.
v.87 They had almost consumed me upon earth, but I forsook not thy precepts.
v.88 (a) | Revive | me after thy loving kindness; so shall I keep the testimony of thy mouth.

LA'MEDH

v.89 (b) Forever, O LORD, thy word is settled in heaven.
v.90 Thy faithfulness is unto all generations; thou hast established the earth, and it abideth.
v.91 They continue this day according to thine ordinances; for all are thy servants.
v.92 Unless thy law had been my delight, I should then have perished in mine affliction.
v.93 I will never forget thy precepts; for with them thou hast (c) | given me life |.
v.94 I am thine; save me; for I have sought thy precepts.

v.95 The wicked have waited for me to destroy me, but I will consider thy testimonies.
v.96 I have seen an end of all perfection, but thy commandment is exceedingly broad.

MEM

v.97 Oh, how love I thy law! (d) It is my meditation all the day.
v.98 Thou, through thy commandments, hast made me (e) wiser than mine enemies; for they are ever with me.
v.99 I have more understanding than all my teachers; for thy (f) testimonies are my meditation.
v.100 I understand more than the (g) ancients, because I kept thy precepts.
v.101 I have (h) | restrained | my feet from every evil way, that I might keep thy word.
v.102 I have not departed from thine (i) | ordinances | ; for thou hast taught me.
v.103 How sweet are thy words unto my taste! Yea, sweeter than honey to my mouth.
v.104 Through thy precepts I get understanding; therefore, I hate every false way.

NUN

v.105 Thy word is a (j) lamp unto my feet, and a light unto my path.
v.106 I have (k) sworn, and I will perform it, that I will keep thy righteous (i) | ordinances | .
v.107 I am afflicted very much; (a) | revive | me, O LORD, according unto thy word.
v.108 Accept, I beseech thee, the (l) freewill offerings of my mouth, O LORD, and teach me thine (i) | ordinances | .
v.109 My soul is continually in my hand; yet do I not forget thy law.
v.110 The wicked have laid a snare for me; yet I erred not from thy precepts.

v.111 (m) Thy testimonies have I taken as an heritage forever; for they are the rejoicing of my heart.
v.112 I have inclined mine heart to perform thy statutes always, even unto the end.

SA'MEKH

v.113 I hate vain thoughts, but thy law do I love.
v.114 Thou art my (n) hiding place and my shield; I hope in thy word.
v.115 (o) Depart from me, ye evildoers; for I will keep the commandments of my God.
v.116 Uphold me according unto thy word. that I may live; and let me not be (p) ashamed of my hope.
v.117 Hold thou me up, and I shall be safe; and I will have respect unto thy statutes continually.
v.118 Thou hast trodden down al those who err from thy statutes; for their deceit is falsehood.
v.119 Thou puttest away all the wicked of the earth (q) like dross; therefore, I love thy testimonies.
v.120 (r) My flesh trembleth for fear of thee, and I am afraid of thy judgments.

A'YIN

v.121 I have (s) | executed justice and righteousness | ; leave me not to mine oppressors.
v.122 Be surety for thy servant for good; let not the proud oppress me.
v.123 Mine eyes fail for thy salvation, and for the word of thy righteousness.
v.124 Deal with thy servant according unto thy mercy, and (t) teach me thy statutes.
v.125 I am thy servant; give me understanding, that I may know thy testimonies.
v.126 It is time for thee, LORD, to work; for they have made void thy law.
v.127 Therefore, I love thy commandments above gold; yea, above fine gold.

v.128 Therefore, I esteem all thy precepts concerning all things to be right, and I hate every false way.

PE

v.129 Thy testimonies are wonderful; therefore doth my soul keep them.
v.130 The entrance of thy words giveth (a) light; it giveth understanding unto the (b) simple.
v.131 I opened my mouth, and (c) panted; for I longed for thy commandments.
v.132 (c) Look thou upon me, and be (e) merciful unto me, as thou (f) | dost | unto those who love thy name.
v.133 Order my steps in thy word, and let not any iniquity have (g) dominion over me.
v.134 (h) Deliver me from the oppression of man; so will I keep thy precepts.
v.135 (i) Make thy face to shine upon thy servant, and teach me thy statutes.
v.136 Rivers of waters run down (j) mine eyes, because they keep not thy law.

TSADHE

v.137 Righteous art thou, O LORD, and upright are thy judgments.
v.138 Thy testimonies that thou hast commanded are righteous and very faithful.
v.139 My zeal hath consumed me, because mine enemies have forgotten thy words.
v.140 Thy word is very (k) pure; therefore, thy servant loveth it.
v.141 I am small and despised; yet do not I forget thy precepts.
v.142 Thy righteousness is an everlasting righteousness, and thy law is the (l) truth.
v.143 Trouble and anguish have taken hold of me; yet thy commandments are my delight.
v.144 The righteousness of thy testimonies is everlasting; give me understanding, and I shall live.

QOPH

v.145 I cried with my whole heart. Hear me, O Lord; will keep thy statutes.
v.146 I cried unto thee. Save me, and I shall keep thy testimonies.
v.147 I (m) | anticipated | the dawning of the (n) morning, and cried; I hoped in thy word.
v.148 Mine eyes (o) | anticipate | the night watches, that I might meditate in thy word.
v.149 Hear my voice, according unto thy loving-kindness; O Lord, (p) | revive | me according to my (q) | justice | .
v.150 They draw (r) | near | that follow after mischief; they are far from thy law.
v.151 Thou art near, O Lord, and all thy commandments are truth.
v.152 Concerning thy testimonies, I have known of old that thou hast founded them forever.

RESH

v.153 (s) Consider mine affliction, and deliver me; for I do not forget thy law.
v.154 (t) Plead my cause, and (u) deliver me; (p) | revive | me according to thy word.
v.155 Salvation is far from the wicked; for they seek thy statutes.
v.156 Great are thy tender mercies, O Lord; (p) | revive | me according to thine (v) | ordinances | .
v.157 Many are my persecutors and mine enemies; yet do I not (w) decline from thy testimonies.
v.158 I beheld the transgressions, and was grieved, because they kept not thy word.
v.159 Consider how I love thy precepts; (p) | revive | me, O Lord, according to thy loving-kindness.
v.160 Thy word Is true from the beginning, and every one thy righteous (v) | ordinances | endureth forever.

SHIN

v.161 (x) Prince have persecuted me without a cause, but my heart standeth in awe of thy word.
v.162 I rejoice at thy word, as one that findeth great spoil.
v.163 I hate and abhor lying, but thy law do I love.
v.164 Seven times a day do I praise thee, because of thy righteous (v) | ordinances | .
v.165 (y) Great peace have they who love thy law, and (z) nothing shall offend them.
v.166 LORD, I have hoped for thy (aa) salvation, and done thy commandments.
v.167 My soul hath kept thy testimonies, and I love them exceedingly.
v.168 I have kept thy precepts and thy testimonies; for all my ways are before thee.

TAV

v.169 Let my cry come near before thee, O LORD; (bb) give me understanding, according to thy word.
v.170 Let my supplication come before thee; deliver me, according to thy word.
v.171 My lips shall utter praise, when thou hast taught me thy statutes.
v.172 My tongue shall speak of thy word; for all thy commandments are righteousness.
v.173 Let thine hand help me; for I have chosen thy precepts.
v.174 I have longed for thy salvation, O LORD, and thy law Is my delight.
v.175 Let my soul live, and it shall praise thee; and let thine (a) | ordinances | help me.
v.176 I have (b) gone astray like a lost sheep. Seek thy servant; for I do not forget thy commandments.

Isa.1:10

v.10 Hear the word of the LORD, ye rulers of Sodom; give ear unto the law of our God, ye people of Gomor'rah.

Ex.19:1

v.1 In the third month, when the children of Israel were gone forth out of the land of Egypt, the same day came they into the wilderness of Sinai.

Gal.3:24

v.24 Wherefore, the law was our schoolmaster to bring us unto Christ, that we might be justified by faith.

v.2 Blessed are they that keep his testimonies and that seek him with the (a) whole heart.

(a) whole heart
(a) Dt.6:5; 10:12; 11:13; 13:3

Dt.6:5

v.5 And thou shalt love the Lord thy God with all thine heart, and with all thy soul, and with all thy might.

Dt.10:12

v.12 And now, Israel, what doth the LORD thy God require of thee, but to fear the LORD thy God to walk in all his ways and to love him, and to serve the LORD thy God with all thy heart and with all thy soul,

Dt.11:13

v.13 And it shall come to pass hearken diligently unto my commandments which I command you this day, to serve him with all your heart and with all your soul,

Dt.13:3

v.3 Thou shalt not hearken unto the words of that prophet, or that dreamer of dreams; for the Lord your

God | testeth | you, to know whether ye love the LORD
your God with all your heart and with all your soul.

v.3 (b) They also do no iniquity; they walk in his ways.

(b) They also
(b) 1 Jn.3:9;5:18

1Jn.3:9

v.9 Whosoever Is born of God doth not commit sin; for
his seed remaineth in him, and he cannot sin, because
he Is born of God.

1Jn.5:18

v.18 We know that whosoever is born of God sinneth not,
but he that is begotten of God keepeth himself, and
that wicked one toucheth him not.

v.4 Thou hast commanded us to keep thy precepts diligently.
v.5 Oh, that my ways were directed to keep thy statutes!
v.6 Then shall I not be ashamed, when I have respect unto all
thy commandments.
v.7 I will praise thee with uprightness of heart, when I shall
have learned thy righteous judgments.
v.8 I will keep thy statutes; oh, forsake me not utterly.

4(119:1) This Psalm, born of love for the law of God, extols the beauties and excellences of the written Word of God in a way found nowhere else in the Bible. God's Word is treated under these designations: (1) law; (2) word (words); (3) ordinances; (4) commandments; (5) precepts; (6) testimonies: (7) statutes; and (8) judgments. "Judgments" and "ordinances" are translations of the same Hebrew word. Only vv. 90,121,122.and 132 do not give a synonym for the law.

The shades of meaning in the words employed are as follows: "Law" is primarily instrution or teaching, then all of God's revelations for life. "Word" is speech or utterance, a general word for the disclosure of God's will. "Ordinance" (also "judgments") refer to legal pronouncements, rules of divine administration. "Commandments" are authoritative orders used as religious principles. "Precepts" relate to man's moral obligations as enjoined by God. "Testimonies" indicate God's own declarations concerning His nature and purpose. "Statutes" refer elsewhere to civil and religious appointments of the Mosaic law. The word "way" is used as a synonym for all of these terms.

BETH
(2)

v.9 Wherefore shall a young man cleanse his ways? By taking heed thereof according to thy word.
v.10 (c) With my whole heart have I sought thee; oh, let me not wander from thy commandments.

(c) With my whole heart
(c) Cp.2Chr.15:15

v.15 And all Judah rejoiced at the oath; for they had sworn with all their heart, and sought him with their whole desire, and he was found by them. And the LORD gave them rest round about.

v.11 Thy word have I hidden in mine heart, that I might not sin against thee.
v.12 Blessed art thou, O LORD; teach me thy statutes.
v.13 With my lips have I declared all the (d) | ordinances | of thy mouth.

(d) | ordinances |
(d) KJV judgments

v.14 I have rejoiced in the way of thy testimonies, as much as in all riches.

v.15 I will meditate in thy precepts, and have respect unto thy ways.

v.16 I will delight myself in thy statutes; I will not forget thy word.

GI'MEL
(3)

v.17 (e) Deal bountiful with thy servant, that I may live, and keep thy word.

(e) deal bountiful
(e) Ps.116:7

v.7 Return unto thy rest, O my soul; for the LORD hath dealt bountifully with thee.

v.18 Open thou mine eyes, that I may behold wondrous things out of thy law.

v.19 I am a (f) | sojourner | in the earth; hide not thy commandments from me.

(f) | sojourner |
(f) KJV stranger.
1Chr.29:15;Ps.39:12;
Heb.11:13;cp.2Cor.5:6

1Chr.29:15

v.15 And they gathered their brethren, and sanctified themselves, and came, according to the commandments of the king, by the words of the LORD, to cleanse the house of the LORD.

Ps.39:12

v.12 Hear my prayer, O LORD, and give ear unto my cry. Hold not thy peace at my tears; for I am a stanger with thee, and a sojourner, as all my fathers were.

Heb.11:13

v.13 These all died in faith, not having received the promises but having seen them afar off, and were persuaded of them, and embraced them, and confessed that they were strangers and pilgrims on the earth.

2Cor.5:6

v.6 Therefore we are always confident, knowing that, while we are at home in the body, we are absent from the Lord

v.20 My soul breaketh for the longing that it hath unto thine (d) | ordinances | at all times.

(d) | ordinances |
(d) KJV judgments

v.21 Thou hast rebuked the proud who are cursed, who do err from thy commandments.
v.22 (g) Remove from me reproach and contempt; for I have kept thy testimonies.

(g) remove from me
(g) Ps.39:8

v.8 Deliver me from all my transgressions; make me not the reproach of the foolish.

v.23 Princes also did sit and speak against me, but thy servant did meditate in thy statutes.
v.24 Thy testimonies also are my delight and my counselors.

DA'LETH
(4)

v.25 My soul (h) | clingeth to | the dust; (i) | revive | me according to thy word.

(h) | clingeth to |
(h) KJV cleaveth unto.
Ps.44:25
(i) | revive | me
(i) KJV quicken.
Ps. 143:11

Ps.44:25

v.25 For our soul is bowed down to the dust; our belly cleaveth unto the earth.

Ps.143:11

v.11 | Revive | me, O LORD, for thy name's sake; for thy righteousness sake bring my soul out of trouble.

v.26 I have declared my ways, and thou heardest me; teach me thy statutes.
v.27 Make me to understand the way of thy precepts; (j) so shall I talk of thy wondrous works.

(j) so shall I talk
(j) Ps.145:5-6

v.5 I will speak of the glorious honor of thy majesty, and thy wondrous works.
v.6 And men shall speak of the might of thy | awe-inspiring | acts; and I will declare thy greatness.

v.28 My soul (k) melteth for heaviness; (l) strengthen thou me according unto thy words.

(k) melteth for
(k) Lit. droppeth
(l) strengthen
(l) Cp.1Pet.5:10

v.10 But the God of all grace, who hath called us unto his

eternal glory by Christ Jesus, after ye have suffered awhile, make you perfect, |establish|, strengthen, settle you.

v.29 Remove from me the way of lying, and grant me thy law graciously.
v.30 I have chosen the way of truth; thine (d) |ordinances| have I had before me.

(d) |ordinances|
(d) KJV judgments

v.31 I have (m) |clung| unto thy testimonies; O LORD, put me not to shame.

(m) |clung|
(m) KJV stuck

v.32 I will run the way of thy commandments, when thou shalt (n) enlarge my heart.

(n) enlarge my heart
(n) Cp. 1Ki.4:29;Isa.60:5;2Cor.6:11

1 Ki.4:29

v.29 And God gave Solomon wisdom and |very| much understanding, and largeness of heart, even as the sand that is on the seashore.

Isa.60:5

v.5 Then thou shalt see, and flow together, and thine heart shall fear, and be enlarged, because the abundance of the sea shall be converted unto thee, the forces of the |nations| shall come unto thee.

2Cor.6:11

v.11 O ye Corinthians, our speech to you is candid, our heart is wide open.

HE
(5)

v.33 Teach me, O LORD, the way of thy statutes, and I shall keep it unto the end.
v.34 (o) Give me understanding, and I shall keep thy law; yea, I shall observe it with my whole heart.

(o) Give me understanding;
(o) v.73;Prov.2:6;Jas.1:5

Ps.119:73

v.73 Thy hands have made me and fashioned me; give me understanding, that I may learn thy commandments.

Prov.2:6

v.6 For the LORD giveth wisdom; out of his mouth cometh knowledge and understanding.

Jas.1:5

v.5 If any of you lack wisdom, let him ask of God, who giveth to all men liberally, and upbraideth not, and it shall be given him.

v.35 Make me to go in the path of thy commandments; for therein do I delight.
v.36 Incline my heart unto thy testimonies, and not to (p) covetousness.

(p) covetousness
(p)Ezek.33:31;Mk.7:21-22;1Tim.6:10;Heb.13:5

Ezek.33:31

v.31 And they come unto thee as the people come, and they sit before thee as my people, and they hear thy words, but they will not do them; for with their mouth they show much love, but their heart goeth after their covetousness.

Mk.7:21-22

v.21 **For from within, out of the heart of men, proceed evil thoughts, adulteries, fornications, adulteries, fornications, murders,**
v.22 **Thefts, covetousness, wickedness, deceit, lasciviousness, an evil eye, blasphemy, pride, foolishness.**

1Tim.6:10

v.10 For the love of money is the root of all evil, which, while some coveted after, they have erred from the faith, and pierced themselves through with many sorrows.

Heb.13:5

v.5 Let your |manner of life| be without covetousness, and be content with such things as ye have; for he hath said, I will never leave thee, nor forsake thee.

v.37 Turn away mine eyes from beholding vanity, and (i)|revive| thou me in thy way.

(i)|revive| thou me
(i) KJV quicken.

Ps.143:11

v.11 |Revive| me, O LORD, for thy name's sake; for thy righteousness sake bring my soul; for I am thy servant.

v.38 (q)|Establish| thy word unto thy servant, who is devoted to thy (r) fear.

(q) |Establish| thy word
(q) KJV Stablish.
Cp.2Sam.7:25
(r) fear;
(r) See Ps.19:9,note
See Ps.23:4 Messianic Psalm

2Sam.7:25

v.25 And now, O LORD God, the word that thou hast spoken concerning thy servant, and concerning his house, establish it forever, and do as thou hast said.

v.39 Turn away my reproach which I fear; for thine (d)|ordinances| are good.

(d)|ordinances|
(d) KJV judgments

v.40 Behold, I have longed after thy precepts; (s) |give me life| in thy righteousness.

(s) |give me life|
(s) KJV quicken me.

VAV
(6)

v.41 Let thy mercies come also unto me, O Lord, even thy salation, according to thy word.
v.42 So shall I have wherewith to answer him that reproacheth me; for I (t) trust in thy word.

(t) trust
(t) See Ps.2:12,note
See Ps.40:4 Messianic Psalm

v.43 And take not the word of truth utterly out my mouth; for I have hoped in thine (d) | ordinances | .

(d) | ordinances |
(d) KJV judgments

v.44 So shall I keep thy law continually forever and ever.
v.45 And I will walk at (a) liberty; for I seek thy precepts.

(a) liberty;
(a) Prov.4:12

v.12 When thou goest, thy steps shall not be | hindered | ; and when thou runnest, thou shalt not stumble.

v.46 (b) I will speak of thy testimonies also before kings, and will not be ashamed.

(b) I will speak
(b) Ps.138:1;cp.Mt.10:18-19;
Acts 26:1-29

Ps.138:1

v.1 I WILL praise thee with my whole heart; before the gods will I sing praise unto thee.

Mt.10:18-19

v.18 **And ye shall be brought before governors and kings for my sake, for a testimony against them and the Gentiles.**

v.19 **But when they deliver you up, |be not anxious| how or what ye shall speak; for it shall be given you in that same hour what ye shall speak.**

Acts 26:1-29

v.1 THEN Agrip'pa said unto Paul, Thou art permitted to speak for thyself. Then Paul stretched forth the hand, and answered for himself:

v.2 I think myself happy, King Agrip'pa, because I shall answer for myself this day before thee |concerning| all the things of which I am accused of the Jews,

v.3 Especially because I know thee to be expert in all customs and questions which are among the Jews; wherefore, I beseech thee to hear me patiently.

v.4 My manner of life from my youth, which was at the first among mine own nation at Jerusalem, know all the Jews,

v.5 Who knew me from the beginning, if they would testify, that after the |strictest| sect of our religion I lived a Pharisee.

v.6 And now I stand and am judged for the hope of the promise made of God unto our fathers,

v.7 Unto which promise our twelve tribes, |earnestly| serving God day and night, hope to come. For which hope's sake, King Agrip'pa, I am accused by the Jews.

v.8 Why should it be thought a thing incredible with you, that God should raise the dead?

v.9 I verily thought within myself, that I ought to do many things contrary to the name of Jesus of Nazareth,

v.10 Which thing I also did in Jerusalem; and many of the saints did I shut up in prison, having received authority from the chief priests. And when they were put to death, I gave my voice against them.

v.11 And I punished them |often| in every synagogue,
and compelled them to blaspheme; and being
exceedingly mad against them, I persecuted them
even unto |foreign| cities.
v.12 Wherefore, as I went to Damascus with authority and
commission from the chief priests,
v.13 At midday, O king, I saw in the way a light from
heaven, above the brightness of the sun, shining
round about me and them who journeyed with me.
v.14 And when we were all fallen to the earth, I heard a
voice speaking unto me, and saying in Hebrew
tongue, **Saul, Saul, why persecutes thou me? It is
hard for thee to kick against the |goads|.**
v.15 And I said, Who art thou, Lord? And he said, **I am
Jesus, whom thou persecutes.**
v.16 **But rise, and stand upon thy feet; for I have appeared
unto thee for this purpose, to make thee a minister
and a witness both of these things which thou hast
seen, and of those things in which I will appear unto
thee;**
v.17 **Delivering thee from the people, and from the
Gentiles, unto whom now I send thee,**
v.18 **To open their eyes, and to turn them from darkness to
light, and from the power of Satan unto God, that they
may receive forgiveness of sins, and inheritance
among them who are sanctified by faith that is in me.**
v.19 Whereupon, O King Agrip'pa, I was not disobedient
unto the heavenly vision,
v.20 But showed first unto them of Damascus, and at Jerusalem,
and throughout all the |borders| of Judaea, and then to
the Gentiles, that they should repent and turn to God, and
do works |fit| for repentance.
v.21 For these causes the Jews caught me in the temple,
and went about to kill me.
v.22 Having, therefore, obtained help from God, I
continue unto this day, witnessing both to small and
great, saying no other things than those which the
prophets and Moses did say should come:

v.23 That Christ should suffer, and that he should be the first that should rise from the dead, and should show light unto the people, and to the Gentiles,
v.24 And as he thus spoke for himself, Festus said with a loud voice, Paul, thou art beside thyself; much learning doth make thee mad.
v.25 But he said, I am not mad, most noble Festus, but speak forth the words of truth and soberness.
v.26 For the king knoweth of these things, before whom also I speak freely; for I am persuaded that none of these things are hidden from him; for this thing was not done in a corner.
v.27 King Agrip'pa, believest thou the prophets? I know that thou believest.
v.28 Then Agrip'pa said unto Paul, Almost thou persuades me to be a Christian.
v.29 And Paul said, I would to God that not only thou but also all that hear me this day were both almost, and altogether, such as I am, except these bonds.

v.47 And I will delight myself in thy commandments, which I have loved.
v.48 My hands also will I lift up unto thy commandments, which I have loved; and I will meditate in thy statutes.

ZA'YIN
(7)

v.49 Remember the word unto thy servant, upon which thou hast caused me to hope.
v.50 This is my comfort in my affliction; for thy word hath (c) |given me life|.

(c) |given me life|
(c) KJV quickened me. v.40

v.40 Behold, I have longed after thy precepts; |give me life| in thy righteousness.

v.51 The proud have had me greatly in derision; yet have I not declined from thy law.
v.52 I remembered thine (d) | ordinances | of old, O LORD, and have comforted myself.

(d) | ordinances |
(d) KJV judgments. v.106

v.106 I have sworn, and I will perform it, that I will keep thy righteous (i) | ordinances |.

v.53 (e) Horror hath taken hold upon me because of the wicked who forsake thy law.

(e) Horror hath taken hold
(e) cp.Ex.32:19;Ezra 9:1-4
Neh.13:25

Ex.32:19

v.19 And it came to pass, as soon as he came | near | unto the camp, that he saw the calf, and the dancing; and Moses' anger | burned |, and he cast the tables out of his hands, and broke them beneath the mount.

Ezra 9:1-4

v.1 Now when these things were done, the princes came to me, saying, The people of Israel, and the priests, and the Levites, have not separated themselves from the people of the lands, doing according to their abominations, of the Ca'naanites, the Hittites, the Periz'zites, the Jeb'u-sites, the Ammonites, the Moabites, the Egyptians, and the Amorites.
v.2 For they have taken of their daughters for themselves, and for their sons, so that the holy seed have | mixed | themselves with the people of those lands; yea, the hand of the princes and rulers hath been | first | in this trespass.

v.3 And when I heard this thing, I |tore| my garment and my mantle, and plucked off the hair of my head and of my beard, and sat down |appalled|.

v.4 Then were assembled unto me everyone who trembled at the words of the God of Israel, because of the transgression of those who had been carried away; and I sat |appalled| until the evening sacrifice.

Neh.13:25

v.25 And I contended with them, and cursed them, and smote certain of them, and plucked off their hair, and made them swear by God, saying, Ye shall not give your daughters unto their sons, nor take their daughters unto your sons, or for yourselves.

v.54 Thy statutes have been my songs in the house of my pilgrimage.

v.55 I have remembered thy name, O LORD, in the night, and have kept thy law.

v.56 This I had, because I kept thy precepts.

KHETH
(8)

v.57 (f) Thou art my portion, O LORD; I have said that I would keep thy words.

(f) Thou art my portion,
(f) Num.18:20Ps.16:5;Lam.3:24

Num.18:20

v.20 And the LORD spoke unto Aaron, Thou shalt have no inheritance in their land, neither shalt thou have any part among them: I am thy part and thine inheritance among the children of Israel.

Ps.16:5

v.5 The Lord is the portion of mine inheritance and of my cup; thou maintainest my lot.

Lam.3:24

v.24 The Lord is my portion, saith my soul; therefore will I hope in him.

v.58 I entreated thy (g) favor with my whole heart; be merciful unto me according to thy word.

(g) favor
(g) Lit. face

v.59 I (h) thought on my ways, and turned my feet unto thy testimonies.

(h) thought on my ways,
(h) Cp. Lk.15:17-18

Lk.15:17-18

v.17 **And when he came to himself, he said, How many of my father's hired servants have bread enough and to spare, and I perish with hunger!**
v.18 **I will arise and go to my father, and will say unto him, Father, I have sinned against heaven, and before thee,**

v.60 I made haste, and delayed not to keep thy commandments.
v.61 The bands of the wicked have robbed me, but I have not forgotten thy law.
v.62 At midnight I will rise to give thanks unto thee, because of thy righteous (d) | ordinances | .

(d) | ordinances |
(d) KJV judgments. v.106
See above v.52

v.63 I am a companion of all those who (i) fear thee, and of those who keep thy precepts.

(i) fear thee,
(i) See Ps.19:9,note
See Ps.23:4 Messianic Psalm

v.64 The earth, O LORD, Is full of thy mercy; teach me thy statutes.

TETH
(9)

v.65 Thou hast dealt well with thy servant, O LORD, according unto thy word.
v.66 Teach me good judgment and (j) knowledge; for I have believed thy commandments.

(j) knowledge;
(j) Phil.1:9

v.9 And this I pray, that your love may abound yet more and more in knowledge and In all judgment;

v.67 Before I was (k) afflicted I went astray, but now have I kept thy word.

(k) afflicted
(k) Prov.3:11;Heb.12:5-11

Prov.3:11

v.11 My son, despise not the chastening of the LORD, neither be weary of his correction;

Heb.12:5-11

v.5 And ye have forgotten the exhortation which speaketh unto you as unto |sons|, My son, despise not thou the chastening of the Lord, nor faint when thou art rebuked of him;

v.6 For whom the Lord loveth he chasteneth, and scourgeth every son whom he receiveth.
v.7 If ye endure chastening, God dealeth with you as with sons; for what son Is he whom the father chasteneth. not?
v.8 But if ye be without chastisement, of which all are partakers, then are ye bastards, and not sons.
v.9 Furthermore, we have had fathers of our flesh who corrected us, and we gave them reverence. Shall we not much rather be In subjection unto the Father of spirits, and live?
v.10 For they verily for a few days chastened us after their own pleasure, but he for our profits, that we might be partakers of his holiness.
v.11 Now no chastening for the present seemeth to be joyous, but grievous; nevertheless, afterward It yielded the peaceable fruit of righteousness unto them who are exercised by it.

v.68 Thou art good, and doest good; teach me thy statutes.
v.69 Thou proud have forged a lie against me, but I will keep thy precepts with my whole heart.
v.70 Their heart is as fat as grease, but I delight in thy law.
v.71 It is good for me that I have been afflicted, that I might learn thy statutes.
v.72 The law of thy mouth Is better unto me than thousands of gold and silver.

YODH
(10)

v.73 Thy hands have made me and (l) fashioned me; give me understanding, that I may learn thy commandments.

(l) fashioned me;
(l) Job 10:8;31:15;
Ps.138:8;139:15-16

Job 10:8

v.8 Thine hands have made me and fashioned me together round about; yet dost destroy me.

Job 31:15

v.15 Did not he who made me in the womb make him?And not one fashion us in the womb?

Ps.138:8

v.8 The LORD will perfect, O LORD, endureth forever; forsake not the works of thine own hands.

Ps.139:15-16

v.15 My substance was not hidden from thee, when I was made in secret, and |intricately| wrought in the lowest parts of the earth.
v.16 Thine eyes did see my substance, yet being |unformed|; and in thy book all my members were written, which in continuance were fashioned, when as yet there was none of them.

v.74 They that (i) fear thee will be (m) glad when they see me, because I have hoped in thy word.

(i) fear
(i) See Ps.19:9, note ;
See Ps.23:4 Messianic Psalm
(m) glad
(m) Ps.107:42;cp.1 Cor.13:6

Ps.107:42

v.42 The righteous shall see it, and rejoice; and all iniquity shall stop her mouth.

1 Cor.13:6

v.6 Rejoiceth not in Iniquity, but rejoiceth in the truth;

v.75 I know, O Lord, that thy judgments are right, and (n) that thou in faithfulness hast afflicted me.

(n) that thou in faithfulness
(n)Heb.12:10

v.10 For they verily for a few days chastened us after their own pleasure, but he for our profit, that we might be partakers of his holiness.

v.76 Let, I pray thee, thy merciful kindness be for my comfort, according to thy word unto thy servant.
v.77 Let thy tender mercies come unto me, that I may live; for thy law In my (o) delight.

(o) delight
(o) vv.24,47,174

v.24 Thy testimonies also are my delight and my counselors.
v.47 And I will delight myself in thy commandments, which I have loved.
v.174 I have longed for thy salvation, O Lord, and thy law is my delight.

v.78 Let the proud be ashamed; for they dealt perversely with me without a cause; but I will meditate in thy precept.
v.79 Let those who fear thee turn unto me, and those who have known thy testimonies.
v.80 Let my heart be sound in thy statutes, that I be not ashamed.

KAPH
(11)

v.81 (p) My soul fainteth for thy salvation, but I hope in thy word.

(p) My soul
(p) Ps.73:26;84:2

Ps.73:26

v.26 My flesh and my heart fail, but God is the strength of my heart, and my portion forever.

Ps.84:2

v.2 My soul longeth, yea, even fainteth for the courts of the LORD; my heart and my flesh cry out for the living God.

v.82 Mine eyes fail for thy word, saying, When wilt thou comfort me?
v.83 For I am become like a (q) | wineskin | in the smoke; yet do I not forget thy statutes.

(q) | wineskin |
(q) KJV bottle.
cp. Job 30:30

v.30 My skin Is black upon me, and my bones burned with heat.

v.84 How many are the days of thy servant? (r) When wilt thou execute judgment on those who persecute me?

(r) When wilt thou
(r) cp. Rev.6:10

v.10 And they cried with a loud voice, saying, How long, O Lord, holy and true, dost thou not judge and avenge our blood on them that dwell on the earth?

v.85 The proud have digged pits for me, which are not after thy law.
v.86 All thy commandments are faithful. They (s) persecute me wrongfully; help thou me.

(s) persecute me;
(s) Ps.38:19;
cp.Mt.5:10

Ps.38:19

v.19 But mine enemies are lively, and they are strong; and they that hate me wrongfully are multiplied.

Mt.5:10

v.10 **Blessed are they who are persecuted for righteousness' sake; for theirs is the kingdom of heaven.**

v.87 They had almost consumed me upon earth, but I forsook not thy precepts.
v.88 (a) |Revive| me after thy loving-kindness; so shall I keep the testimony of thy mouth.

(a) |Revive| me;
(a) KJV Quicken, v.88; quicken,v.107
See the above: v.88

v.107 I am afflicted very much; (a) |revive| me, O LORD, according unto thy word.

LA'MEDH
(12)

v.89 (b) Forever, O LORD, thy word Is settle in heaven.
(b) Forever;
(b) Ps.89:2;Mt.24:34-35;1 Pet.1:25

Ps.89:2

v.2 For I have said, Mercy shall be built up forever; thy faithfulness shalt thou establish in the very heavens.

Mt.24:34-35

v.34 **Verily I say unto you, This generation shall not pass, till all these things be fulfilled.**
v.35 **Heaven and earth shall pass away, but my words shall not pass away.**

1 Pet.1:25

v.25 But the word of the Lord endureth forever. And this is the word which by the gospel is preached unto you.

v.90 Thy faithfulness Is unto all generations; thou hast established the earth, and it abideth.
v.91 They continue this day according to thine ordinances; for all are thy servants.
v.92 Unless thy law had been my delight, I should then have perished in mine affliction.
v.93 I will never forget thy precepts; for with them thou hast (c) |given me life|.

(c) |given me life|;
(c) KJV quickened me. v.40

v.40 Behold, I have longed after thy precepts; |give me life| in thy righteousness.

v.94 I am thine; save me; for I have sought thy precepts.
v.95 The wicked have waited for me to destroy me, but I will consider thy testimonies.
v.96 I have seen an end of all perfection, but thy commandment is exceedingly broad.

MEM
(13)

v.97 Oh, how love I thy law! (d) It is my meditation all the day.

(d) It is my meditation
(d) Ps.1:2

v.2 But his delight is in the law of the LORD; and in his law doth he meditate day and night.

v.98 Thou, through thy commandments, hast made me (e) wiser than mine enemies; for they are ever with me.

(e) wiser
(e)Dt.4:6

v.6 Keep, therefore, and do them; for this is your wisdom and your understanding In the sight of the nation, who shall hear all these statutes and say, Surely this great nation is a wise and understanding people.

v.99 I have more understanding than all my teachers; for thy (f) testimonies are my meditation.

(f) testimonies
(f) cp.2 Tim.3:14-15

v.14 But continue thou in the things which thou hast learned and hast been assured of, knowing of whom thou hast learned them, v.15 And that from a child thou hast known the holy scriptures, which are able to make thee wise unto salvation through faith which is in Christ Jesus.

v.100 I understand more than the (g) ancients, because I keep thy precepts.

(g) ancients
(g) Job 32:7-9

v.7 I said, Days should speak, and multitude of years should teach wisdom.
v.8 But there Is a spirit in man; and the inspiration of the Almighty giveth them understanding.
v.9 Great men are not always wise; neither do the aged understand |justice|.

v.101 I have (h)|restrained| my feet from every evil way, that I might keep thy word.

(h)| restrained|
(h) KJV refrained. Cp.1 Ki.3:14; 8:25;9:4;11:38;2 Chr.7:17-18

1 Ki3:14

v.14 And if thou wilt walk In my ways, to keep my statutes and my commandments, as thy father, David, did walk, then I will lengthen thy days.

1 Ki.8:25

v.25 Therefore now, LORD God of Israel, keep with thy servant David, my father, that which thou promisedst him, saying, There shall not fail thee a man in my sight to sit on the throne of Israel; so that thy children take heed to their way, that they walk before me as thou hast walked before me.

1 Ki.9:4

v.4 And If thou wilt walk before me, as David, thy father, walked, in integrity of heart, and in uprightness, to do according to all that I have commanded thee, and wilt keep my statutes and mine |ordinances|,

1 Ki.11:38

v.38 And It shall be, If thou wilt hearken unto all that I command thee, and wilt walk in my ways, and do what is right in my sight, to keep my statutes and my commandments, as David, my servant, did, that I will be with thee, and build thee a sure house, as I built for David, and will give Israel unto thee.

2 Chr.7:17-18

v.17 And as for thee, if thou wilt walk before me, as David, thy father, walked, and do according to all that I have commanded thee, and shalt observe my statutes and mine |ordinances|,
v.18 Then will I |establish| the throne of thy kingdom, according as I have covenanted with David, thy father, saying, There shall not fail thee a man to be ruler in Israel.

v.102 I have not departed from thine (i) |ordinances|; for thou hast taught me.

(i) |ordinances;
(i) KJV judgments

vv.52,56

v.52 I remembered thine (d) |ordinances| of old, O Lord, and have comforted myself.
v.56 This I had, because I kept thy precepts.

v.103 How sweet are thy words unto my taste! Yea, sweeter than honey to my mouth.

v.104 Through thy precepts I get understanding; therefore, I hate every false way.

NUN

(14)

v.105 Thy word is a (j) lamp unto my feet, and a light unto my path.

(j) lamp unto
(j) Prov.6:23

v.23 For the commandment is a lamp, and the law is light, and reproofs of Instruction are the way of life.

v.106 I have (k) sworn, and I will perform it, that I will keep thy righteous (i) | ordinances | .

(k) swore
(k) cp.Neh.10:29
(i) | ordinances |
(i) KJV vv.52,56
See: above v. 102

v.29 They did cleave to their brethren, their nobles, and entered into a curse, and into an oath, to walk in God's law, which was given by Moses, the servant of God, and to observe and do all the commandments of the LORD, our Lord, and his | ordinances | and his statutes.

v.107 I am afflicted very much; (a) | revive | me, O LORD, according unto thy word.

(a) | revive | me
(a) KJV Quicken,v.88; quicken, v.107
See: above v.88; 107

v.108 Accept, I beseech thee, the (l) free-will offerings of my mouth, O LORD, and teach me thine (i) | ordinances | .

(l) free-will
(l) Hos.14:2;Heb.13:15
(i) | ordinances |
(i) KJV judgments.vv.52,56;See above v.106

v.109 My soul Is continually In my hand; yet do I not forget thy law.
v.110 The wicked have laid a snare for me; yet I erred not from thy precepts.
v.111 (m) Thy testimonies have I taken as an heritage forever; for they are the rejoicing of my heart.

(m) Thy testimonies
(m) Dt.33:4

v.4 Moses commanded us a law, even the inheritance of the congregation of Jacob.

v.112 I have inclined mine heart to perform thy statutes always, even unto the end.

SA'MEKH
(15)

v.113 I hate vain thoughts, but thy law do I love.
v.114 Thou art my (n) hiding place and my shield; I hope in thy word.

(n) hiding place
(n) Ps.32:7;91:1

Ps.32:7

v.7 Thou art my hiding place; thou shalt preserve me from trouble; thou shalt compass me about with songs of deliverance. Selah.

Ps.91:1

v.1 HE who dwelleth in the secret place of the Most High shall abide under the shadow of the Almighty.

v.115 (o) Depart from me, ye evildoers; for I will keep the commandments of my God.

(o) depart from me,
(o) Ps.6:8;139:19;Mt.7:23

Ps.6:8

v.8 Depart from me, all ye workers of iniquity; for the LORD hath heard the voice of my weeping.

Ps.139:19

v.19 Surely, thou wilt slay the wicked, O God; depart from me therefore, ye bloody men.

Mt.7:23

v.23 **And then will I profess unto them, I never knew you; depart from me, ye that work iniquity.**

v.116 Uphold me according unto thy word. That I may live; and let me not be (p) ashamed of my hope.

(p) ashamed
(p)Ps.25:2;Rom.5:5;9:33;10:11

Ps.25:2

v.2 O my God, I trust in thee; let me not be ashamed, let not mine enemies triumph over me.

Rom.5:5

v.5 And hope maketh not ashamed, because the love of God Is shed abroad in our hearts by the Holy |Spirit| who is given unto us.

Rom.9:33

v.33 As it Is written, Behold, I lay in zion a stumbling stone and rock of offense; and whosoever believeth on him shall not be ashamed.

Rom.10:11

v.11 For the scripture saith, Whosoever believeth on him shall not be ashamed.

v.117 Hold thou me up, and I shall be safe; and I will have respect unto thy statutes continually.
v.118 Thou hast trodden down all those who err from thy statutes; for their deceit Is falsehood.
v.119 Thou puttest away all the wicked of the earth (q) like dross; therefore, I love thy testimonies.

(q) like dross;
(q) cp.Ezek.22:18

v.18 Son of man, the house of Israel is to me become dross; all they are |bronze|, therefore, I will gather you into the midst of Jerusalem.

v.120 (r) My flesh trembleth for fear of thee, and I am afraid of thy judgments.

(r) my flesh trembleth
(r) Hab.3:16

v.16 When I heard, my belly trembled, my lips quivered

at the voice; rottenness entered into my bones, and I trembled in myself, that I might rest in the day of trouble. When he cometh up unto the people, he will invade them with his troops.

A'YIN
(16)

v.121 I have (s) | executed justice and righteousness | ; leave me not to mine oppressors.

(s) | executed justice and righteousness | ;
(s) KJV done judgment and justice

v.122 Be surety for thy servant for good; let not the proud oppress me.
v.123 Mine eyes fail for thy salvation, and for the word of thy righteousness.
v.124 Deal with thy servant according unto thy mercy, and (t) teach me thy statutes.

(t) teach
(t) v.12

v.12 Blessed art thou, O LORD; teach me thy statutes.

v.125 I am thy servant; give me understanding, that I may know thy testimonies.
v.126 It Is time for thee, LORD, to work; for they have made void thy law.
v.127 Therefore, I love thy commandments above gold; yea, above fine gold.
v.128 Therefore, I esteem all thy precepts concerning all things to be right, and I hate every false way.

PE
(17)

v.129 Thy testimonies are wonderful; therefore doth my soul keep them.

v.130 The entrance of thy words giveth (a) light; it giveth understanding unto the (b) simple.

(a) light;
(a) Prov.6:23
(b) simple;
(b) Ps.19:7;Prov.1:4

Prov.6:23

v.23 For the commandment is a lamp, and the law Is light, and reproofs of instruction are the way of life,

Ps.19:7

v.7 All the brethren of the poor do hate him. How much more do his friends go far from him! He pursueth them with words, yet they are |lacking| to him.

Prov.1:4

v.4 To give |prudence| to the simple, to the young man knowledge and discretion.

v.131 I opened my mouth, and (c) panted; for I longed for thy commandments.

(c) panted;
(c) Ps.42:1

v.1 BLESSED is he that considereth the poor; the LORD will deliver him In time of trouble.

v.132 (d) Look thou upon me, and be (e) merciful unto me, as thou (f) |dost| unto those who love thy name.

(d) Look thou upon me,
(d) Ps.106:4
(e) merciful
(e) Ps.51:1

(f) |dost|
(f) KJV usest to do

Ps.106:4

v.4 Remember me, O LORD, with the favor that thou bearest unto thy people; oh, visit me with thy salvation,

Ps.51:1

v.1 HAVE mercy upon me, O God, according to thy loving-kind-ness; according unto the multitude of thy tender mercies blot out my transgressions.

v.133 Order my steps in thy word, and let not any Iniquity have (g) dominion over me.

(g) dominion
(g) Ps.19:13;Rom.6:12,14

Ps.19:13

v.13 Keep back thy servant also from presumptuous sin; let them not have dominion over me. Then shall I be upright, and I shall be Innocent from the great transgression.

Rom.6:12,14

v.12 Let not sin, therefore, reign in your mortal body, that ye should obey it in lusts.
v.14 For sin shall not have dominion over you; for ye are not under the law but under grace.

v.134 (h) Deliver me from the oppression of man; so will I keep thy precepts.

(h) Deliver me
(h) Lk.1:74

v.74 That he would grant unto us that we, being delivered out of the hand of our enemies, might serve him without fear,

v.135 (i) Make thy face to shine upon thy servant, and teach me thy statutes.

(i) make thy face to shine
(i) Ps.4:6

v.6 There are many that say, Who will show us any good? LORD, lift thou up the light of thy countenance upon us.

v.136 Rivers of waters run down (j) mine eyes, because they keep not thy law.

(j) mine eyes;
(j) Jer.9:1;14:17;cp.Ezek.9:4

Jer.9:1

v.1 OH, that my head were waters, and mine eyes a fountain of tears, that I might weep day and night for the slain of the daughter of my people!

Jer.14:17

v.17 Therefore, thou shalt say this word unto them, Let mine eyes run down with tears night and day, and let them not cease; for the virgin daughter of my people is broken with a great breach, with a very grievous blow.

Ezek.9:4

v.4 And the LORD said unto him, Go through the midst of the city, through the midst of Jerusalem, and set a mark upon the foreheads of men that sigh and that cry for all the abominations that are done in the midst of it.

TSADHE'
(18)

v.137 Righteous art thou, O LORD, and upright are thy judgments,
v.138 Thy testimonies that thou hast commanded are righteous and very faithful.
v.139 My zeal hath consumed me, because mine enemies have forgotten thy words.
v.140 Thy word is very (k) pure; therefore, thy servant loveth it.

(k) pure;
(k) Lit. tried or refined

v.141 I am small and despised; yet do not I forget thy precepts.
v.142 Thy righteousness, is an everlasting righteousness, and thy law is the (l) truth.

(l) truth;
(l) v.151;Ps.19:9;Jn.17:17

v.151 Thou art near, O LORD, and all thy commandments are truth.

Ps.19:9

v.9 The fear of the LORD is clean, enduring forever; the |ordinances| of the LORD are true and righteous altogether.

Jn.17:17

v.17 **Sanctify them through thy truth; thy word is truth.**

v.143 Trouble and anguish have taken hold of me; yet thy commandments are my delight.
v.144 The righteousness of thy testimonies is everlasting; give me understanding, and I shall live.

QOPH
(19)

v.145 I cried with my whole heart. Hear me, O Lord; I will keep thy statutes.
v.146 I cried unto thee. Save me, and I shall keep thy testimonies.
v.147 I (m) | anticipated | the dawning of the (n) morning, and cried; I hoped in thy word.

(m) | anticipated |
(m) KJV prevented
(n) morning
(n) Ps.5:3;88:13;130:6

Ps.5:3

v.3 My voice shalt thou hear in the morning, O Lord; in the morning will I direct my prayer unto thee, and will look up.

Ps.88:13

v.13 But unto thee have I cried, O Lord; and in the morning shall my prayer | come before | thee.

Ps.130:6

v.6 My soul waiteth for the Lord more than they that watch for the morning; I say, more than they that watch for the morning.

v.149 Mine eyes (o) | anticipate | the night watches, that I might meditate in thy word.

(o) | anticipate |
(o) KJV judgment

v.150 They draw (r) |near| that follow after mischief; they are far from thy law.

(r) |near|
(r) KJV nigh.
Cp. Ps.145:18

v.18 The LORD is |near| unto all those who call upon him, to all who call upon him in truth.

v.151 Thou art near, O LORD, and all thy commandments are truth.
v.152 Concerning thy testimonies, I have known of old that thou hast founded them forever.

RESH
(20)

v.153 (s) Consider mine affliction, and deliver me; for I do not forget thy law.

(s) Consider
(s) Lam.5:1

v.1 REMEMBER, O LORD, what is come upon us; consider, and behold our reproach.

v.154 (t) Plead my cause, and (u) deliver me; (p) |revive| me according to thy word.

(t) Plead my cause,
(t) Cp. 1 Sam.24:15
(u) deliver me;
(u) Redemption (kinsman type:v.154;
Ps.130:7 (Gen.48:16;Isa.59:20,note)

See: Ps.72:14 Messianic Psalm
(p) | revive | me
(p) KJV quicken. vv.25,107

1 Sam.24:15

v.15 The Lord, therefore, be judge, and judge between me and thee, and see, and plead my cause, and deliver me out of thine hand

Ps.119:154

v.154 (t) Plead my cause, and (u) deliver me; (p) | revive | me according to thy word.

Ps.130:7

v.7 Let Israel hope in the Lord; for with the Lord there is mercy, and with him is plenteous redemption.

Gen.48:16

v.16 | An angel | who redeemed me from all evil, bless the lads; and let my name be named on them, and the name of my fathers, Abraham and Isaac; and let them grow into a multitude in the midst of the earth.

See: Redemption (kinsman type) Isa.59:20,note
See: Ps.72:14 Messianic Psalm

Ps.119:25

v.25 My soul (h) | clingeth to | the dust; (i) | revive | me according to thy word.

Ps.119:107

v.107 I am afflicted very much; (a) | revive | me, O LORD, according unto thy word.

v.155 Salvation is far from the wicked; for they seek not thy statutes.
v.156 Great are thy tender mercies, O LORD; (p) | revive | me according to thine (v) | ordinances | .

(p) | revive | me
(p) KJV quicken vv.25,107
See: above v.Ps.119:149
(v) | ordinances |
(v) KJV judgments

v.157 Many are my persecutors and mine enemies; yet do I not (w) decline from thy testimonies.

(w) decline
(w) v.51;Ps.44:18

v.51 The proud have had me greatly in derision; yet have I not declined from thy law.

Ps.44:18

Our heart is not turned back, neither have our steps declined from thy way;

v.158 I beheld the transgressors, and was grieved, because they kept not thy word.
v.159 Consider how I love thy precepts; (p) | revive | me, O LORD, according to thy loving-kindness.

(p) | revive | me,
(p) KJV quicken.vv.25,107
See: above v. Ps.119:149

v.160 Thy word is true from the beginning, and every one of thy righteous (v) | ordinances | endureth forever.

(v) | ordinances |
(v) KJV judgments

SHIN
(21)

v.161 (x) Princes have persecuted me without a cause, but my heart standeth in awe of thy word.

(x) Princes have persecuted
(x) v.23;cp.1 Sam.24:11,14;26:18

Ps.119:23

v.23 Princes also did sit and speak against me, but thy servant did meditate in thy statutes.

1 Sam.24:11,14

v.11 Moreover, my father, see, yea, see the skirt of thy robe in my hand; for in that I cut off the skirt of thy robe, and killed thee not, know thou and see that there not, know thou and see that there is neither evil nor transgression in mine hand, and I have not sinned against thee; yet thou huntest my soul to take it.
v.14 After whom is the king of Israel come out? After whom dost thou pursue? After a dead dog! After a flea!

1 Sam.26:18

v.18 And he said, | Why | doth my Lord thus pursue after his servant? For what have I done? Or what evil is in mine hand?

v.162 I rejoice at thy word, as one that findeth great spoil.

v.163 I hate and abhor lying, but thy law do I love.
v.164 Seven times a day do I praise thee, because of thy righteous (v) | ordinances | .

(v) | ordinances |
(v) KJV judgments

v.165 (y) Great peace have they who love thy law, and (z) nothing shall offend them.

(y) Great peace
(y)Prov.3:2;Isa.32:17
(z) nothing
(z) Lit. they shall have no stumbling block

Prov.3:2

v.2 For length of days, and long life, and peace, shall they add to thee.

Isa.32:17

v.17 And the work of righteousness shall be peace, and the effect of righteousness, quietness and assurance forever.

v.166 LORD, I have hoped for thy (aa) salvation, and done thy commandments.

(aa) salvation,
(aa) v.174; Gen.49:18

v.174 I have longed for thy salvation, O LORD, and thy law is my delight.

Gen.49:18

v.18 I have waited for thy salvation, O LORD.

v.167 My soul hath kept thy testimonies, and I love them exceedingly
v.168 I have kept thy precepts and thy testimonies; for all my ways are before thee.

TAV
(22)

v.169 Let my cry come near before thee, O LORD; (bb) give me understanding, according to thy word.

(bb) give me understanding
(bb) v.144

v.144 The righteousness of thy testimonies is everlasting; give me understanding, and I shall live.

v.170 Let my supplication come before thee; deliver me, according to thy word.
v.171 My lips shall utter praise, when thou hast taught me thy statutes.
v.172 My tongue shall speak of thy word; for all thy commandments are righteousness.
v.173 Let thine hand help me; for I have chosen thy precepts.
v.174 I have longed for thy salvation, O LORD, and thy law is my delight.
v.175 Let my soul live, and it shall praise thee; and let thine (a) | ordinances | help me.

(a) | ordinances |
(a) KJV judgments Ps.18:22

v.22 For all his | ordinances | were before me, and I did not put away his statutes from me.

v.176 I have (b) gone astray like a lost sheep. Seek thy servant; for I do not forget thy commandments.

(b) gone astray
(b) Isa.53:6;1Pet.2:25; cp.Lk.15:4

Isa.53:6

v.6 All we like sheep have gone astray; we have turned every one to his own way, and the LORD hath laid on him the iniquity of us all.

1Pet.2:25

v.25 For ye were as sheep going astray, but are now returned unto the Shepherd and Bishop of your souls.

Lk.15:4

v.4 **What man of you, having an hundred sheep, if he lose one of them, doth not leave the ninety and nine in the wilderness, and go after that which is lost, until he find it?**

VII

PILGRIM PSALMS-120-134

ASCENT JOY CAPTIVITY TO JERUSALEM

A CRY OF DISTRESS

A SONG OF ׀DEGREES

PSALM 120

v.1 IN my distress I cried unto the LORD, and he heard me.
v.2 Deliver my soul, O LORD, from lying lips, and from a deceitful tongue.
v.3 What shall be given unto thee? Or what shall be done unto thee, thou false tongue?
v.4 Sharp arrows of the mighty, with coals of juniper!
v.5 Woe is me, that I sojourn in (c) Me'shech, that I dwell in the tents of (d) Kedar!

(c) Me'shech;
(c) Gen.10:2;Ezek.27:13
(d) Kedar;
(d) Gen.25:13;Jer.49:28-29

Gen.10:2

v.2 The sons of Ja'pheth: Gomer, and Magog, and Ma'dai, and Ja-van, and Tubal, and Me'shech, and Ti'ras.

Ezek.27:13

v.13 Ja'van, Tubal, and Me'shech were thy merchants; they traded the persons of men and vessels of |bronze| in thy market.

Gen.25:13

v.13 And these are the names of the sons of Ishmael, by their names, according to their generations: the first—born of Ishmael, Neba'joth; and Kedar, and Adbeel, and Mibsam,

Jer.49:28-29

v.28 Concerning Kedar, and concerning the kingdoms of Hazor, which Nebuchadrez'zar, king of Babylon, shall smite, thus saith the LORD: Arise ye, go up to Kedar, and spoil the men of the east.
v.29 Their tents and their flocks shall they take away; they shall take to themselves their curtains, and all their vessels, and their camels; and they shall cry unto them, Fear is on every side.

v.6 My soul hath long dwelt with him that hateth peace.
v.7 I am for peace; but when I speak, they are for war.

1(120-134, inscriptions) Fifteen Psalms (Ps.120-134) are called "Songs of Ascents," "ascents" being the correct rendering of the word translated "degrees." The view most generally accepted is that these Psalms were either sung by pilgrims on the ascending march from the Babylonian captivity to Jerusalem, or ` that they were sung by worshipers from all parts of Palestine as they went up to Jerusalem for the great festivals (Dt.16:16). An alternate view is that the headings "A Song of Ascents," refer to the fifteen steps leading to the Court of Israel in the Temple, and that these Psalms were sung on these steps

THE TRAVELER'S PSALM

A SONG OF ı DEGREES

PSALM 121

v.1 I WILL lift mine eyes unto the hills, From whence cometh my help?

v.2 My help (e) cometh from the LORD, who made heaven and earth.

(e) cometh from
(e)Jer.3:23

v.23 Truly in vain is salvation hoped for from the hills, and from the multitude of mountains; truly in the LORD, our God, is the salvation of Israel.

v.3 He will not suffer thy (f) foot to be moved; he who (g) keepeth thee will not slumber.

(f) foot to be moved;
(f) 1 Sam.2:9;Prov.3:23,26
(g) keepeth
(g) Ps.34:19-20;Prov.24:12

1 Sam.2:9

v.9 He will keep the feet of his saints, and the wicked shall be silent in darkness; for by strength shall no man prevail.

Prov.3:23,26

v.23 Then shalt thou walk in thy way safely, and thy foot shall not stumble.
v.26 For the LORD shall be thy confidence, and shall keep thy foot from being taken.

Ps.34:19-20

v.19 Many are the afflictions of the righteous; but the LORD delivereth him out of them all.
v.20 He keepeth all his bones; not one of them is broken.

Prov.24:12

v.12 If thou sayest, Behold, we knew it not; doth not he that |weigheth| the heart consider it? And he that keepeth thy soul, doth not he know it? And shall not he render to every man according to his works?

v.4 Behold, he who keepeth Israel shall neither slumber nor sleep.
v.5 The LORD is thy keeper; the LORD is thy (h) shade upon thy (i) hand.

(h) shade
(h)Isa.25:4
(i) hand
(i)Ps.16:8;109:31

Isa.25:4

v.4 For thou hast been a strength to the poor, a strength to the needy in his distress, a refuge from the storm, a shadow from the heat, when the blast of the terrible ones is like a storm against the wall.

Ps.16:8

v.8 I have set the LORD always before me; because he is at my right hand, I shall not be moved.

Ps.109:31

v.31 For he shall stand at the right hand of the poor, to save him from those that condemn his soul.

v.6 (j) The sun shall not smite thee by day, nor the moon by night.

(j) the sun
(j) Ps.91:5;Isa.49:10;Rev.7:16

Ps.91:5

v.5 Thou shalt not be afraid for the terror by night, nor for the arrow that flieth by day.

Isa.49:10

v.10 They shall not hunger nor thirst, neither shall the heat nor sun smite them; for he who hath mercy on them shall lead them, even by the springs of water shall he guide them.

Rev.7:16

v.16 They shall hunger no more, neither thirst any more; neither shall the sun light on them, nor any heat.

v.7 The LORD shall preserve thee from all evil; he shall (k) preserve thy soul.

(k) preserve
(k) Ps.41:2;97:10;145:20

Ps. 41:2

v.2 The LORD will preserve him, and keep him alive; and he shall be blessed upon the earth, and thou wilt not deliver him unto the will of his enemies.

Ps.97:10

v.10 Ye who love the LORD, hate evil. He preserveth the souls of his saints; he delivereth them out of the hand of the wicked.

Ps.145:20

v.20 The LORD preserveth all those who love him, but all the wicked will he destroy.

v.8 The LORD shall (l) preserve thy going out and thy coming in from this time forth, and even for evermore.

(l) preserve thy going
(l) Dt.28:6;Prov.2:8;3:6

Dt.28:6

v.6 Blessed shalt thou be when thou comest in, and blessed shalt thou be when thou goest out.

Prov.2:8

v.8 He keepeth the paths of |justice|, and preserveth the way of his saints.

Prov.3:6

v.6 In all thy ways acknowledge him, and he shall direct thy paths.

See: A Song of 1 degrees—Psalm 120

JOYFUL ANTICIPATION OF JERUSALEM

A SONG OF ı DEGREES OF DAVID

PSALM 122

v.1 I WAS glad when they said unto me; (m) Let us go into the house of the LORD.

(m) Let us go
(m) Cp. Isa.2:3;Zech.8:21

Isa.2:3

v.3 And many people shall go and say, Come ye, and let us go up to the mountain of the LORD, to the house of the God of Jacob; and he will teach us of his ways, and we will walk in his paths; for out of Zion shall go forth the law, and the word of the LORD from Jerusalem.

Zech.8:21

v.21 And the inhabitants of one city shall go to another, saying, Let us go speedily to pray before the LORD, and to seek the LORD of hosts; I will go also.

v.2 Our feet shall stand within thy gates, O Jerusalem.
v.3 Jerusalem is builded as a city that is (n) compact together,

(n) compact together,
(n) Cp. 2 Sam.5:9

v.9 So David dwelt in the fort, and called it the city of David. And David built round about from Millo and inward.

v.4 (o) Whither the tribes go up, the tribes of the LORD, unto the testimony of Israel, to give thanks unto the name of the LORD.

(o) Whither the tribes
(o) Ex.23:17;Dt.16:16

Ex.23:17

v.17 Three times in the year all thy males shall appear before the Lord God.

Dt.16:16

v.16 Three times in a year shall all thy males appear before the LORD God in the place which he shall choose: in the feast of unleavened bread, and in the feast of weeks, and in the feast of tabernacles; and they shall not appear before the LORD empty.

v.5 For there are (p) set thrones of judgment, the thrones of the house of David.

(p) set thrones of judgment,
(p) Dt.17:8;2 Chr.19:8

Dt.17:8

v.8 If there arise a matter too hard for thee in judgment, between blood and blood, between plea and plea, and between stroke and stroke, being matters of controversy within thy gates, then shalt thou arise, and get thee up into the place which the LORD thy God shall choose;

2 Chr.19:8

v.8 Moreover, in Jerusalem did Jehosh'aphat set of the Levites, and of the priests, and of the |heads| of the fathers of Israel, for the judgment of the LORD, and for controversies, when they returned to Jerusalem.

v.6 Pray for the peace of Jerusalem; they shall prosper who love thee.
v.7 Peace be within thy walls, and prosperity within thy palaces.
v.8 For my brethren and companions' sakes, I will now say, Peace be within thee.
v.9 Because of the house of the LORD our God, I will seek thy good.

See: A Song of 1 degrees of David—Psalm 120

LOOKING FOR GOD'S MERCY

A SONG OF I DEGREES

PSALM 123

v.1 UNTO thee (q) lift I up mine eyes, O thou who dwellest in the heavens.

(q) lift mine eyes,
(q) Ps.121:1-2;141:8

Ps.121:1-2

v.1 I WILL lift up mine eyes unto the hills. From whence cometh my help?
v.2 My help cometh from the LORD, who made heaven and earth.

Ps.141:8

v.8 But more eyes are unto thee, O God, the Lord; in thee is my trust; leave not my soul destitute.

v.2 Behold, as the eyes of servants look unto the hand of their masters, and as the eyes of maiden unto the hand of her mistress, (r) so our eyes wait upon the LORD our God, until he has mercy upon us.

(r) so our eyes;
(r)Ps.25:15

v.15 Mine eyes are ever toward the LORD; for he shall pluck my feet out of the net.

v.3 Have mercy upon us, O LORD, have mercy upon us; for we are exceedingly filled with contempt.
v.4 Our soul is exceedingly filled with the (s) | scoffing | of those who are at ease, and with the contempt of the proud.

(s) | scoffing |
(s) KJV scorning.
Cp. Neh.2:19;4:1-5

Neh.2:19

v.19 But when Sanbal'lat, the Horonite, and Tobiah, the servant, the Ammonite, and Geshem, the Arabian, heard it, they laughed us to scorn, and despised us, and said, What is this thing that ye do? Will ye rebel against the king?

Neh.4:1-5

v.1 But it came to pass that, when Sanbal'lat heard that we were building the wall, he was | angry |, and | felt | great indignation, and mocked the Jews.
v.2 And he spoke before his brethren and the army of Samaria, and said, What are these feeble Jews doing? Will they fortify themselves? Will they sacrifice? Will they | finish | in a day? Will they revive the stones out of the heaps of the rubbish, seeing they are burned?
v.3 Now Tobian, the Ammonite, was by him, and he said, Even that which they build, if a fox go up, he shall break down their stone wall.
v.4 Hear, O our God; for we are despised; and turn their reproach upon their own head, and give them for a | spoil | in the land of captivity.

v.5 And cover not their iniquity, and let not their sin be blotted out from before thee; for they have provoked thee to anger before the builders.

See: A Song of 1 degrees—Psalm 120

GOD ON THE SIDE OF HIS PEOPLE

A SONG OF DEGREES

PSALM 124

v.1 IF it had not been the LORD who was on our (t) side, now may Israel say,

(t) side, now may Israel say,
(t) Ps.118:6;Rom.8:31

Ps.118:6

v.6 The LORD is on my side; I will not fear. What can man do unto me?

Rom.8:31

v.31 What shall we then say to these things? If God be for us, who can be against us?

v.2 If it had not been the LORD who was on our side, when men rose up against us;
v.3 (a) Then they had swallowed us up (b) | alive |, when their wrath was kindled against us;

(a) Then they had swallowed
(a) Ps.56:1-2;57:3;Prov.1:12

(b) |alive|
(b) KJV quick

Ps.56:1-2

v.1 BE merciful unto me, O God; for man would swallow me up; he, fighting daily, oppresseth me.
v.2 Mine enemies would daily swallow me up; for they are many that fight against me, O thou Most High.

Prov.1:12

v.12 Let us swallow them up alive as |sheol|, and whole, as those that go down into the pit;

v.4 Then the waters had overwhelmed us, the stream had gone over our soul;
v.5 Then the proud waters had gone over our soul.
v.6 Blessed be the LORD, who hath not given us a prey to their teeth.
v.7 (c) Our soul is escaped (d) like a bird out of the snare of the fowlers; the snare is broken, and we are escaped.

(c) Our soul is escaped
(c) Ps.91:3
(d) like a bird:
(d) Prov.6:5

Ps.91:3

v.3 Surely he shall deliver thee from the snare of the fowler, and from the noisome pestilence.

Prov.6:5

v.5 Deliver thyself like a roe from the hand of the hunter, and like a bird from the hand of the fowler.

v.8 Our (e) help is in the name of the LORD, who made heaven and earth.

(e) help is in the name of the LORD,
(e) Ps.121:2

v.2 My help cometh from the LORD; who made heaven and earth.

See: A Song of 1 degrees of David—Psalm 120

THE LORD'S ENCOMPASSING PROTECTION

A SONG OF f DEGREES

PSALM 125

v.1 THEY who (g) trust in the LORD shall be as Mount Zion, which cannot be removed, but abideth forever.

(g) trust
(g) Faith: v.1;Jon.3:5.
(Gen.3:20;Heb.11:39,note)
See above v.1

Jon.3:5

v.5 So the people of Nin'eveh believed God, and proclaimed a fast, and put on sackcloth, from the greatest of them even to the least of them.

Gen.3:20

v.20 And Adam called his wife's name Eve, because she was the mother of all living.

Heb.11:39,note

v.39 And these all, having |received witness| through faith, received not the promise,

Note: 3(11:39) Faith, Summary: The essence of faith consists in believing and receiving what God has revealed, and may be defined as that trust in the God of the Scriptures and in Jesus Christ whom He has sent, which receives Him as Lord and Savior and impels to loving obedience and good works (Jn.1:12; Jas.2:14-26). The particular uses of faith give rise to its secondary definitions:

(1) For salvation, faith is personal trust, apart from meritorious works, in the Lord Jesus Christ as delivered because of our offenses and raised again because of our justification (Rom.4:5,23-25;5:1).
(2) As used in prayer, faith is the "confidence that we have in him, that if we ask anything according to his will, he heareth us" (1 Jn.5:14-15).
(3) As used in reference to unseen things of which Scripture speaks, faith gives "substance" to them so that we act upon the conviction of their reality (Heb.11:1-3). And
(4) as a working principal in life, the uses of faith are illustrated in this chapter.

v.2 As the mountains are round about Jerusalem, so the LORD is round about his people from henceforth even forever.
v.3 For the (h) rod of the wicked shall not rest upon the lot of the righteous, lest the righteous put forth their hands unto iniquity.

(h) rod
(h) Or scepter

Isa.14:5

v.5 The LORD hath broken the staff of the wicked, and the scepter of the rulers.

v.4 Do good, O LORD, unto those who are good, and those who are upright in their hearts

v.5 As for such as turn aside unto their crooked ways, the LORD shall lead them forth with the workers of iniquity; but peace shall be upon Israel.

See: A Song of f degrees—Psalm 120

REMEMBRANCE OF PAST BLESSING

A SONG OF f DEGREES

PSALM 126

v.1 (i) WHEN the LORD turned again the captivity of Zion, (j) we were like them that dream.

(i) WHEN the LORD turned again the captivity
(i)Ps.53:6;85:1;Hos.6:11;Joel 3:1
(j) we
(j) Cp. Acts 12:9

Ps.53:6

v.6 Oh, that the salvation of Israel were come out of Zion! When God bringeth back the captivity of his people, Jacob shall rejoice, and Israel shall be glad.

Ps.85:1

v.1 LORD, thou hast been favorable unto thy land; thou hast brought back the captivity of Jacob.

Hos.6:11

v.11 Also, O Judah, he hath set an harvest for thee, when I returned the captivity of my people.

Joel 3:1

v.1 FOR, behold, in those days, and in that time, when I shall bring again the captivity of Judah and Jerusalem,

Acts 12:9

v.9 And he went out, and followed him, and |knew| not that it was true which was done by the angel, but thought he saw a vision.

v.2 Then was our mouth filled with laughter, and our tongue with singing; then said they among the (k)|nations|, The LORD hath done great things for them.

(k)|nations|
(k) KJV heathen

v.3 The LORD hath done great things for us, whereof we are glad.
v.4 Turn again our captivity, O LORD, like the streams in the (l)|Ne'gev|.

(l)|Ne'gev|
(l) KJV south.
See Gen.12:9,note

v.12 And Abram journeyed, going on still toward the |Ne'gev|.

Note: 4(12:9)Negev (also spelled Negeb and translated "south" in K.J.V.) is the transliteration of a Hebrew word meaning dry. It is a geographical term which refers to a specific section of Palestine (e.g. Gen.13:1) located between Debir and the Arabian Desert. It is an arid region most of the year. Since this area was south of the larger part of Israel, the word also came to be used to denote that direction 9cp. Gen.13:14; Dan.8:4,9;11:5, etc.).

v.5 They that sow in tears shall (m) reap in (n) joy.

(m) reap
(m) Gal.6:9
(n) joy
(n) Or singing.
Cp.Neh.12:43

Gal.6:9

v.6 And let us not be weary in well doing; for in due season we shall reap, if we faint not.

Neh.12:43

v.43 Also that day they offered great sacrifices, and rejoiced; for God had made them rejoice with great joy. And the women and the children rejoiced, so that the joy of Jerusalem was heard even afar off.

v.6 He that goeth forth and weepeth, bearing precious seed, shall doubtless come again with (o) rejoicing, bringing his sheaves with him.

(o) rejoicing
(o) Isa.61:3

v.3 To appoint unto those who mourn in Zion, to give unto them beauty for ashes, the oil of joy for mourning, the garment of praise for the spirit of heaviness, that they might be called trees of righteousness, the planting of the LORD, that he might be glorified.

See: A Song of f degrees—Psalm 120

CHILDREN ARE GOD'S HERITAGE

A SONG OF f DEGREES OF SOLOMON

PSALM 127

v.1 EXCEPT the LORD build the house, they labor in (p) vain that
build it; (q) except the LORD keep the city, the watchman
waketh but in vain.

(p) vain that build it;
(p) Cp.Lev.26:20
(q) except the LORD
(q) Ps.121:1-5

Lev.26:20

v.20 And your strength shall be spent in vain; for your land shall not yield her increase, neither shall the trees of the land yield their fruits.

Ps.121:1-5

v.1 I WILL lift up mine eyes unto the hills. From whence cometh my help?
v.2 My help cometh from the LORD, who made heaven and earth.
v.3 He will not suffer thy foot to be moved; he who keepeth thee will not slumber.
v.4 Behold, he who keepeth Israel shall neither slumber nor sleep.

v.5 The Lord is thy keeper; the Lord is thy shade upon thy right hand.

v.2 It is vain for you to rise up early, to sit up late, to (r) eat the bread of sorrows; for so he giveth his beloved sleep.

(r) ear the bread of sorrow;
(r) Cp. Gen.3:17-19

Gen.3:17-19

v.17 And unto Adam he said, Because thou hast hearkened unto the voice of thy wife, and hast eaten of the tree, of which I commanded thee, saying, Thou shalt not eat of it: cursed is the ground for thy sake; in sorrow shalt thou eat of it all the days of thy life;
v.18 Thorns also and thistles shall it bring forth to thee; and thou shalt eat the herb of the field.
v.19 In the sweat of thy face shalt thou eat bread, till thou return unto the ground; for out of it wast thou taken: for dust thou art, and unto dust shalt thou return.

v.3 Lo, (s) children are a heritage from the Lord; and the (t) fruit of the womb is his (u) reward.

(s) children are a heritage from the Lord
(s) Gen.33:5;48:4;Josh.24:3-4
(t) fruit
(t) Dt.28:4
(u) reward Ps.113:9

Gen.33:5

v.5 And he lifted up his eyes, and saw the women and the children; and said, Who are those with thee? And he said, The children whom God hath graciously given thy servant.

Gen.48:4

v.4 And said unto me, Behold, I will make thee fruitful, and multiply thee, and I will make of thee a multitude of people; and will give this land to thy seed after thee for an everlasting possession.

Josh.24:3-4

v.3 And I took your father, Abraham, from the other side of the |river|, and led him throughout all the land of Ca'naan, and multiplied his seed, and gave him Isaac.
v.4 And I gave unto Isaac, Jacob and Esau. And I gave unto Esau, Mount Seir, to possess it; but Jacob and his children went down into Egypt.

Dt.28:4

v.4 Blessed shall be the fruit of thy body, and the fruit of thy ground, and the fruit of thy cattle, the increase of thy |cows|, and the flocks of thy sheep.

Ps.113:9

v.9 He maketh the barren woman to keep house, and to be a joyful mother of children. Praise ye the LORD.

v.4 As arrows are in the hand of a mighty man, so are children of one's youth.
v.5 (v) Happy is the man who hath his quiver full of them; they shall not be ashamed, but they shall speak with the enemies in the gate.

(v) happy is the man
(v) Ps.128:2-3

v.2 For thou shalt eat the labor of thine hands; happy shalt thou be, and it shall be well with thee.
v.3 Thy wife shall be as a fruitful vine by the sides of thine house; thy children like olive plants round about thy table.

See: A Song of f degrees—Psalm 120

BLESSINGS OF THE HOME OF THE GOD-FEARING

A SONG OF f DEGREES

PSALM 128

v.1 BLESSED is every one that (w) feareth the LORD, that walketh in his ways.

(w) feareth the LORD,
(w) See Ps.19:9,note
See Messianic Psalm 23:4

v.2 For thou shalt eat the labor of thine hands; happy shalt thou be, and it shall be (x) well with thee.

(x) well with thee
(x) Dt.4:40;Isa.3:10

Dt.4:40

v.40 Thou shalt keep, therefore, his statutes, and his commandments, which I command thee this day, that it may go well with thee, and with thy children after thee, and that thou mayest prolong thy days upon the earth, which the LORD thy God giveth thee, forever.

Isa.3:10

v.10 Say to the righteous, that it shall be well with them; for they shall eat the fruit of their doings.

v.3 Thy wife shall be (y) as a fruitful vine by the sides of thine house; thy (z) children (aa) like olive plants round about thy table.

(y) as a fruitful vine
(y)Ezek.19:10
(z) children;
(z)Ps.127:3-5
(aa) like olive;
(aa) Ps.52:8;144:12

Ezek.19:10

v.10 Thy mother is like a vine in thy blood, planted by the waters; she was fruitful and full of branches by reason of many waters.

Ps.127:3-5

v.3 Lo, children are an heritage from the Lord; and the fruit of the womb is his reward.
v.4 As arrows are in the hand of a mighty man, so are children of one's youth.
v.5 Happy is the man who hath his quiver full of them; they shall not be ashamed, but they shall speak with the enemies in the gate.

Ps.52:8

v.8 But I am like a green olive tree in the house of God; I trust in the mercy of God forever and ever.

Ps.144:12

v.12 That our sons may be like plants grown up in their youth; that our daughters may be like cornerstones, polished after the similitude of a palace;

v.4 Behold, that thus shall the man be blessed who feareth the LORD.
v.5 The LORD shall bless thee out of Zion, and thou shalt see the good of Jerusalem all the days of thy life.
v.6 Yea, (bb) thou shalt see thy children's children, and peace upon Israel.

(bb) thou shalt see
(bb) Cp. Gen.50:23;Job 42:16

Gen.50:23

v.23 And Joseph saw E'phraim's children of the third generation: the children also of Ma'chir, the son of Manas'seh, were brought up upon Joseph's knees.

Job 42:16

v.16 After this lived Job an hundred and forty years, and saw his sons, and his sons' sons, even four generations.

See A Song of f degrees Psalm 120

A PLEA FROM THE PERSECUTED

A SONG OF f DEGREES

PSALM 129

v.1 MANY a time have they afflicted me (cc) from my youth, may Israel now say,

(cc) from my youth,
(cc) Jer.1:19;15:20;
Mt.16:18;2 Cor.4:8-9

Jer.1:19

v.19 And they shall fight against thee, but they shall not prevail against thee; for I am with thee, saith the LORD, to deliver thee.

Jer.15:20

v.20 And I will make thee unto this people a |fortified bronze| wall; and they shall fight against thee, but they shall not prevail against thee; for I am with thee to save thee and to deliver thee, saith the LORD.

Mt.16:18

v.18 **And I say also unto thee, That thou art Peter, and upon this rock I will build my church, and the gates of |hades| shall not prevail against it.**

2 Cor.4:8-9

v.8 We troubled on every side, yet not distressed; we are perplexed, but not in despair;
v.9 Persecuted, but not forsaken; cast down, but not destroyed;

v.2 Many a time have they afflicted me from my youth; yet they have (cc) not prevailed against me.

(cc) not prevailed
(cc) See above v.1

v.3 The plowers plowed upon my back; they made long their furrows.
v.4 The LORD is righteous; he hath cut asunder the cords of the wicked.
v.5 Let them all be confounded and turned back that hate Zion.
v.6 Let them be (a) like the grass upon the housetops, which withered (b) |before| it growth up,

(a) like the grass
(a) Ps.37:2
(b) |before|
(b) KJV afore

Ps.37:2

v.2 For they shall soon be cut down like the grass, and wither like the green herb.

v.7 Wherewith the mower filleth not his hand, nor he that bindeth sheaves his bosom.
v.8 Neither do they who go by say, The blessing of the LORD be upon you; we (c) bless you in the name of the LORD.

(c) bless you
(c) Cp. Ruth 2:4

v.4 And, behold, Boaz came from Bethlehem, and said unto the reapers, The Lord be with you, And they answered him, The Lord bless thee.

See: A Song of d degrees Psalm 120

WAITING FOR THE MORNING

PSALM 130

v.1 Out of the depths have I cried unto thee, O LORD.
v.2 Lord, hear my voice; let thine ears be attentive to the voice of my supplications.
v.3 If thou LORD, shouldest mark iniquities, O Lord, who shall (e) stand?

(e) who shall stand?
(e) Nah.1:6

Nah.1:6

v.6 Who can stand before his indignation? And who can abide in the fireceness of his anger? His fury is poured out like fire, and the rocks are thrown down by him.

v.4 But there is forgiveness with thee, that thou mayest be feared?

(f) that thou mayest be feared?;
(f) 1Ki.8:39-40;
See Ps.19:9,note;Messianic Ps.16

I Ki.8:39-40

v.8 Then hear thou in heaven, thy dwelling place, and forgive, and do, and give to every man according to his ways, whose heart thou knowest (for thou, even thou only, knowest the hearts of all the children of men),

v.40 That they may fear thee all the days that they live in the land which thou gavest unto our fathers.

v.5 I wait for the LORD, my soul doth wait, and in his word do I hope.
v.6 (g) My soul waited for the Lord more than they that watch for
the morning; I say, more than they that watch for the morning.

(g) My soul waited for the Lord
(g) Ps.33:20;40:1;Isa.8:17

Ps.33:20

v.20 Our soul waited for the LORD; he is our help and our shield.

Ps.40:1

v.1 I WAITED patiently for the LORD, and he inclined unto me, and heard my cry.

Isa.8:17

v.17 And I will wait upon the LORD, who hideth his face from the house of Jacob, and I will look for him.

v.7 Let Israel (h)hope in the LORD; for with the LORD (i) there is mercy, and with him is plenteous (j) redemption.

(h) hope in the LORD;
(h) Ps. 131:3
(i) there is mercy,
(i) Ps.86:5,15;Isa.55:7
(j) with him is plenteous redemption,
(j) Redemption (kinsman type):vv.7-8;
Prov.23:11.(Gen.48:16;Isa.59:20, note)

Ps.131:3

v.3 Let Israel hope in the Lord from henceforth and forever.

Ps.86:5,15

v.5 For thou, Lord, art good, and ready to forgive, and plenteous in mercy unto all those who call upon thee.
v.15 But thou, O Lord, art a God full of compassion, and gracious, long-suffering, and plenteous in mercy and truth.

Isa.55:7

v.7 Let the wicked forsake his way, and the unrighteous man his thoughts, and let him return unto the Lord, and he will have mercy upon him; and to our God; for he will abundantly pardon.
v.7 Let Israel (h) hope in the Lord; for with the LORD (i) there is mercy, and with him is plenteous (j) redemption.
v.8 And he shall redeem Israel from all his iniquities.

Prov.23:11

v.11 For their redeemer is mighty; he shall plead their cause with thee.

Gen.48:16

v.16 |An angel| who redeemed me from all evil, bless the lads; and let my name be named on them, and the name of my fathers, Abraham and Isaac; and let them grow into a multitude in the midst of the earth.

Isa.59:20,note (see note in Messianic Ps.72)

v.20 And the Redeemer shall come to Zion, and unto those who turn from transgression in Jacob, saith the LORD.

v.8 And he shall redeem Israel from all his iniquities.

See A Song of d degrees—Psalm 120

GROWING IN GRACE

A SONG OF d DEGREES OF DAVID

PSALM 131

v.1 LORD, my heart is not haughty, nor mine eyes lofty; neither do I exercise myself in great neither matters, or in things too high for me.
v.2 Surely I have behaved and quieted myself, like a child that is weaned of his mother; my soul is even like a weaned child.
v.3 Let Israel hope in the LORD from henceforth and forever.

See A Song of d degrees—Psalm of David

TRUST IN THE GOD OF DAVID

A SONG OF d DEGREES

PSALM 132

v.1 LORD, remember David, and all his afflictions;
v.2 How he swore unto the LORD, and vowed unto the mighty God of Jacob: Surely I will not come into the tabernacle of my house, nor go up into my bed;
v.4 I will not give sleep to mine eyes, or slumber to mine eyelids,
v.5 (k) Until I find out a place for the LORD, an habitation for the Mighty God of Jacob.

(k) Until I find out a place for the LORD,
(k) Acts 7:46

v.46 Who found favor before God, and desired to find a tabernacle for the God of Jacob.

v.6 Lo, we heard of it at (l) Eph'rathan; we found it in the fields of (m) the wood.

(l) Eph'rathan;
(l) Or Ephraim
(m) the wood;
(m) Or Jaar, 1 Chr.13:5

v.5 So David gathered all Israel together, from Shi'hor of Egypt even unto the |entrance| of He'math, to bring the ark of God from Kiribati—je'arim.

v.7 (n) We will go into his tabernacles; we will worship at his footstool.

(n) We will go into his tabernacles;
(n) Ps.121:1-2

v.1 I WILL lift up mine eyes unto the hills. From whence cometh my help?
v.2 My help cometh from the LORD, who made heaven and earth.

v.8 Arise, O LORD, into thy rest, thou, and the ark of thy strength.
v.9 Let thy priests be clothed with (o) righteousness, and let thy saints shout for joy.

(o) righteousness,
(o) Righteousness (garment): v.9;
Isa.11:5.(Gen.3:21;Rev.19:8)
See above v. 9

Isa.11:5

v.5 And righteousness shall be the girdle of his loins, and faithfulness the girdle of his |waist|.

Gen.3:21

v.21 For Adam also and for his wife did the LORD God make coats of skins, and clothed them.

Rev.19:8

v.8 And to her was granted that she should be arrayed in fine linen, clean and white; for the fine linen is the |righteousness| of saints.

v.10 For thy servant David's sake turn not away the face of thine anointed.

v.11 (p) The LORD hath swore in truth onto David; he will not turn from it: (q) Of the fruit of thy body will I set upon thy throne.

(p) The LORD hath swore
(p) Ps.89:3-4,33;110:4
(q) Of the fruit
(q) 2 Sam.7:12;1Ki.8:25;
2 Chr.6:16;Lk.1:69;Acts 2:30

Ps.89:3-4

v.3 I have made a covenant with my chosen, I have sworn unto David, my servant:
v.4 Thy seed will I establish forever, and build up thy throne to all generation. Selah.
v.33 Nevertheless, my loving-kind-ness will I not utterly take from him, nor |allow| my faithfulness to fail.

Ps.110:4

v.4 The LORD hath sworn, and will not repent, Thou art a priest forever after the order of Melchiz'edek.

2 Sam. 7:12

v.12 And when thy days be fulfilled, and thou shalt sleep with thy fathers, I will set up thy seed after thee, which shall proceed out of |thine own body|, and I will establish his kingdom.

1 Ki.8:25

v.25 Therefore now, LORD God of Israel, keep with thy servant David, my father, that which thou promisedst him, saying, There shall not fail thee a man in my sight to sit on the throne of Israel; so that thy children take heed to their way, that they walk before me as thou hast walked before me.

2 Chr.6:16

v.16 Now therefore, O LORD God of Israel, keep with thy servant David, my father, that which thou hast promised him, saying, There shall not fail thee a man in my sight to sit upon the throne of Israel, | if only | thy children take heed to their way to walk in my law, as thou hast walked before me.

Lk.1:69

v.69 And hath raised up an horn of salvation for us in the servant, David;

Acts 2:30

v.30 Therefore, being a prophet, and knowing that God had sworn with an oath to him, that of the fruit of his loins, according to the flesh, he would raise up Christ to sit on his throne;

v.12 If thy children will keep my covenant and my testimony that I shall teach them, their children shall also sit upon thy throne for evermore.
v.13 (r) For the LORD hath chosen Zion; he hath desired it for his habitation.

(r) For the LORD hath chosen Zion;
(r) Ps.48:1-2

v.1 GREAT is the LORD, and greatly to be praised in the city of our God, in the mountain of his holiness.
v.2 Beautiful for situation, the joy of the whole earth, is Mount Zion, on the sides of the north, the city of the great king.

v.14 (s) This is my rest forever; here will I dwell; for I have desired it.

(s) This is my rest forever;
(s) Ps.68:16

v.16 Why leap ye, ye high hills? This is the hill which God desireth to dwell in; yea, the LORD will dwell in it forever.

v.15 I will abundantly bless her provision; I will satisfy her poor with bread.
v.16 (t) I will also clothe her priests with salvation; and her saints shall (u) shout aloud for joy.

(t) I will also clothe her priests
(t) 2 Chr.6:41;Ps.132:9;149:4
(u) shout
(u) 1 Sam.4:5

2 Chr.6:41

v.41 Now, my God, let, I beseech thee, thine eyes be open, and let thine ears be |attentive| unto the prayer that is made in this place.

Ps.132:9

v.9 Let thy priest be clothed with righteousness, and let thy saints shout for joy.

Ps.149:4

v.4 For the LORD taketh pleasure in his people; he will beautify the meek with salvation.

v.17 There will I make the (w) horn; of David to bud; I have ordained a (x) lamp for mine anointed.

(w) horn;
(w) See Dt.33:17,note—See—Messianic Ps. 89:17

(x) lamp
(x) 1 Ki.11:36;15:4; 2Chr.21:7

1 Ki.11:36

v.36 And unto his son will I give one tribe, that David, my servant, may have a light always before me in Jerusalem, the city which I have chosen to put my name there.

1 Ki.15:4

v.4 Nevertheless, for David's sake, did the LORD his God give him a lamp in Jerusalem, to set up his son after him, and to establish Jerusalem,

2 Chr.21:7

v.7 Howbeit, the LORD would not destroy the house of David, because of the covenant that he had made with David, and as he promised to give a light to him and to his sons forever.

v.18 His enemies will I (y) clothe with shame, but upon himself shall his crown flourish.

(y) clothe with shame,
(y) Ps.35:26;109:29

Ps.35:26

v.26 Let them be ashamed and brought to confusion together who rejoice at mine hurt; let them be clothed with shame and dishonor who magnify themselves against me.

See A Song of d degrees—Psalm 120

THE BLESSEDNESS OF BROTHERLY LOVE

A SONG OF d DEGREES OF DAVID

PSALM 133

v.1 BEHOLD, how good and how pleasant it is for (z) brethren to dwell together in unity!

(z) brethren
(z)Heb.13:1;
cp. Gen.13:8

Heb.13:1

v.1 Let brotherly love continue.

Gen. 13:8

v.8 And Abram said unto Lot, Let there be no strife, I pray thee, between me and thee, and between my herdsmen and thy herdsmen; for we are brethren.

v.2 It is like the precious ointment upon the head, that ran down upon the beard, even Aaron's beard; that went down to the skirts of his garments,
v.3 Like the dew of (aa) Hermon, and like the dew that descended upon the mountains of Zion; for (bb) there the LORD commanded the blessing, even life for evermore.

(aa) Hermon
(aa) Dt.4:48
(bb) there the LORD
(bb) Lev.25:21;Dt.28:8;Ps.42:8

Dt.4:48

v.48 From Aro'er, which is by the bank of the river Arnon, even unto Mount Sion, which is Hermon,

Lev.25:21

v.21 Then I will command my blessing upon you in the sixth year, and it shall bring forth fruit for three years.

Dt.28:8

v.8 The LORD shall command the blessing upon thee in thy storehouses, and in all that thou settest thine hand unto; and he shall bless thee in the land which the LORD thy God giveth thee.

Ps.42:8

v.8 Yet the LORD will command his loving—kindness in the daytime, and in the night his song shall be with me, and my prayer unto the God of my life.

PRAISE BY NIGHT

A SONG OF a DEGREES

PSALM 134

v.1 BEHOLD, bless ye the LORD, all ye servants of the LORD, who by night stand in the house of the LORD.
v.2 Lift up your hands in the sanctuary, and bless the LORD.
v.3 The LORD, who made heaven and earth, bless thee out of Zion.

VIII
THANKSGIVING PSALMS
118 AND 136

CHRIST AS THE STONE OR ROCK

PSALM 118

v.1 OH, give thanks unto the LORD, for he is good; (p) because
his mercy endureth forever.

(p) because his mercy endureth forever.
(p) Ps.136:1-26

v.1 OH, give thanks unto the LORD, for he is good; for
his mercy endureth forever.
v.2 Oh, give thanks unto the God of gods; for his mercy
endureth forever.
v.3 Oh, give thanks unto the Lord of lords; for his mercy
endureth forever;

v.4 To him who alone doeth great wonders; for his mercy endureth forever;
v.5 To him who by wisdom made the heavens; for his mercy endureth forever;
v.6 To him who stretched out the earth above the waters; for his mercy endureth forever;
v.7 To him who made great lights; for his mercy endureth forever;
v.8 The sun to rule by day; for his mercy endureth forever;
v.9 The moon and stars to rule by night; for his mercy endureth forever;
v.10 To him who smote Egypt in their first-born; for his mercy endureth forever;
v.11 And brought out Israel from among them; for his mercy endureth forever;
v.12 With a strong hand, and with | an outstretched | arm; for his mercy endureth forever;
v.13 To him who divided the Red Sea into parts; for his mercy endureth forever;
v.14 And made Israel to pass through the midst of it; for his mercy endureth forever;
v.15 But overthrew Phar'aoh and his host in the Red Sea; for his mercy endureth forever;
v.16 To him who led his people through the wilderness; for his mercy endureth forever;
v.17 To him who smote great kings; for his mercy endureth forever;
v.18 And slew famous king's for his mercy endureth forever;
v.19 Sihon, king of the Amorites; for his mercy endureth forever;
v.20 And Og, the king of Bashan; for his mercy endureth forever;
v.21 And gave their land for an heritage; for his mercy endureth forever;
v.22 Even an heritage unto Israel, his servant; for his mercy endureth forever;
v.23 Who remembered us in our low estate; for his mercy endureth forever;

v.24 And hath redeemed us from our enemies; for his mercy endureth forever;
v.25 Who giveth food to all flesh; for his mercy endureth forever;
v.26 Oh, give thanks unto the God of heaven; for his mercy endureth forever;

v.2 Let Israel now say that his mercy endureth forever.
v.3 Let the house of Aaron now say that his mercy endureth forever;
v.4 Let them now who (b)fear the LORD say that his mercy endureth forever.

(b) fear
(b) Ps.19:9,note

v.9 The fear of the LORD is clean, enduring forever; the |ordinances| of the LORD are true and righteous altogether.

2(19:9) "The fear of the LORD" is an O.T. expression meaning reverential trust, includind the hatred of evil.

v.5 I called upon the LORD in distress; the LORD answered me, and set me in a large place.
v.6 The (q) LORD is on my side; I will not fear. What can a man do unto me?

(q) LORD is on my side;
(q) Ps.56:9;Rom.8:31;Heb.13:6

Ps.56:9

v.9 When I cry unto thee, then shall mine enemies turn back: this I know; for God is for me.

Rom.8:31

v.31 What shall we then say to these things ? If God be for us, who can be against us?

Heb.13:6

v.6 So that we may boldly say, The Lord is my helper, and I will not fear what man shall do unto me.

v.7 The LORD taketh my part with those who help me; therefore shall I see my desire upon those who hate me.
v.8 It is better to trust in the LORD than to put confidence in (r) man.

(r) man;
(r) Cp. 2Chr.32:7-8;Isa. 31:1-3

2Chr.32:7-8

v.7 Be strong and courageous, be not afraid nor for all the king of Assyria, nor for all the multitude who are with him; for there are more with us than with him.
v.8 With him is an arm of flesh; but with us is the LORD, our God, to help us, and to fight our battles. And the people rested themselves upon the words of Hezeki'ah, king of Judah.

Isa.31:1-3

v.1 Woe to those who go down to Egypt for help, and |rely| on horses, and trust in chariots, because they are many; and in horsemen, because they are very strong; but they look not unto the Holy One of Israel, neither seek the LORD!
v.2 Yet he also is wise, and will bring evil, and will not call back his words, but will arise
v.3 Now the Egyptians are men, and not God; and their horses flesh, and not God; and their horses flesh, and not spirit. When the LORD shall stretch out his hand, both he that helpeth shall fall down, and he that is |helped| shall fall down, and they all shall fail together.

v.9 It is better to (a) trust in the LORD than to put trust confidence in princes.

(a) trust,
(a)Ps.2:12,note

v.12 Kiss the Son, lest he be angry, and ye perish from the way, when his wrath is kindled but a little. Blessed are they who put their trust in him.

Note 1(2:12) Trust is the characteristic O.T. word the N.T. "faith," and "believe." It occur 152 times in the O.T., and is the rendering of Hebrew words signifying to take refuge (e.g. Ruth 2:12); to lean on (e.g. Ps.56:3); to roll on (e.g. Ps. 22:8); to wait for (e.g. Job.35:14).

v.10 All nations compassed me about, but in the name of the LORD will I destroy them.
v.11 (s) They compassed me about; yea, they compassed me about, but in the name of the LORD I will destroy them.

(s) They compassed me about;
(s) Ps.88:17

Ps. 88:17

v.17 They came round about me daily like water; they compassed me about together.

v.12 They compassed me about like (t) bees; they are quenched (u) like the fire of thorns, for in the name of the LORD I will destroy them.

(t) bees;
(t) cp. Dt.1:44
(u) like the fire of thorns,
(u) cp.Nah.1:10

Dt.1:44

v.44 And the Amorites, who dwelt in that mountain, came out against you, and chased you as bees do, and destroyed you in Seir, even unto Hormah.

Nah.1:10

v.10 For while they are |entangled| together like thorns, and while they are drunk like drunkards, they shall be devoured like stubble fully dry.

v.13 Thou hast thrust (v)|hard| at me that I might fall, but the LORD helped me.

(v) |hard|
(v) KJV sore

v.14 The (a) Lord is my strength and song, and is become my salvation.

(a) Lord is my strength
(a) Ex.15:2; Isa.12:2

Ex.15:2

v.2 The Lord is my strength and song, and he is become my salvation; he is my God, and I will prepare him an habitation; my father's God, and I will exalt him.

Isa.12:2

v.2 Behold, God is my salvation; I will trust, and not be afraid; for the Lord, even |the LORD|, is my strength and my song; he also is become my salvation.

v.15 The voice of rejoicing and salvation is in the tabernacles of the righteous; the right hand of the Lord doeth valiantly.

v.16 The right hand of the LORD is exalted; the right hand of the LORD doeth valiantly.
v.17 I shall (b) not die, but live, and declare the works of the LORD.

(b) not die,
(b) Ps.116:8-9;cp.Ps.6:5;Hab.1:12

Ps.116:8-9

v.8 For thou hast delivered my soul from death, mine eyes from tears, and my feet from falling.
v.9 I will walk before the LORD in the land of the living.

Ps.6:5

v.5 For in death there is no remembrance of thee; in |sheol| who shall give thee thanks?

Hab.1:12

v.12 Art thou not from everlasting, O LORD, my God, mine Holy One? We shall not die. O LORD, thou hast ordained them for judgment; and, O Mighty God, thou hast established them for correction.

v.18 The LORD (c) hath chastened me (d)|very much|, but he hath not given me over unto death.

(c) hath chastened me
(c) 2Cor.6:9
(d)|very much,
(d) KJV sore

2Cor.6:9

v.9 As unknown, and yet always well known; as dying, and, behold, we live; as chastened, and not killed; rejoicing

v.19 (e) Open to me the gates of righteousness; I will go into them, and I will praise the LORD,

(e) Open to me the gate
(e) Isa.26:2;cp. Ps.24:7

Isa.26:2

v.2 Open ye gates, that the righteous nation that keepeth the truth may enter in.

Ps.24:7

v.7 Lift up your heads, O ye gates; and be ye lifted up, ye everlasting doors; and the king of glory shall come in.

v.20 This gate of the LORD, (f) into which the righteous shall enter.

(f) into which the righteous shall enter;
(f) Isa.35:8;Rev.21:27;22:14-15

Isa.35:8

v.8 And an highway shall be there, and a way, and it shall be called The way of holiness; the unclean shall not pass over it, but it shall be for those; the wayfaring men, though fools, shall not err therein.

Rev.21:27

v.27 And there shall in no |way| enter into it anything that defileth, neither he that worketh abomination, or maketh a lie, but they who are written in the Lamb's book of life.

Rev.22:14-15

v.14 Blessed are they that |wash their robes|, that they may have right to the tree of life, and may enter in through the gates into the city.

v.15 For |outside| are dogs, and sorcerers, and |fornicators|, and whosoever loveth and maketh a lie.

v.21 I will praise thee; for thou hast heard me, and art become my salvation.

v.22 The 1(g) stone which the builders refused is become the head of the corner.

1(g) stone which the builders refused
(g) 1(118:22) Christ (Stone):v.22;
Isa.8:14.(Gen.49:24;1Pet.2:8).

Ps. 118 looks beyond the rejection of the Stone (Christ) to His final exaltation in the kingdom, See above,v.22

Isa.8:14

v.14 And he shall be for a sanctuary; but for a stone of stumbling and for a rock of offense to both the houses of Israel, for a |trap| and for a snare to the inhabitants of Jerusalem.

Gen.49:24

v.24 But his bow abode strength, and the arms of his hands were made strong by the hands of the mighty God of Jacob (from there is the shepherd, the stone of Israel),

1 Pet.2:8

v.8 And a stone of stumbling, and a rock of defense, even to them who stumble at the word, being disobedient; whereunto also they were appointed.

v.23 (h) This is the LORD's doing; it is marvelous in our eyes.

(h) This is the LORD's doing;
(h) lit. This is from the LORD

v.24 This is the day which the LORD hath made; we will rejoice and be glad in it.

v.25 Save now, I beseech thee, O LORD! O LORD, I beseech thee, send now prosperity!
v.26 (i) Blessed is he that cometh in the name of the LORD; we have blessed you out of the house of the LORD.

(i) Blessed is he that cometh
(i) Mt.21:9;23:39;Mk.11:9;
Lk.13:35;19:38;Jn.12:13

Mt. 21:9

v.9 And the multitudes that went before, and that followed, cried, saying, Hosanna to the Son of David! Blessed is he that cometh in the name of the Lord! Hosanna in the highest!

Mt.23:39

v.39 **For I say unto you, Ye shall not see me henceforth, till ye shall say, Blessed is he that cometh in the name of the Lord.**

Mk.11:9

v.9 And they that before, and they that followed, cried, saying, Hosanna! Blessed is he that cometh in the name of the Lord.

Lk.13:35

v.35 **Behold, your house is left unto you desolate; and verily I say unto you, Ye shall not see me, until the time come when ye shall say, Blessed is he that cometh in the name of the Lord.**

Lk.19:38

v. 38 Saying, Blessed be the king who cometh in the name of the Lord; peace in heaven, and glory in the highest.

Jn.12:13

v.13 Took branches of palm trees, and went forth to meet him, and cried, Hosanna! Blessed is the King of Israel, cometh in the name of the Lord.

v.27 God is the LORD, who hath shown us light; bind the sacrifice with cords, even unto the horns of the altar.
v.28 Thou art my God, and I will praise thee; thou art my God, I will exalt thee.
v.29 2 Oh, give thanks unto the LORD, for he is good; for his mercy endureth forever.

2(118:29) The Messianic Psalms: Summary. That the Psalms contain a testimony to Christ, our Lord Himself affirmed (Lk.24:44,etc.), and the N.T. quotations from the Psalter point unerringly to those Psalms which have the Messianic character. A similar spiritual and prophetic character identifies others. See Ps.2:1,note.

(1) Christ is seen in the Psalms in two general attitudes: as suffering (e.g. Ps.22), and as entering into His kingdom glory (e.g.Ps.2 and 24. Cp.Lk.24:25-27).

(2) Christ is seen in His Person as (a) Son of God (Ps.2:7), and very God (Ps.45:6-7;102:25;110:1); (b) Son of man (Ps.8:4-6); and (c) Son of David (Ps.89:3-4,27,29).

(3) Christ is seen in His offices as (a) Prophet (Ps.22:22,25;40:9-10);(b) Priest (Ps.110:4);and (c) king (e.g.Ps.2 and 24).

(4) Christ is seen in His varied work, As Priest He offers Himself in sacrifice (Ps.22;40:6-8,with Heb.10:5-12), and, in resurrection, as the Priest—Shepherd, ever living to make intercession (Ps.23, with Heb.7:21-25; 13:20). As Prophet He proclaims the name of the LORD as Father (Ps.22:22, with Jn.20:17). As King He fulfills the Davidic Covenant (Ps.89) and restore alike the dominion of man over creation (Ps.8:4-8;Rom.8:17-21) and the Father over all (1Cor.15:25-28).

(5) The Messianic Psalms give also the inner thoughts, the exercises of soul, of Christ in His earthly experiences (e.g. Ps.16:8-11;22:1-21;40:1-17)

118—Messianic Psalm—Scofield
Hallelujah (Hallel)—Scofield
Thanksgiving—King James Study Bible (Nelson)

THE LORD'S ENDURING MERCY

PSALM 136

v.1 OH, give thanks unto the LORD, for he is good; (t) for his mercy endureth forever.

(t) for his mercy;
(t) 1 Chr.16:34,41; 2Chr.20:21

1 Chr.16:34,41

v.34 Oh, give thanks unto the LORD; for he is good; for his mercy endureth forever.
v.41 And with them Heman and Jedu'thun, and the rest who were chosen, who were |mentioned| by name, to give thanks to the LORD, because his mercy endureth forever.

2 Chr.20:21

v.21 And when he had consulted with the people, he appointed singers unto the LORD, who should praise the beauty of holiness, as they went out before the army, and to say, Praise the LORD; for his mercy endureth forever.

v.2 Oh, give thanks unto (u) the God of gods; for his mercy endureth forever.

(u) the God of gods;
(u) Cp.Dt.4:35,39; Isa.44:8;
45:5;46:9; 1 Cor.8:5-6;
See Ps.16:4,note

Dt.4:35

v.35 Unto thee it was shown, thou mightest know that the LORD, he is God; there is none else beside him.
v.39 Know therefore this day, and consider it in thine heart, that the LORD, he is God in heaven above, and upon the earth beneath; there is none else.

Isa.44:8

v.8 Fear not, neither be afraid; have not I told thee from that time, and have declared it? Ye are even my witnesses. Is there a God beside me? Yea, there is no God; I know not any.

Isa.45:5

v.5 I am the LORD, and there is none else, there is no God beside me; I girded thee, though thou hast not known me,

Isa.46:9

v.9 Remember the former things of old; for I am God, and there is none else; I am God, and there is none like me,

1 Cor.8:5-6

v.5 For though there be that are called gods, whether in heaven or in earth (as there are gods many, and lords many),
v.6 But to us there is but one God, the Father, of whom are all things, and we in him.; and one Lord Jesus Christ, by whom are all things, and we by him.

Ps.16:4,note

v.16 Their sorrows shall be multiplied, who hasten after another god; their drink offerings of blood will I not offer, nor take up their names into my lips.

Note: 1(16:4) Of course there is only one God (1 Cor.8:5-6). The pagans had, however, those whom they called "gods" e.g. in David's day, Dagon and Baal. Then and now, whatever preempts the place in one's heart that belongs to the true God may be said to be a god, e.g. self and the pleasures of this world (2 Tim.3:2,4).

v.3 Oh, give thanks to the Lord of lords; for his mercy endureth forever;
v.4 To him who alone doeth great wonders; for his mercy endureth forever;
v.5 (v) To him who by wisdom made the heavens; for his mercy endureth forever;

(v) To him who by wisdom
(v) Gen.1:1,6-8;Prov.3:19;Jer.51:15

Gen.1:1,6-8

v.1 IN the beginning God created the heaven and the earth.
v.6 And God said, Let there be a firmament in the midst of the waters, and let it divide the waters from the waters.
v.7 And God made the firmament, and divided the waters which were under the firmament from the waters which were above the firmament: and it was so.
v.8 And God called the firmament Heaven. And the evening and the morning were the second day.

Prov.3:19

v.19 The LORD by wisdom hath founded the earth; by understanding hath he established the heavens.

Jer.51:15

v.15 He hath made the earth by his power; he hath established the world by his wisdom, and hath stretched out the heavens by his understanding v.6 (w) To him who stretched out the earth above the waters; for his mercy endureth forever;

(w) To him who stretched
(w) Gen.1:9;Ps.24:2;Jer.10:12

Gen.1:9

v.9 And God said, Let the waters under the heaven be gathered together unto one place, and let the dry land appear: and it was so.

Ps.24:2

v.2 For he hath founded it upon the seas, and established it upon the floods.

Jer.10:12

v.12 He hath made the earth by his power; he hath established the world by his wisdom, and hath stretched out the heavens by his |understanding|.

v.7 (x) To him who made great lights; for his mercy endureth forever;

(x) To him who made great lights;
(x) Gen.1:14

v.14 And God said, Let there be lights in the firmament of the heaven to divide the day from the night; and let them be for signs, and for seasons, and for days, and years;

v.8 (y) The sun to rule by day; for his mercy endureth forever;

(y) The sun to rule
(y) Gen.1:16

v.16 And God made two great lights; the greater light to rule the day, and the lesser light to rule the night: he made the stars also.

v.9 The moon and stars to rule by night; for his mercy endureth forever;
v.10 (z) To him who smote Egypt in their first-born; for his mercy endureth forever;

(z) To him who smote Egypt in their first-born;
(z) Ex.12:29;Ps.135:8

Ex.12:29

v.29 And it came to pass, that at midnight the LORD smote all the first-born in the land of Egypt, from the first-born of Phar'aoh who sat on his throne unto the first-born of the captive who was in the dungeon; and all the first-born of cattle.

Ps.135:8

v.8 Who smote the first-born of Egypt, both of man and beast;

v.11 (aa) And brought out Israel from among them; for his mercy endureth forever.

(aa) And brought out Israel
(aa) Ex.12:51;13:3,16

Ex.12:51

v.51 And it came to pass the |very same| day, that the LORD did bring the children of Israel out of the land of Egypt by their armies.

Ex.13:3,16

v.3 And Moses said unto the people, Remember this day, in which ye came out from Egypt, out of the house of bondage; for by strength of hand the Lord brought you out from this place; there shall no leavened bread be eaten.

v.16 And it shall be for a token upon thine hand, and for frontlets between thine eyes; for by strength of hand the LORD brought us forth out of Egypt.

v.12 With a strong hand, and with (bb) |an outstretched | arm; for his mercy endureth forever;

(bb) |an outstretched | arm;
(bb) KJV a stretched out

v.13 (cc) To him who divided the Red Sea into parts; for his mercy endureth forever;

(cc) To him who divided
(cc) Ex.14:21-22;Ps.78:13

Ex.14:21

v.21 And Moses stretched out his hand over the sea; and the Lord caused the sea to go back by a strong east wind all that night, and made the sea dry land, and the waters were divided.

v.22 And the children of Israel went into the midst of the sea upon the dry ground; and the waters were a wall unto them on their right hand, and on their left.

Ps.78:13

v.13 He divided the sea, and caused them to pass through; and he made the waters to stand as an heap.

v.14 And made Israel to pass through the midst of it; for his mercy endureth forever.

v.15 (dd) But overthrew Phar'aoh and his host in the Red Sea; for his mercy endureth forever;

(dd) But overthrew
(dd) Ex.14:27;Ps.135:9

Ex.14:27

v.27 And Moses stretched forth his hand over the sea, and the sea returned to its strength when the morning appeared; and the Egyptians fled against it; and the LORD overthrew the Egyptians in the midst of the sea.

Ps.135:9

v.9 Who sent |signs| and wonders into the midst of thee, O Egypt, upon Phar'aoh, and upon all his servants;

v.16 To him who led his people through the wilderness; for his mercy endureth forever;
v.17 (ee) To him who smote great kings; for his mercy endureth forever;

(ee) To him who smote
(ee) Ps.135:10-11

Ps.135:10-11

v.10 Who smote great nations, and slew mighty kings:
v.11 Sihon, king of the Amorites, and Og, king of Bashan, and all the kingdoms of Ca'naan,

v.18 (a) And slew famous kings; for his mercy endureth forever:

(a) And slew
(a) Dt.29:7

v.7 And when ye came unto this place, Sihon, the king of Heshbon, and Og, the king of Bashan, came out against us unto battle, and we smote them.

v.19 (b) Sihon, king of the Amorites; for his mercy endureth forever;

(b) Sihon, king
(b) Num.21:21

v.21 And Israel sent messengers unto Sihon, king of the Amorites, saying,

v.20 And (c) Og the king of Bashan; for his mercy endureth forever;

(c) Og the king
(c) Num.21:33

v.33 And they turned and went up by the way of Bashan: and Og, the king of Bashan, went out against them, he, and all his people, to the battle at Ed'rei.

v.21 (d) And gave their land for an heritage; for his mercy endureth forever;

(d) And gave their land
(d) Josh.12:1;Ps.135:12

Josh.12:1

v.1 Now these are the kings of the land, whom the children of Israel smote and possessed their land on the other side of the Jordan toward the rising of the sun, from the river Arnon unto Mount Hermon, and all the |Ar'abah| on the east:

Ps.135:12

v.12 And gave their land for an heritage, an heritage unto Israel, his people.

v.22 Even an heritage unto Israel, his servant; for his mercy endureth forever;

v.23 (e) Who remembered us in our low estate; for his mercy endureth forever;

(e) Who remembered us
(e) Gen.8:1;Dt.32:36;Ps.113:7

Gen.8:1

v.1 AND God remembered Noah, and every living thing, and all the cattle that was with him in the ark: and God made a wind to pass over the earth, and the waters |subsided|;

Dt.32:36

v.36 For the LORD shall judge his people, and repent himself for his servants, when he seeth that their power is gone, and there is none shut up or left.

Ps.113:7

v.7 He raiseth up the poor out of the dust, and lifteth the needy out of the dunghill.

v.24 And hath (f) redeemed us from our enemies; for his mercy endureth forever;

(f) redeemed us
(f) Ps.44:7

v.7 But thou hast saved us from our enemies, and hast put them to shame who hated us.

v.25 Who giveth food to all flesh; for his mercy endureth forever.
v.26 Oh, give thanks unto the God of heaven; for his mercy endureth forever.

Reflections

IX. THE SUMMATION PSALM 150—

THE SUMMATION OF GOD'S PRAISE

THE SUMMATION OF GOD'S PRAISE

PSALM 150

v.1 (x) PRAISE ye the LORD. Praise God in his sanctuary; praise him in the firmament of his power.

(x) PRAISE ye the LORD.
(x) Ps.145:5-6

v.5 I will speak of the glorious honor of thy majesty, and of thy wondrous works.
v.6 And men shall speak of the might of thy |awe-inspiring| acts; and I will declare thy greatness.

v.2 Praise him for his mighty acts; praise him according to his excellent (y) greatness.

(y) greatness
(y) Dt.3:24

v.24 O Lord God thou hast begun to show thy servant thy greatness, and thy mighty hand. For what God is there in heaven or in earth, who can do according to thy works, and according to thy might?

v.3 Praise him with the sound of the (z) trumpet; praise him with the (aa) psaltery and (q) harp.

(z) trumpet;

(z) Heb. shofar, the horn of a cow or ram
(aa) psaltery
(aa) Probably a harp or guitar
(q) harp
(q) Probably a zither or lyre

v.4 Praise him with the (p) timbrel and dance; praise him with stringed instruments and (bb) |flutes|.

(p) timbrel and dance;
(p) Probably a tambourine
(bb) KJV organs

v.5 Praise him upon the loud cymbals; praise him upon the high sounding cymbals.
v.6 Let everything that hath breath praise the Lord. Praise ye the Lord.

APPENDIX

GOD'S ALL-SEEING EYE AND INESCAPABLE PRESENCE—PSALM 139

Dedicated to the late Rev. Rudolph Robinson,
St. Paul Chapel Baptist Church
Philadelphia, Pa.

GOD'S ALL–SEEING EYE AND INESCAPABLE PRESENCE

PSALM 139

v.1 O LORD, thou hast (s) searched me, and known me.

(s) searched me
(s) Cp.Ps.139:23

v.23 Search me, O God, and know my heart; try me, and know my thoughts;

v.2 (t) Thou knowest my downsitting and mine uprising; thou (u) understandest my thought afar off.

(t) Thou knowest my downsitting and mine uprising
(t) Cp. 2 Ki.19:27
(u) understandest my thought afar off.
(u) Cp. Mt.9:4;Jn.2:24-25

2 Ki.19:27

v.27 But I know thy abode, and thy going out, and thy coming in, and thy rage against me.

Mt.9:4

v.4 And Jesus, knowing their thoughts, said, **Why think ye evil in your hearts?**

Jn.2:24-25

v.24 But Jesus did not commit himself unto them, because he knew all men,
v.25 And needed not that any should testify of man; for he knew what was in man.

v.3 Thou compassest my path and my lying down, and art acquainted with all my ways.
v.4 For there is not a word in my tongue, but, lo, LORD, (v) thou knowest it altogether.

(v) thou knowest it altogether.
(v) Heb.4:13

v.13 Neither is there any creature that is not manifest in his sight, but all things are naked and opened unto the eyes of him with whom we have to do.

v.5 Thou hast beset me behind and before, and laid thine hand upon me.
v.6 (w) Such knowledge is (x) too wonderful for me; it is high, I cannot attain unto it.

(w) Such knowledge is
(w) Job 42:3;Ps.40:5
(x) too wonderful for me;
(x) Cp. Rom.11:33

Job. 42:3

v.3 Who is he who hideth counsel without knowledge? Therefore have I uttered that which I understood not; things too wonderful for me, which I knew not.

Ps.40:5

v.5 Many, O LORD, my God, are thy wonderful works which thou hast done, and thy thoughts which are | towards us | ; they cannot be reckoned up in order unto thee, If I would declare and speak of them, they are more than can be numbered.

Rom.11:33

v.33 Oh, the depth of the riches both of the wisdom and knowledge of God! How unsearchable are his judgments, and his ways past finding out!

v.7 (y) Whither shall I go from thy (z) Sprit? Or whither shall I flee from thy presence?

(y) Whither shall I go from thy
(y) Jer.23:24; Amos 9:2-4;cp.Jon.1:3
(z) Spirit?
(z) Holy Spirit (O.T.):v.7; Ps.143:10.
(Gen.1:2;Zech.12:10)

Jer.23:24

v.24 Can any hide himself in secret places that I shall not see him? saith the LORD. Do not I fill heaven and earth? saith the LORD.

Amos 9:2-4

v.2 Though they dig into | sheol |, | there | shall mine hand take them; though they climb up to heaven, | from there | will I bring them down;
v.3 And though they hide themselves in the top of Carmel, I will search and take them out | from there | ; and though they be hidden from my sight in the

bottom of the sea, |there| will I command the serpent, and he shall bite them;

v.4 And though they go into captivity before their enemies, |there| will I command the sword, and it shall slay them; and I will set mine eyes upon them for evil, and not for good.

Jon.1:3

v.3 But Jonah rose up to flee unto Tar'shish from the presence of the LORD, and went down to Joppa, and he found a ship going to Tarshish; so he paid the fare, and went down into it, to go with them unto Tarshish from the presence of the LORD. See the above Ps.139:7

Ps.143:10

v.10 Teach me to do thy will; for thou art my God. Thy Spirit is good; lead me into the land of uprightness.

Gen.1:2

v.2 And the earth was without form, and void; and darkness was upon the face of the deep. And the Spirit of God moved upon the face of the waters.

Zech.12:10

v.10 And I will pour upon the house of David, and upon the inhabitants of Jerusalem, the Spirit of grace and of supplications; and they shall look upon me whom they have pierced, and they shall mourn for him, as one mourneth for his only son, and shall be in bitterness for him, as one that is in bitterness for his first—born.

v.8 If I ascend up into heaven, thou art there; if I make my bed in (aa) |sheol|, behold, thou art (bb) there.

(aa) |sheol|
(aa) KJV hell. See Hab.2:5,note;cp.Lk.16:23,note
See Ps.16 :10 Messianic Psalm
(bb) there
(bb) Amos 9:2-4 See above v.7

v.9 If I take the wings of the morning, and dwell in the uttermost parts of the sea,
v.10 Even there shall thy hand lead me, and thy right hand shall hold me.
v.11 If I say, Surely the darkness shall cover me; even the night shall be light about me.
v.12 Yea, the (cc) darkness hideth not from thee, but the night shineth as the day; the darkness and the light are both alike to thee.

(cc) darkness hideth not from thee,
(cc) Job 26:6;34:22;Dan.2:22;Heb.4:13

Job 26:6

v.6 |Sheol| is naked before him, and destruction hath no covering.

Job 34:22

v.22 There is no darkness, nor shadow of death, where the workers of iniquity may hide themselves.

Dan.2:22

v.22 He revealed the deep and secret things; he knoweth what is in the darkness, and the light dwelleth with him.

Heb.4:13

v.13 Neither is there any creature that is not manifest in his sight, but all things are naked and open unto the eyes of him with whom we have to do.

v.13 For thou hast possessed my (a) |inward parts|; thou hast covered me in my mother's womb.

(a) |inward parts|;
(a) KJV reins

v.14 I will praise thee; for I am fearfully and wonderfully made. Marvelous are thy works, and that my soul knoweth right well.
v.15 (b) My substance was not hidden from thee, when I was made in secret, and (c) |intricately| wrought in the lowest parts of the earth.

(b) My substance was not hidden from thee,
(b) Job 10:8-9;Eccl.11:5
(c) |intricately| wrought in the lowest parts of the earth.
(c) KJV curiously

Job 10:8-9

v.8 Thine hands have made me and fashioned me together round about; yet thou dost destroy me.
v.9 Remember, I beseech thee, that thou hast made me as the clay. And wilt thou bring me into dust again?

Eccl.11:5

v.5 As thou knowest not what is the way of the |wind|, nor how the bones grow in the womb of her who is with child, even so thou knowest not the works of God, who maketh all.

v.16 Thine eyes did see my substance, yet being (d) |unformed|; and in thy book all my members were written, which in continuance were fashioned, when as yet there was none of them.

(d) |unformed|
(d) KJV unperfect

v.17 (e) How precious also are thy thoughts unto me, O God! How great is the sum of them!

(e) How precious also are thy thoughts
(e) Rom.11:33

v.33 Oh, the depth of the riches both of the wisdom and knowledge of God! How unsearchable are his judgments, and his ways past finding out!

v.18 If I should count them, they are more in number than the sand; when I awake, I am still with thee.
v.19 (f) Surely, thou wilt slay the wicked, O God; depart from me therefore, ye bloody men.

(f) Surely
(f) Isa.11:4

v.4 But with righteousness shall he judge the poor, and reprove with equity for the meek of the earth; and he shall smite the earth with the rod of his mouth, and with the breath of his lips shall he slay the wicked.

v.20 For they (g) speak against thee wickedly, and thine enemies take thy name in vain,

(g) speak against thee wickedly,
(g) Jude 15

v.15 To execute judgment upon all, and to |convict| all

that are ungodly among them of all their ungodly deeds which they have ungodly committed, and of all their hard speeches which ungodly sinners have spoken against him.

v.21 Do not I hate them, O LORD, that hate thee? And am not I grieved with those who rise up against thee?
v.22 I hate them with perfect hatred; I count them mine enemies.
v.23 (h) Search me, O God, and know my heart; (i) try me, and know my thoughts,

(h) Search me,
(h) Job 31:6;Ps.26:2
(i) try me,
(i) Test—tempt: vv.23-24; Prov.1:10.
(Gen.3:1;Jas.1:14)

Job 31:6

v.6 Let me be weighed in an even balance, that God may know mine integrity.

Ps. 26:2

v.2 Examine me, O LORD, and prove me; |test| my |heart| and my |mind|.

Ps.139:23-24

v.23 (h) Search me, O God, and know my heart; (i) try me, and know thoughts,
v.24 And see if there be any wicked way in me, and (j) lead me in the way everlasting.

Prov.1:10

v.10 My son, if sinners entice thee, consent thou not.

Gen.3:1

v.1 Now the serpent was more subtle than any beast of the field which the LORD God had made. And he said unto the woman, yea, hath God said, Ye shall not eat of every tree of the garden?

Jas.1:14

v.14 But every man is tempted, when he is drawn away of his own lust, and enticed.

v.24 And see if there be any wicked way in me, and (j) lead me in the way everlasting.

(j) lead me in the way everlasting.
(j) Ps.5:8;143:10

Ps.5:8

v.8 Lead me, O LORD, in thy righteousness because of mine enemies; make thy way straight before my face.

Ps.143:10

v.10 Teach me to do thy will; for thou art my God. Thy Spirit is good; lead me into the land of uprightness.

[dedicated to the late Rev. Rudolph Robinson,
St. Paul Chapel Baptist Church, Philadelphia, Pa.
Pastor and Friend]
[who often quoted this Psalm before Preaching]

Reflections

INDEX TO ANNOTATIONS

INDEX TO ANNOTATIONS

REFERENCE BOOKS

Henry, Matthew

Commentary of the Bible

Nelson - King James Study Bible

Scofield - Reference Bible

Strong's Analytical Concordance

Thompson's Chain Reference Bible